Section 27 and Freedman's Village
in Arlington National Cemetery

ALSO BY RIC MURPHY
AND FROM McFARLAND

*Rear Admiral Larry Chambers, USN:
First African American to Command
an Aircraft Carrier* (2018)

Section 27 and Freedman's Village in Arlington National Cemetery

The African American History of America's Most Hallowed Ground

RIC MURPHY *and*
TIMOTHY STEPHENS

McFarland & Company, Inc., Publishers
Jefferson, North Carolina

LIBRARY OF CONGRESS AND BRITISH LIBRARY
CATALOGUING DATA ARE AVAILABLE

Library of Congress Control Number 2020006105

ISBN 978-1-4766-7730-9 (print)
ISBN 978-1-4766-3641-2 (ebook)

© 2020 Ric Murphy and Tim Stephens. All rights reserved

No part of this book may be reproduced or transmitted in any form or by any means, electronic or mechanical, including photocopying or recording, or by any information storage and retrieval system, without permission in writing from the publisher.

Front cover: photograph of the plaque marking Section 27 at Arlington National Cemetery (photograph by and courtesy of Ric Murphy)

Printed in the United States of America

McFarland & Company, Inc., Publishers
Box 611, Jefferson, North Carolina 28640
www.mcfarlandpub.com

To the known and unknown of Arlington Heights,
who once lived, worked, and liberated this hallowed land,
and to all those who are buried in the Arlington National Cemetery

Acknowledgments

OUR RESEARCH OWES MUCH to the cooperation of archivists, curators, librarians, and historians who freely shared their time and expertise. We wish to thank Sam Anthony, office of the chief of staff and to the National Archives; John Liebertz, historic preservation planner, Arlington County Department of Community Planning, Housing & Development; the staffs of the Library of Virginia, the Virginia Historical Society, and the Arlington Public Library's Center for Local History, and the Alexandria Public Library's Collections Division.

We are also grateful to Paul Sluby for his knowledge of African American cemeteries in the Washington, D.C., area; to Matt Penrod of the National Park Service and to Roderick Gainer of the Department of the Army. And, a special thanks to Craig Syphax and Stephen Hammond for their insights on the Custis-Carter-Syphax families; and to Dr. Cheryl Janifer LaRoche, Dr. John Walsh, and Jake Wynn for their professional expertise in their review of the manuscript.

Finally, we wish to pay tribute to the more than 3,800 men, women and children who with courage and bravery and against all odds attempted to live a life of freedom and in the pursuit of happiness, in our nation's capital Washington, District of Columbia. While they were never able to pass on to their descendants their heroic deeds, we hope by sharing the story of how they happened to be buried in Arlington National Cemetery, that their story will no longer be forgotten to history. Thank you for your service.

Table of Contents

Acknowledgments — vi
Images, Tables, Figures and Maps — ix
"Bury Me in a Free Land" by Frances Ellen Watkins Harper — xii
Introduction — 1

1. The Men Who Shaped Arlington — 9
2. A City Under Siege — 15
3. Arlington Plantation — 23
4. Enslavement at Arlington — 35
5. Civil War — 56
6. Washington's Contraband — 65
7. Health and Medical Care — 76
8. Freedman's Village — 92
9. National Cemeteries — 103
10. United States Colored Troops — 113
11. The Contraband Cemetery — 128
12. The Forgotten Union Blue — 134
13. Eviction — 145
14. Reconstruction, Reconciliation and Retribution — 153

Epilogue — 172
   APPENDIX I. CHRONOLOGY — 177
   APPENDIX II. INVENTORY OF SLAVES AT ARLINGTON

PLANTATION BELONGING TO G.W.P. CUSTIS,
JANUARY 1, 1858 183
APPENDIX III. EMANCIPATION BY R.E. LEE OF
G.W.P. CUSTIS' ENSLAVED 184
APPENDIX IV. GROWTH OF EMPLOYMENT IN
WASHINGTON, D.C., FROM 1850 TO 1870 186
APPENDIX V. AN AFRICAN AMERICAN WALKING TOUR
OF ARLINGTON CEMETERY 188

Chapter Notes 193
Bibliography 209
Index 219

Images, Tables, Figures and Maps

List of Images

Image 1: James Parks	11
Image 2: Contraband Going North "Wagon Fording the Rappahannock River"	16
Image 3: The Washington Family	25
Image 4: Charles Syphax	39
Image 5: Living Room of the Custis-Lee Mansion	41
Image 6: Mary Custis Lee	59
Image 7: General Robert E. Lee (CSA)	59
Image 8: Mrs. Selena Gray	61
Image 9: Union Soldiers at Arlington	62
Image 10: General Butler Contemplating Fate of Enslaved Men	67
Image 11: Stampede of Slaves to Fortress Monroe	69
Image 12: Freedman's Village School, Washington, D.C.	74
Image 13: Emancipation Proclamation	79
Image 14: Camp Convalescent	83
Image 15: Dr. Anderson R. Abbott, MD	87
Image 16: Alexander Thomas Augusta, MD	87
Image 17: The Emancipation of the Custis Enslaved by R. E. Lee	93
Image 18: Plan of Freeman's Village	96
Image 19: Freedman's Village Regulations	97
Image 20: 107th Regiment, United States Colored Troops	98
Image 21: Sojourner Truth	100
Image 22: Carnage of the Battle of Antietam	106

Image 23: Section 27 First Burials	109
Image 24: United States Colored Troops Recruiting Poster	114
Image 25: 54th Regiment Massachusetts Volunteer Infantry Assault	115
Image 26: General Lee Meets General Grant at Appomattox	125
Image 27: The Unknowns	131
Image 28: The Enslaved Shed Their Slave Names and Took Names of Important People	132
Image 29: Formerly Enslaved Men Named After Presidents	133
Image 30: Section 27 Medal of Honor Recipients	139
Image 31: Robert E. Lee's Amnesty Oath	159
Image 32: Civil War Unknowns Memorial	161
Image 33: Confederate Memorial	169
Image 34: Confederate Monument Relief Panel: "Mammy"	170
Image 35: Confederate Monument Relief Panel: "Faithful Servant Following Young Master"	171
Image 36: Tomb of General Montgomery C. Meigs	174
Image 37: Honored Citizen James Parks Grave Site	175

List of Tables

Table 1: 1800 to 1870 District of Columbia Ten-Year Population Growth	78
Table 2: Consolidated Statement of Contraband Tax	95

List of Figures

Figure 1: Enslaved Within the Family	39
Figure 2: Will of George Washington Parke Custis	44–45
Figure 3: Washington Bureau, *Boston Traveler* Newspaper	46–47
Figure 4: *New York Times*, "The Will of Mr. Custis"	47–48
Figure 5: Letter from R.E. Lee: "[T]wo women belonging to the Estate of G.W.P. Custis"	49–50
Figure 6: Letter on the Treatment of the Enslaved at Arlington House	52–53
Figure 7: The Hypocrisy of Enslavement at Arlington House	54
Figure 8: Sojourner Truth Appointment	99
Figure 9: Grant Letter of Suggestion to General Lee of Surrender	123

Figure 10: General Lee's Letter Response Relative to Terms of
    Surrender   123
Figure 11: General Grant's Terms of Surrender   124–125
Figure 12: Requesting to Serve His Country in the United States
    Colored Troops   141
Figure 13: A Letter Requesting Appointment as Surgeon to Some
    of the Colored Regiments   142
Figure 14: White Medical Officers Complain About Black Doctor   143

List of Maps

Map 1: Present-day Arlington National Cemetery   8
Map 2: Arlington Heights National Cemetery Grounds   43

Bury Me in a Free Land
by
Frances Ellen Watkins Harper

Make me a grave where'er you will,
In a lowly plain, or a lofty hill;
Make it among earth's humblest graves,
But not in a land where men are slaves.
I could not rest if around my grave
I heard the steps of a trembling slave;
His shadow above my silent tomb
Would make it a place of fearful gloom.
I could not rest if I heard the tread
Of a coffle gang to the shambles led,
And the mother's shriek of wild despair
Rise like a curse on the trembling air.
I could not sleep if I saw the lash
Drinking her blood at each fearful gash,
And I saw her babes torn from her breast,
Like trembling doves from their parent nest.
I'd shudder and start if I heard the bay
Of bloodhounds seizing their human prey,
And I heard the captive plead in vain
As they bound afresh his galling chain.
If I saw young girls from their mother's arms
Bartered and sold for their youthful charms,
My eye would flash with a mournful flame,
My death-paled cheek grow red with shame.
I would sleep, dear friends, where bloated might
Can rob no man of his dearest right;
My rest shall be calm in any grave
Where none can call his brother a slave.
I ask no monument, proud and high,
To arrest the gaze of the passers-by;
All that my yearning spirit craves,
Is bury me not in a land of slaves.

First published in the *Anti-Slavery Bugle* on November 20, 1858.

Introduction

THE LAND OF ARLINGTON NATIONAL CEMETERY has ever been held in deep reverence and is a standing testament to those who have fought for freedom. The landscape at Arlington, Virginia, of regular white marble rows is one of the most recognized and visited places in the country and has been for most of the nation's history.[1] The Civil War consecrated the land, transforming it from a slave plantation owned by the descendants of George Washington's family to the last resting place for the Union dead.

The solid, walled permanence of the fields today hide the fact the land's boundaries and uses have never been fixed. Its occupants, alive and dead, were subject to being (re)moved, renamed and evicted. Arlington was a plantation, a village, a farm, and a commercial picnic ground. Arlington has had homes, camps, cemeteries, and forts scattered across its hills before becoming the preeminent national cemetery for Americans who served with honor. Changes are still afoot; on Memorial Day 2018 it was reported that the Department of the Army is considering restricting burials to those killed in action.[2]

The area that comprises Arlington National Cemetery was a privately owned plantation before it was seized from the Custis family for national security purposes. The Custises were one of the distinguished families of the Virginia planter class, connected to George Washington through his marriage to Martha Custis. Post–Civil War Arlington was not solely a cemetery, but also a farm and home to nearly 1,000 tenant farmers, living in the model Freedman's Village. The ground has been split many times over between owners and was frequently considered by many diverse voices to have special healing powers.[3] The deep history and the forgotten stories of Arlington National Cemetery are as rich and diverse as the national story of the United States itself.

The entire hallowed terrain, which was once a part of the District of Columbia, played an important role during the Civil War as a defensive bulwark to the national capital and as a major transportation intersection. The main turnpike between the District of Columbia's Georgetown and Virginia's

1

Alexandria traversed Arlington's bottomland, and today the same right-of-way enables the Washington Metro to take visitors to the cemetery. George Washington had a vision for a canal connecting the Potomac River to the Ohio country; and the local portion cut through the Arlington Plantation and is still visible on the approach to the visitor center. The Long Bridge (located near the path of today's 14th Street Bridge/Interstate-395) terminated at the far southeast of the property. The Long Bridge was the last step in the escape to freedom from slavery for Civil War refugees. The Washington-Virginia Railway Company had lines running along the eastern and western sides of the cemetery in the early twentieth century.[4]

Arlington was developed, sustained, and made seemingly permanent by the system of economic slavery in the United States. The mansion was built by enslaved people, the land was cleared and tamed by the enslaved to make a plantation, and mortgages were secured by the ownership of the enslaved. The cash inheritances of heirs were paid by selling the enslaved. And the enslaved who escaped to Union lines became the support labor that sustained the troops who were billeted at Arlington, thus ensuring their freedom by sustaining an army they would eventually be allowed to fight in.

The plantation was inherited in 1857 by Mary Custis Lee, wife of Colonel Robert E. Lee. Mary Custis Lee was the great-granddaughter of President George and Martha Washington; Arlington Plantation came to Lee's control only by marriage. The Custis family had owned the 1,100-acre parcel via land grant since 1751, and their enslaved people had farmed the land continuously. Mary inherited the plantation in 1857 from her father, George Washington Parke Custis (G.W.P. Custis), who also willed her 196 slaves, including the 63 who were present at Arlington.

Robert E. Lee was named the executor of the estate but found the estate and farm operation lacking. Lee sought a court extension of the will's directive emancipating the enslaved people and sought a new overseer to ensure the enslaved would do their "duty."[5] Colonel Lee would sell the enslaved people or rent them out to other plantations to raise cash for the inheritances bestowed on G.W.P. Custis' white nieces and nephews. In 1859, enslaved Mary and Wesley Norris escaped the Arlington Plantation only to be captured, returned and punished. The New York press reported that Lee ordered particularly vicious punishment; the nature of the punishment began to define Lee's reputation as a symbol of the Lost Cause.[6]

An earlier grant of land went to the mixed-race Maria Carter Syphax, Mary Custis Lee's half-sister, for a 17-acre tract in the southwest corner of the estate in 1826. Though important to the history of Arlington Cemetery, the Syphax family is not the focus of this text. However, the Syphax story illustrates and intersects with many of the themes of our book: government takings, duty to family and country, the public health emergency brought on by the Civil War, and the defense of inalienable rights, resilience, and the preservation of history and its artifacts.

A book about James Parks, the former slave who worked as an Arlington Cemetery grave digger, would be equally compelling, given his life at Arlington spans from 1843 to 1929 and covers all the major formations and changes. There is, however, too little documentation to reveal and fully describe his true contribution. We know he was born enslaved to G.W.P. Custis and that he remained at Arlington laboring in support of the Union Army, becoming a leader of the men who dug the graves. We know his parents and siblings are buried in the slave cemetery now lost under the streets of Rosslyn. We know he led the replanting of the trees (many of which survive to provide shade today) cut by Union troops to improve sightlines and provide fuel and materials for housing. He would live at Freedman's Village, paying his rent and presumably farming a ten-acre plot. His interview by the *Washington Star* in 1928 provides intriguing details about the character of G.W.P. Custis, Lee and the earlier days at Arlington. James Parks is buried in Section 15E, Grave 2.

At the start of the Civil War, Colonel Lee had to decide: remain loyal to the nation his family had defended for generations or take up arms with the secessionists to defend his native state of Virginia. In mid–March 1861, Confederate Secretary of War LeRoy Pope Walker[7] offered Lee a command as a brigadier-general. The United States Army also made it clear they wanted his continued service. On March 28, Lee's mentor General Winfield Scott promoted Lee to full colonel, whereon Lee pledged allegiance to the new commander-in-chief, President Lincoln.[8]

Colonel Lee was at Arlington before, during and after Abraham Lincoln arrived in Washington to assume the presidency. Lee was presented to the president once at a military reception at the White House on March 12, the only time they would meet. Despite being skeptical of secession, Lee resigned his commission on April 20, 1861, a day after President Abraham Lincoln's proxies had offered Lee field command of the U.S. Army. Lee pledged his allegiance to the Confederacy as head of the Virginia state military and assumed the rank of major general, Confederate States of America (CSA), three days later. Lee would exchange letters with his wife, mourning the loss of "old Arlington" and urging her to leave. On May 13, Mary Custis vacated the family plantation at Arlington House to take up residence in Richmond, Virginia. Mary left unsure whether she or her heirs would ever see one of her childhood homes again.

At the onset of the Civil War, there were fewer than 100 surgeons in the U.S. Army and there was no training program for nurses. During the war twice as many soldiers would die of infection than battlefield wounds. The Civil War was a time of great medical innovation, which led to an enormous expansion of hospital capacity, the regularizing of embalming, and the first widespread use of women in paid care. Many nursing leaders emerged, including Clara Barton, Dorothea Dix and Sojourner Truth. However, the expansion of care would not be delivered to the escaped enslaved and would remain largely segregated. Outbreaks of whooping cough, measles and yellow fever would occur in the fog of war, even as authorities had prevention methods available. Fugitive enslaved were arriving in the federal city in tattered clothing, with innumerable diseases and close to starvation. They arrived in a city without a reliable clean water supply and exacerbated the already raging public health emergency.

The beautiful, healthful hills of Arlington Heights would be part of the answer to the public health emergency brought on by the Civil War. Once Virginia formally seceded from the Union, U.S. troops seized the Heights and began digging fortifications. The Custis Mansion became the headquarters for General McDowell, whose troops shared the grounds with former enslaved people escaping the public health emergency in the capital. A formal settlement, Freedman's Village, was established on May 15, 1863, by order of Secretary of War Stanton and an official recognition ceremony occurred on December 4. Freedman's Village would provide a roof for some thousand African Americans.

The village was designed as a model with a church, hospital and school surviving for thirty years before an eviction expanded the footprint of the cemetery in the 1890's, and the landscape came under more military control. Freedman's Village was celebrated because it existed on the very land forfeited to the Union because of the "treason" of its former occupant, General Robert E. Lee (CSA).[9] In 1864 a further transformation of the property occurred after President Lincoln asked General Montgomery C. Meigs (the Union Army's quartermaster) to find a solution to the burden of burying soldiers in the capital's cemeteries, which were now full.

On May 15, 1864, the first Union soldier, William Christman was buried. Christman, a poor Pennsylvanian laborer, enlisted as a private into Company G, 67th Pennsylvania Volunteer Infantry, to take advantage of the recruitment bonuses and help his family financially. Having served only a month, Christman became infected with the highly contagious rubella virus. He was laid to rest in a pauper's grave at Arlington, in what would become Section 27, because his family did not have the resources to have his remains sent home. A month later General Meigs ordered burials to be made in Mary Custis Lee's treasured rose garden to demonstrate the Union resolve in taking control of the land. The genesis of Arlington as a National Cemetery was born in the undoing of slavery as an economic system.

At the close of the Civil War, nearly 16,000 of the war's dead were buried on the property, including 4,000 whose name were "unknown." African-

American soldiers who served as part of the United States Colored Troops, some whom served with distinction in fighting for their nation, were segregated into a separate section of the cemetery for burial. Arlington would become two largely segregated cemeteries. The lower cemetery, where William Christman was interred, was located in the northeast of the property and would fill with the graves of 3,800 former enslaved who could no longer be accommodated in the cemeteries of Washington, D.C. This area, now known as Section 27, also filled with 1,500 U.S. Colored Troops (USCT). Later the racial segregation was extended when General Meigs allowed Confederate graves to be moved away from the predominantly African American graves.

The former enslaved, often referred to as contraband, buried in Section 27 were instrumental in the construction and maintenance of Washington's defenses during the Civil War and the building of the capital city after the war. As former slave and segregated cemeteries all across the South today are disappearing due to neglect, abandonment and development, Section 27 holds a unique and rich history of African American war dead. In life and death, the men of the United States Colored Troops faced discrimination, segregation and disrespect, even during the time of their passing and burial.

By May 1863, African Americans were being actively recruited into the Union Army. The USCT participated primarily in the Eastern Theater of the war and were in a number of regiments that marched into Richmond as Confederate President Jefferson Davis fled the burning city. More than 4,000 USCT were on hand at Appomattox when General Robert E. Lee surrendered on April 9, 1865, to General Grant. During the war, the USCT war dead would be sent north, and 1,800 of them would be interred at Arlington in the segregated northeast corner across the gravel road from the contraband cemetery. The roads that run through Section 27 are named for Union Generals Weitzel and Ord, who commanded the USCT.

At the conclusion of the Civil War, Arlington was a residential community for former fugitive slaves, and some 200 acres of the tract had been designated as the final resting place for the nation's heroes. The rest of the plantation was subdivided into 10-acre farms, Fort Whipple (now Fort Myer), and the Syphax property. Until 1883 the cemetery was known as the U.S. Military Cemetery and occupied less than 20 percent of the original Custis' land purchase.[10]

Arlington was the site of the first Decoration Day in 1868, a unique holiday that devoted time to remember the fallen. The day is now formalized as the national Memorial Day holiday. At the 1871 Arlington Decoration Day, Frederick Douglass declared, "We must never forget that the loyal soldiers who rest beneath this sod flung themselves between the nation and the nation's destroyers."[11] The Civil War decided the legal basis of slavery in the Union, but there was massive resistance in the South to beat back Reconstruction and the establishment of civil rights for all citizens. In 1874 Secretary of War Belknap communicated in an open letter that Arlington should welcome all "orderly persons who desire to decorate any of the graves in the enclosure," specifically to address the local concerns for Confederate graves.[12] The honorable resting place of the Union was becoming accessible to the enemies who had fought to maintain the system of slavery.

In the immediate aftermath of the Civil War the victorious Republican Party and Union had a paramount hold over the national capital and national narrative. In the latter part of the nineteenth century Washington, D.C., was filling its avenues, circles and pocket-triangle parks with statues of Union Admirals and Generals—Farragut, Grant, Logan, Scott—that still define the neighborhoods of the city. Prior to the war Washington was barely a city and had very few monuments. Jefferson (1847) and Jackson (1853) had statues near the White House, but General Washington's statue would not fill Washington Circle until February 1860, and the obelisk that now dominates the Mall was unfinished at the time of the conflict.[13] Arlington would rise in prominence as its fields were chosen by the Union officer class as their burial ground.

The Grand Army of the Republic (GAR) would become the most prized political endorsement sought by Republican candidates for high office and was a key ally in ensuring USCT soldiers were honored alongside the white regiments. In 1873 it took the urging of the GAR for Congress to appropriate $1 million to replace the military headboards with permanent marble stones in Section 27. The GAR initiated numerous gatherings, marched troops through the Capital, became a formidable lobbying organization, managed a successful publication[14] and was instrumental in securing benefits and pensions for Union servicemen that amounted to 40 percent of federal revenues by 1893.[15]

Numerous re-interments and organizational fluctuations would occur before Arlington took on its modern form, including changes in burial practices, selection criteria and interment of presidents. Widows, generals and citizens would lead marches from the District of Columbia to "bind the nation's wounds," to demonstrate the brotherhood of Union and Confederate warriors, and to mark the path to freedom. The National Cemetery would come to include a special burial section and the leaders of the Lost Cause eventually succeeded in putting a monument to the Confederacy at Arlington.

On December 4, 1882, the Supreme Court of the United States determined the federal government had taken the land from the Custis-Lee family without due process. Mary Custis Lee's son, George Washington Custis Lee, then turned around and sold the property (all 624 acres minus the Syphax claim) back to the government. Maps from this period show the area as the U.S. Military Reservation, when the burial function began to take precedence over other uses.

Freedman's Village has disappeared from the landscape of Arlington; it is recognized only by a storyboard in a park outside of the National Cemetery and a bridge that spans Columbia Pike, the road that marked the southern border of the original property. Years after George Washington Custis Lee took $125,000 from the federal government for his claim to Arlington, the village and its tenants were threatened with eviction. Many moved a few hundred yards south to create the African American neighborhood of Nauck, keeping their church congregations intact, and the final few left around 1900, after a monetary settlement with the federal government.

By 1900 the white resistance had recovered political power across the South and the era of Jim Crow segregation took hold. No African Americans were elected to Congress for the next 28 years, and none from former Confederate states until 1973. Arlington was not immune to these forces; a monument to the Confederacy was installed and ceremoniously unveiled by President Woodrow Wilson on the birthday of Jefferson Davis, June 4, 1914. Arlington would remain a segregated burial ground until President Harry Truman ordered the Army integrated.

The Grand Army of the Republic had to fight off efforts by the United Daughters of the Confederacy to claim ownership of the Arlington Mansion in the 1920s. The GAR was not able to overcome Congress, which designated that Arlington House be renamed as a "memorial" to Robert E. Lee. Congress, in the spirit of "ensuring the correct interpretation of its history,"[16] in 1955 and 1972 chose to lock this part of Arlington into a single framework, an updated version of the Lost Cause. There are many more "correct interpretations" that are on less-than-full display—the unknown contraband who walked to freedom, groundskeeper James Parks, the unknown soldiers whose records have been lost by administrative changes, Freedman's Village, Section 27—we have tried to bring these freedom stories further forward.

Our purpose here is to describe how the people and their uses of the land at Arlington Heights transformed it from renowned fishing ground for the native tribes along the Potowmack (Potomac River) to a slave plantation, to a military camp and tenant farm community, to the National Cemetery. These stories are instrumental to understanding the full meaning of this hallowed ground. The book illustrates how all of the varied uses of the Custis tract contribute to our understanding of the magnificent freedom Arlington Cemetery symbolizes. To accomplish this, we explore the genesis of the first burial tract, Section Twenty 27, and examine how the forgotten (and in most cases undocumented) labors of African Americans are at the center of the financing, constructing and reconstructing of this special American landscape.

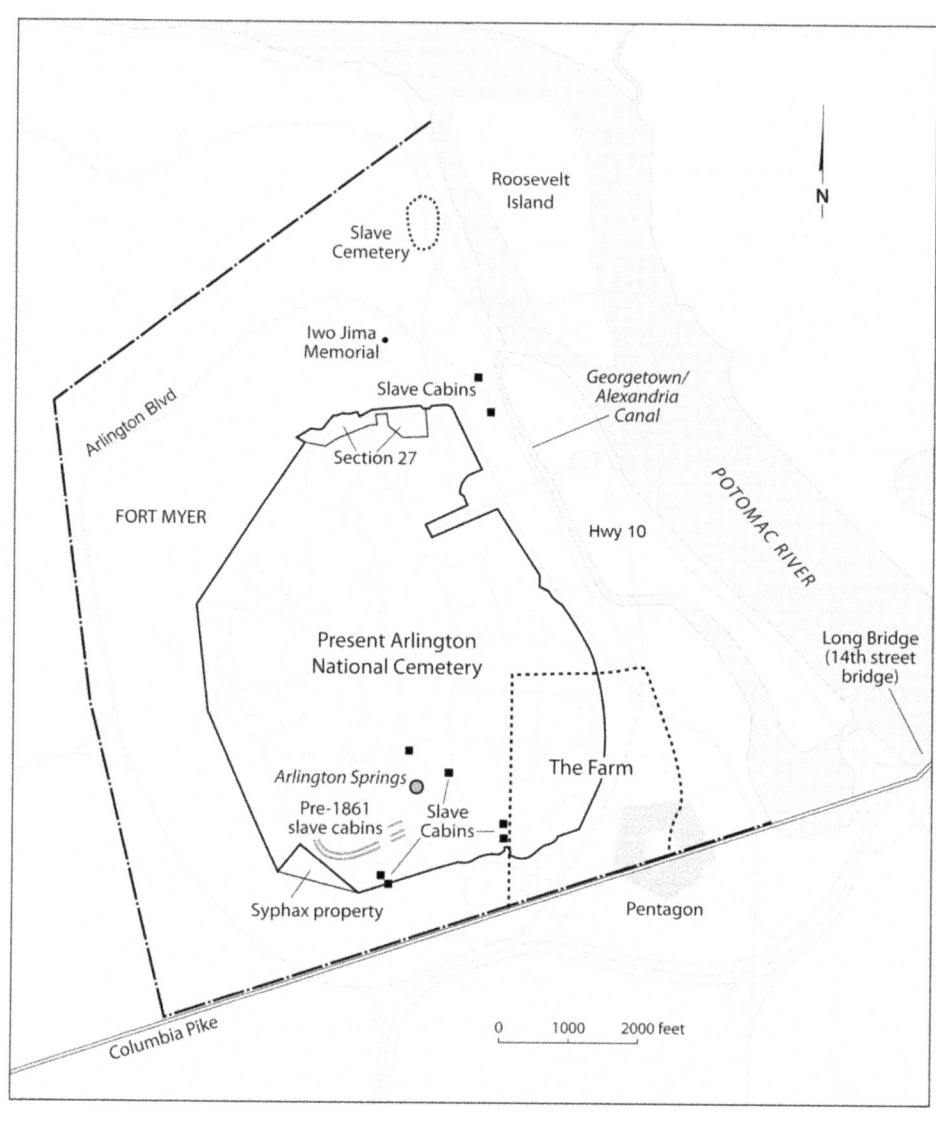

Present-day Arlington National Cemetery and environs, today encircled by Arlington Blvd. to the west and Highway 10 to the east, adjacent to the former Fort Myer U.S. Army post. Location of the tenant farm community is shown by the dotted line. The former route of Columbia Pike is shown, passing through what is today the Pentagon.

CHAPTER 1

The Men Who Shaped Arlington

IN THE LATE MUGGY SUMMER OF 1928, more than 70 years after the death of George Washington Parke Custis, the fascination with Arlington National Cemetery was only growing. The war dead from the Civil War, the Indian Wars, the Spanish-American War and now World War I were buried on this hallowed ground. The picturesque rolling hills were dotted with marble headstones representing the once vibrant lives of men who fought for the American Constitution and its founding principles. Section 27, the first of 60 sections to be laid, contained the bodies of the very first burials including military dead and those they fought for, over 3,800 fugitive enslaved men, women and children who risked their lives to become free Americans.

With each passing year, the mystique of Major George Washington Parke Custis only grew. The adopted son of our nation's first President, George Washington, and the natural-born grandson of his wife Martha Custis Washington, George Washington Parke Custis was considered the closest thing America had to royalty:

> As a child he met all of the great actors participating in the American Revolution, and when Washington became President, he was taken along with him to New York to live in the old Osgood House on Cherry Street and later to Philadelphia. In both places he frequently came in contact with the pioneers in the building of this great republic, as well as the most cultured and refined elements with which the First President continually surrounded himself.[1]

All the advantages afforded to him in his youth only piqued the citizenry's curiosity about him during his adulthood. The swirling rumors about Major Custis were as complex as they were interesting. In his declining years, his great wealth seemed to evaporate. It was said that at the time of his grandmother's marriage in 1759 to George Washington, whom he was named after, she brought to the marriage an estate valued at $100,000, including "30,000 pounds sterling, consisting of certificates of deposit on the Bank of England, enclosed in a small iron chest," which in later years was in the custody of Major Custis.[2] He was a strong proponent of the abolitionist Colonization Society, yet he enslaved almost 200 African Americans; many of the families originated from his grandmother's estate upon her passing. There was even a multi-racial family by the name of Syphax, purportedly descended from the Washingtons, who lived nearby on land reportedly given to them by Custis.

The Custis family dated back to the earliest days of the Virginia colony, and many wondered what Major Custis would think of having the northernmost portion of his beloved plantation now serving as the final resting place for approximately 1,500 United States Colored Troops, and 3,800 fugitive enslaved. These were the enslaved who fled his friends' and family's plantations, heading north to escape the institution of slavery, the same institution that helped Custis' friends and family build their wealth. Many also wondered if he would approve of the Confederate monument built 14 years prior, such a tall edifice as to dwarf any man standing next to it. The changes to the property were enormous, and many wondered what Major G.W.P. Custis would think of them and how much his family had lost during the Civil War.

Enoch Aquila Chase, a reporter from the *Washington Star*, wanted to know more about Major Custis. He initially believed that there was no one left alive who could answer questions about Custis or provide insight as to who the Major really was and what he thought about all the changes to his property. But the reporter soon learned that there was an old former slave of Mr. Custis still living up near the property, and the remarkable rumor was that he had known Mr. Custis personally.

After arrangements were made, Chase approached the modest home of Mr. James Parks. The elderly Parks was waiting for his guest and "sitting in a rickety old chair under a gnarled apple tree beside the chicken yard, as several grandchildren" were playing nearby.[3] As the journalist approached, he couldn't believe that this tall, dignified old man with a full head of gray hair and dressed in pressed overalls was once an enslaved man at Arlington Plantation. If James Parks was who many claimed he was, this would certainly be a prized interview. The only other man who saw more of a transformation of the former Arlington Plantation was Parks' original slaveholder, George Washington Park Custis, the adopted son of the first president of the United States, George Washington.

As any good journalist would do, Chase conducted his due-diligence before the interview. He went to see Mr. Robert Dye, superintendent at Arlington National Cemetery, and asked if he knew James Parks. Dye responded, "Why, that old fellow can tell you more about this place than anyone living.... He surely was a slave to George Washington Parke Custis.... I don't know how old he is, but he must be close to a hundred. When I came to

Arlington in 1893, he looked just as old as he does today."[4] For a reporter this bit of information was important, adding credibility to Mr. Parks as a source of information on the former plantation, its original owner and its transformation into the now revered national cemetery.

Parks and Chase met and exchanged pleasantries, but then entered the awkward period of assessing each other's trustworthiness. The journalist needed to determine if the information to be provided by Mr. Parks was credible, particularly because of his advanced years. Chase opened by asking, "I understand you were born a slave at Arlington many years ago?"[5]

As much as Chase wanted to appraise Mr. Parks' cognitive skills and reliability for an interesting story for his newspaper, old Mr. Parks needed to take stock of this young man who was going to ask him a whole bunch of questions about his life. After all he had seen in his lifetime, he really wasn't sure if he felt like talking about it, particularly to this young stranger. Parks, who was born about 1843, confirmed that he was born a slave and said nothing more. Although it was reported that Parks had what was referred to as "rheumy" eyes, the two men looked at each other—one waiting for an old man to ramble on, the other waiting for a young man to get to the point.

This was the first of a number of interviews that provided an unique, personalized history of the northern Virginia plantation, its original owner, and its transformation from the home of one of America's most important historical figures, George Washington Parke Custis—along with his ancestors, his descendants, and the enslaved people he owned—to the land we now know as Arlington National Cemetery.

"Uncle Jim" Parks, as he was known, helped to transform the plantation's stately grounds first into a Freedman's Village where he once lived, then to a pauper's cemetery for the poor and enslaved, and finally to a military cemetery for the Civil War dead. His family was steeped in the history of the Washington and Custis families as their enslaved people. According to Parks:

James Parks, born enslaved on the property, dug many of the first graves in Arlington National Cemetery and its Section 27 (courtesy National Park Service Arlington House).

> [He] ... was born on Arlington plantation ... his father, mother, brothers and sisters were all slaves of the Custis family; and his grandfather was for many years head cook at the mansion house, he lived to be more than a hundred years old. All his folks are buried in the slave burial grounds, down in the grove of trees near the river shore, on that part of Arlington reservation now under the jurisdiction of the Department of Agriculture as an experimental farm.[6]

As a young man, Parks initially lived with his parents and siblings in the slave quarters in the lower portion of the property. When Mr. Custis died, Parks, at 15 or 16 years old, was present at his burial. He recalled that he stood "with the other black folks apart from the white folks, when they laid Mr. Custis beneath his own trees not far from the big house that stands today overlooking the Potomac and the Capital City."[7] Parks had tremendous respect for his former slaveholder.

Throughout the years, many have questioned the circumstances under which the enslaved people at each of George Washington Parke Custis' properties were set free, and whether it was done by the last will and testament of G.W.P. Custis or by the stroke of the pen of President Abraham Lincoln signing the Emancipation Proclamation. As captured in the interview by the reporter Enoch Aquila Chase, there was no question in James Parks' mind as to when and how he obtained his freedom:

> Mr. Custis had provided in his will for the liberation of all his slaves within five years after his death. Such indeed is a fact, but as he died in October, 1857, and as President Lincoln's final Emancipation Proclamation was issued January 1, 1863, there might possibly have been some doubt as to which of these two documents was responsible for the freedom of the Arlington slaves. Nevertheless, Jim Parks has no doubt in his own mind; it was his old master's will and not the famous proclamation that set him free.[8]

The Civil War brought tremendous change to Arlington Heights and to its neighbor to the east, the city of Washington, D.C. When the war broke out, it dramatically changed the farmlands of northern Virginia, the site of many catastrophic battles. As Union and Confederate armies crisscrossed the landscape, they left devastation in their wake. White Virginians fled south behind the safety and protection of Confederate lines, while many enslaved Virginians fled north behind the safety of the Union Army where they were protected and could seek freedom.

At the beginning of the war, three enslaved men escaped and sought asylum at Fort Monroe. When their Confederate slaveholder came for his "property" pursuant to the 1850 Fugitive Slave Act, Union General Benjamin Butler refused to return them, arguing that they were now the "contraband of war." Once the United States Congress passed the Confiscation Act, signed by President Lincoln on August 6, 1861, Union troops were permitted to confiscate any property being used to support the independence of the Confederate states, including confiscating and freeing slaves who reached Union lines. The Confiscation Act set in motion the escape of thousands of enslaved fleeing North seeking asylum as contraband of war.

The once tranquil environment of Arlington Heights would be transformed forever more. James Parks would see Major Custis' daughter, Mary Custis Lee, heir to Arlington Plantation, flee from the only home she had ever known to the safety of Richmond. He would witness the Union Army move into the abandoned family mansion and convert the property into a military camp. Parks would be one of the many men who helped to build "the Civil War earthen ramparts of which stood on the present gate of Fort Myer." He remembered the cannons placed on the property and said that "he had helped to build Fort McPherson, which is still preserved within the walled cemetery enclosure."[9]

One can image that Parks witnessed much for a man of his advanced years, including the arrival of thousands of enslaved men, women and children fleeing their enslavers' plantations as they made their way to Washington. He likely heard from the other Arlington blacks who worked in Washington about the horrendous conditions that the contraband faced when they arrived in the nation's capital only to be placed into overcrowded contraband camps. In August 1862, after the second Battle of Bull Run, "some four hundred slaves arrived in the capital city over a two-day period."[10] The slight chance of freedom attracted more and more contraband to the city. The city of Washington was soon under siege due to a rapidly growing fugitive slave population, many of whom were malnourished, sickly and disease-prone. The weight of a quickly increasing population of unskilled impoverished people forced city and military leaders in Washington to seek relief somewhere—anywhere.

The serenity and "open air" of Arlington Heights across the river was selected as a viable location to redistribute the rising numbers of enslaved people coming to Washington. In June 1863, a federally funded Freedman's Village was constructed next to the property given to the mixed-race woman, Maria Syphax, by her father G.W.P. Custis; this property became a camp of 100 unit homes for the Civil War contraband. Several of the original Custis enslaved families, including James Parks and his young family, moved into one of the units at the village. As a resident of Freedman's Village and in order to make it self-sufficient, Parks was required, like all the other able-bodied persons, to be gainfully employed and worked on several projects on the property as it transitioned from a plantation to a multi-use site.

While the housing at Freedman's Village at Arlington benefited those fortunate enough to escape Washington, it did little to stem the overcrowding and escalating number of deaths in the contraband camps in the city. In the city, "the highest mortality rate, on average [was] ... five per day in the contraband camp in Washington."[11] The increasing numbers of contraband took a toll on the city, and the increasing deaths overwhelmed city services and available resources for burial. Once again the vacant land across the Potomac was deemed to be a viable alternative. General Montgomery Cunningham Meigs had just begun the burial of indigent Civil War dead in Section 27. General Meigs was the chief architect to transform the once idyllic plantation of G.W.P. Custis, and the home of his daughter and son-in-law, Confederate General Robert E. Lee, into the cemetery that we have all come to recognize.

Meigs was a protégé of General Lee in the early 1850s. He felt betrayed by his close friend and former mentor, after Lee denounced his commission with the United States Army and enlisted in the Army of the Confederate States. As far as Meigs was concerned, there was no greater treasonous act that to turn one's back on the United States government and profess one's loyalty to the secessionist government.[12] In retribution, Meigs was determined to contaminate the land and underground drinking wells of the Arlington Estate with bodies found dead in the area. The very first graves at Arlington National Cemetery's Section 27 were dug by James Parks and other men from Freedman's Village.

General Lee's treasonous act and the burial of countless dead men wearing the Union blue uniform set in motion the initial transformation of Arlington Heights from a plantation originally designed by G.W.P. Custis, to a cemetery for poor and indigent farm boys turned soldiers and for those who were once deemed chattel property turned escaped freedmen and women, into the most revered land in the United States, what we now know as Arlington National Cemetery.

Chapter 2

A City Under Siege

AFTER CONGRESS FREED THE ENSLAVED residing within the borders of Washington, D.C., in April 1862, slaves from both southern Maryland and northern Virginia made their way there for shelter and employment.[1] The montage of horse-, mule- and oxen-drawn wagons rolled slowly towards the city of Washington. The animals walked slowly because most were old and sickly, much like the overburdened human cargo they carried. On the more traveled roads, it was not unusual to see the carcass of a dead animal tossed to the side of the road. In the caravan of wagons huddled the infirm, the elderly and the near dead. They were now fugitives, having left in the dark of night, seeking freedom in response to President Abraham Lincoln's Emancipation Proclamation in the nation's capital city of Washington, D.C.

Despite their hunger pangs, the children walked alongside the adults, all of their clothes torn. The fabric was so worn that during the winter months it barely kept them warm. The weathered wagons were of all sizes and shapes, and most were of such deplorable condition that the slaveholders had long ago ordered they be dismantled for firewood to be used in the cold and drafty slave cabins. But the inhabitants of the once-discarded wagons had hoped that this day would come and kept the wagons out of sight and well hidden from their slaveholders and overseers, in the event an opportunity for escape would present itself.

They walked for days on end, evading the Confederate soldiers, and worse yet, the roaming slave catchers. They feared if caught, the men would be beaten and taken from their family to be sold further south, and the children would be stolen from the grasp of their mother's hands. The women were always in fear of what lay in store for them if separated from the group.

The fugitive enslaved were leaving the plantations that surrounded the city. They left Charles, Talbot, Worcester counties, the Eastern Shore and other locations in Maryland. They are reported to have come from James Island, Accomack, King George, and Lancaster County, Virginia, and Sussex County, Delaware.[2] Their search for freedom came in response to President Abraham

16　Section 27 and Freedman's Village in Arlington National Cemetery

Contraband Going North. "Wagon Fording the Rappahannock River" (courtesy the Gilder Lehrman Collection, New York, Reference Number: GLC 5111.01 #926).

Lincoln signing the District of Columbia Emancipation Act on April 16, 1862, freeing all the enslaved people in the nation's capital city.[3] The fugitive enslaved were willing to risk everything to get behind the protection of the Union lines and make it to Washington.

Many from these plantations would end up buried in Washington's cemeteries, some reinterred in Section 27 of Arlington National Cemetery. Details of their lives are meager: "From eight miles this side of Nottingham [Maryland]" and "arrived in Washington four or five months before death. Father was deceased" being some of the most detailed descriptions of those buried at Arlington National Cemetery.[4]

Being an enslaved man, woman or child was never easy, but once slave importation to the United States was prohibited in 1808, it became more difficult for the enslaved because it required even higher productivity. Falling tobacco prices and the depletion of the soil from continuous single crop (tobacco) planting meant plantation slavery was not as profitable in Virginia as it had been in previous years. More profits were embedded in the selling of the enslaved to other parts of the nation.

Slavery began on the shores of Point Comfort in the colony of Virginia 40 to 50 years after the arrival of the first documented Africans in 1619. The trans–Atlantic slave trade was the largest forced movement of people in world history; 12.5 million captives were taken from the continent of Africa to other continents around the world, including British North America and what became the United States of America.[5] Between 1619 and 1865, the United States economy benefited from innumerable hours of free slave labor as a direct correlation of the United States Middle Passage. Approximately 10 million out of the 12.5 million captured Africans reached a port in the Americas, and only 305,326 came to the United States directly from Africa. These enslaved would become the foundational component of the American economy, and were bought, sold, bred, traded, and used as capital and collateral for loans.[6]

The location and concentration of the enslaved changed as profits were realized from their labor. Cotton was king—the crop from which the greatest value could be derived—and the locus of production moved to the fertile lands along the Mississippi.[7] In 1790, the total number of enslaved in the United States exceeded 690,000; the greatest enslaving state was Virginia where there were more than 290,000. Virginia's slaveholders had more than North Carolina, South Carolina, Georgia, Kentucky and the Southwest territory combined. By 1810, the nation's enslaved population grew to more than 1,191,000, primarily from reproduction; to be born to a slave meant you were enslaved. In 1860, the census recorded 3,950,258 enslaved men, women and children.[8] By 1860 the economics of slavery and the country had changed, and Virginia was "devoted to raising cotton-pickers, not cotton," producing enslaved to be sold south or to collateralize loans.[9]

Between 1800 and 1860, the second largest involuntary movement of African—descended enslaved took place. Prior to the invention of Eli Whitney's cotton gin, cotton was handpicked; the gin separated the bolls and debris. With Whitney's cotton gin, the process of getting cotton to market became more profitable. As cotton became more profitable, slaveholders required more slaves to process more cotton for more profits. The locus of production moved away from Virginia and the eastern shore; and by 1850, 75 percent of the enslaved were engaged in the cotton industry in the Deep South. Slave plantations in Virginia had more enslaved people than they could economically afford and began to sell them, generating tremendous profits:

> Between 800,000 and 1 million slaves were moved westward: some were taken along as the owners moved toward new land opening up on what was then the frontier in Kentucky or Tennessee, and then further south to Mississippi and Alabama; others were sold by their owner or their owner's heirs to the great cotton and rice plantations in the deep South. Slaves were no longer needed in large numbers in Virginia, but to the west their price rose as the need for slave labor soared. Exporting slaves became industry—male slaves were marched in coffles of forty or fifty, handcuffed to each other in pairs, with a long chain through the handcuffs passing down the column to keep it together, closely guarded by mounted slave traders and followed by an equal number of female slaves and their children. Most of them were taken to Wheeling,

Virginia, the "busiest slave port" in the United States, and from there were transported by steamboat to New Orleans, Natchez, and Memphis.[10]

The power and influence of southern slaveholders expanded further south and west, and the new states of Alabama, Arkansas, and Mississippi were forged from the profits of slavery. Their political power was enhanced by counting the enslaved as two-thirds of a (non-voting) life in the enumeration of a state's population. The enslaved were the single largest asset in the economy, valued at $3.5 billion in 1860. The lower Mississippi valley, where cotton growing was the most extensive, had the largest number and concentration of millionaires (all plantation owners) in the nation. Estimates of the net value of the country's slaveholders range into the hundreds of billions by today's standards.[11]

The Constitution had given additional representation to the enslaving states. The enslaved had no franchise (let alone pathway to citizenship), but were counted in the census. They represented two-thirds of a person in this enumeration and increased the power of the slave interests in American politics. Eleven of the 15 presidents before Lincoln owned slaves; seven of those presidents were from Virginia and only Van Buren came from a northern state.

Throughout the early nineteenth century the politics of the United States turned on slavery, where it would or could expand, and who was responsible for enforcing the laws of enslavement. In 1808 Congress ended the practice of importing slaves. In 1820 it passed the Missouri Compromise, which set a limit at 36°30' (the location of Missouri's southern border) as the northern limit of future slave states. In 1836 southerners filibustered Michigan's entry into the Union until Arkansas be allowed to enter as a slave state. The 1854 Kansas-Nebraska Act and the 1857 Dred Scott decision would bring an end to these locational compromises and restrictions.[12]

The jettisoning of the compromises and restriction of the westward expansion of slavery reignited Abraham Lincoln's interest in politics, bringing him "roaring back" into the arena.[13] His core beliefs in the "self-made man" contradicted benefitting from free slave labor, and Lincoln's moral opposition to slavery was aroused. He would stay engaged and run for the newly formed Republican Party, one of four candidates in the presidential election of 1860. The election divided the national Democratic Party into a Northern (Stephens Douglas) and Southern (John Breckenridge, Buchanan's Vice President) faction, while John Bell ran as a Southern Whig.[14]

Lincoln never campaigned in the South and won the election with less than 40 percent of the popular vote, but he had an overwhelming Electoral College advantage, carrying 18 states, all above the Mason-Dixon Line. The southern political hegemony began to break down as their representatives stopped participating in Congress in early 1861, before Lincoln was sworn into office. The strong secessionist instincts of these representatives and opposition to Lincoln were as apparent as his commitment to the Union.[15] Virginia's Senator Robert Hunter was sure war was coming, and proposed that the Union "retrocede the jurisdiction of all forts, magazines, arsenals" to the States to meet his "doctrine of peaceable secession."[16]

The compromises inherent in the articles of the Union were now expressed in regional sectarian rhetoric in a partisan press. The regional outlooks were very divergent; newspapers across the divide described issues in strikingly different terms, ascribing harsh motives to the opposite side while claiming God for their own. The harshness of the rhetoric went uninterrupted from the election into fomenting a war and carried right on through the years of conflict.[17]

On the Union side, Confederate motives and tactics were questioned: "Jeff Davis and his Confederate traitors having, in pursuance of a deep-laid conspiracy, precipitated the Southern States into rebellion, are aiming to carry it through by the same system of secret plotting in the North...."[18] From the southern press, equally harsh words were thrown back about General Scott's defense of Washington, D.C., calling it "nonsense" and "an impudent attempt to create a military dictatorship":

> It is not easy to write seriously upon a subject so essentially ridiculous as the notion of "protecting Washington," and taking care of Mr. Lincoln in advance of his arrival.... As for Mr. Lincoln's inauguration, who cares a straw? Who proposes to meddle with him? Secession will not be stopped by his appearance here. And though he be crowned King on the Capitol steps, "who's afraid?"[19]

By the time President Lincoln was sworn into office, seven southern states had seceded from the Union. The nation's capital was being transformed from a small, southern, semi-rural city to the complex national headquarters for the Union Army's military logistics, medical facilities, and as a transportation hub. In 1850, the city had 51,687 inhabitants, by 1860 the population grew to 75,080, and in the 1870 Census it swelled to 131,700.[20]

When the state of Virginia seceded from the Union and joined the Confederate states, the city of Washington was surrounded by slave-holding states, vulnerable to a rebellious attack from the Confederate Army via the Potomac River. Maryland, where slavery was legal, provided no certain protection, even as it had not seceded (nor ever would as Lincoln's border-state strategy succeeded). The first casualty of the Civil War was Nicholas Biddle in the Battle of Baltimore. Biddle was a former slave and one of the Pennsylvania First Defenders who responded to Lincoln's call for a volunteer militia.[21] As they marched through Baltimore, they were attacked with bricks and bottles by citizens of the city. Generals Irvin McDowell and Benjamin Butler were leading efforts to move this militia to defend Fort Monroe, as the fort was key to defending the Chesapeake, the Potomac and the U.S. naval assets in Newport and Hampton, Virginia.

Under the command of Major General George B. McClellan, commander of the Department of the Potomac, an elaborate complex of defenses was built around Washington for its protection, including taking control of the nearby city of Alexandria, Virginia, and erecting fortresses in area highlands. As the city evolved into a military headquarters for the war effort, large numbers of soldiers moved into Washington and surrounding areas to man the forts. Maryland, a slave state filled with people hostile to the new president, would remain a focus throughout the war. Washington was the most heavily fortified city in the nation, with 68 forts, more than 1,100 guns and 32 new miles of military roads. Some of these fortifications, such as Fort Ward in Alexandria, are still visible and can be visited, but none of the fortifications at Arlington have survived.[22]

As soldiers from the northeast were brought to the war front, an elaborate military logistics system and a railway infrastructure were extended to transport the men and their weapons, food and support animals. The provisioning of the military attracted entrepreneurs and profiteers seeking contracts to build the new warehouses, barracks, slaughterhouses and supplies. Fatalities from the battlefields would be sent to Washington, but the city was not organized to accommodate the war dead.

The rapid transformation of the capital created a city under siege. The city had no reliable clean water source, so most people were getting their water from wells or streams, where sewage, dead animals and other waste products would mix. The siege was compounded as thousands of fugitive enslaved men, women and children poured into the city seeking refuge. Mary Todd Lincoln's servant and former slave Elizabeth Keckley observed:

> In the summer of 1862, freedmen began to flock into Washington from Maryland and Virginia. They came with a great hope in their hearts, and with all their worldly goods on their backs. Fresh from the bonds of slavery, fresh from the benighted regions of the plantation, they came to the Capital looking for liberty, and many of them not knowing it when they found it. Many good friends reached forth kind hands, but the North is not warm and impulsive.[23]

She added that the former enslaved did not all adapt well, not showing the requisite work ethic expected in a free labor environment and described them as having "extravagant wants."

The fugitive enslaved risked so much to achieve their freedom; many arrived too sick to survive the long ordeal, and many died on the streets of Washington. Life expectancy was significantly different: the 1850 census estimated African American average age at death was 21.4 years, whites 25.5 years.[24] Differences in health status on arrival were compounded by differences in opportunity and risks. These differences were a common story that resulted in the noticeably varying death rates by race for soldiers in the war. The survivors of the long journey were herded into concentrated camps, with little food and no clean water source to sustain them. The survivors, having shown amazing resilience making their journey, were now too sick or malnourished to survive the communicable diseases—such as whooping cough, measles, yellow and typhoid fever—that often swept through the camps with disastrous results. The residents of the city of Washington complained bitterly about the new conditions brought by the military, profiteers and fugitive enslaved. Their city services could not provide the ample water needed: "Great complaint is made in consequence of the muddy condition of the hydrant water at the present time. For washing purposes, either of the person or of clothing it is worse than useless. And for either cooking or drinking it is disgusting in its appearance...."[25]

The law enforcement system was inadequate to manage the new challenges to social order. The district had a large and growing freed black population, yet these people were still subject to a 10:00 p.m. curfew and morality laws. Freed blacks demanded that rights for the newly arriving escaped enslaved be respected by their local government.

Senator Wilson of Massachusetts, chair of the Senate committee on military affairs, reported that the jail was "such a scene of degradation and inhumanity I have never witnessed" and sought changes:

> I have been called upon repeatedly by colored persons of the most respectable character in this District, and asked if, in organizing the police of the District, we intended to oppress them as a class, and they said that they had never been so oppressed as during the last few months.... I find a list of the persons who have made these arrests, and that they are county constables.... I hope, sir, in the first instance, that these persons will be discharged as speedily as possible; and then that a law will be passed punishing anybody for arresting such persons, and that all the laws in the District of Columbia, oppressive or degrading to any portion of the people, will be wiped from the statute-book.[26]

The mayor of the city was arrested for failure to pledge allegiance to the Union cause, and the police were reorganized.[27] The newspapers would fill with notices of police actions, an explosion in crime, and the different treatment between the races:

> On Saturday night about 9 o'clock, Sergeant Downer with the detachment of the metropolitan police of the Second Ward, made a descent upon a house kept by Jas. Kelly.... A few of the colored prisoners were dismissed, there being no reason to hold them, and the remainder were fined $5.58 each; and the proprietor, for selling liquor to negroes, was fined $16.58.[28]

While other officers were dealing with a white horse-rustler:

> Yesterday Patrolmen Fenwick and Leach arrested a well-known youth named Bobby Garcia, whose deeds have attracted the especial attention of the police for some time

past. A few days ago he was arrested for stealing a saddle and bridle, but was let go on his promise to get the property to return to the owner—a promise he failed to redeem.[29]

Military control was exerted over the brothels and other entertainment indulgences of the soldiers. Gambling houses, taverns and other "places of public amusement were subject to the suppression of marauding and depredations and ... drunkenness" by the Provost Marshall under General Orders No. 69.[30]

The District of Columbia would become the national laboratory for the emancipation experiment, being the closest and easiest location for Congress to manage.[31] Washington could not sustain the growing and diverse population of newcomers straining its resources. The city was forced to expand its boundaries to meet the expanding needs of its populace. Cemeteries were started on the northern (Harmony) and southeastern edges (Giesboro) of the city to accommodate the bodies of the fugitive enslaved.[32] Food, wood and fuel were brought in from further and further away, and the military authorities looked across the river to the pristine land known as Arlington Heights as a possible solution to the city's challenges.

Chapter 3

Arlington Plantation

The land we now call Arlington National Cemetery was once owned by three of the most prominent families in the Commonwealth of Virginia: the Custis, Lee and Washington families. Each was able to trace their lineage to the earliest days of colonial Virginia, and all were part of the planter class. Their forefathers came from England and brought their concepts of feudal land ownership, class relations, and privileges flowing from inheritance with them. Virginia Governor William Berkeley (appointed by King Charles I) recruited these families from the ranks of the Royalists in England, which was divided by civil war in the 1640s. For a short time, England was a republic, after the Royalists lost the war and their leader Charles I was executed. The victorious English parliamentarians forced Berkeley to resign as governor in 1652. He retreated to Green Spring Plantation, his home just west of Williamsburg, Virginia, where he provided refuge for elite exiles during the time of the English Commonwealth.

There was a remarkable concentration of power among very few Virginia families, all of whom were interconnected and had similar, privileged outlooks. The restored monarch, Charles II, reappointed Berkeley as governor of Virginia in 1660. A slaveholder himself, Berkeley re-established the singular planter class control: "As early as 1660 every seat on the ruling Council of Virginia was held by members of five interrelated families, and as late as 1775 every council member was descended from one of the 1660 councilors."[1] The concept of blood and soil is hardwired into the Virginia social formation. The system of enslavement to serve the tobacco planting class was established by these families in their commercial relationships with their English forefathers and cousins. They developed and then embraced a code of behavior and self-perception as natural rulers with little regard for democratic or civil rights. Inter-marrying with astonishing regularity, they held land ownership paramount, to the exclusion of new settlers. Those new settlers would be pushed west to new encounters with the native populations and would largely develop economic systems less dependent on slavery.

The landownership model (and the plantation need for the enslaved) was pervasive and excluded newcomers and outsiders. When the last original colony, Georgia, was being established in 1733, it initially and explicitly rejected the Virginia model. The Oglethorpe Plan for Georgia laid out small plots farmed by free yeoman and barred slavery. The plan in Georgia would not survive the Spanish invasion or the development of a planter class that envied the riches being derived by enslavement across the border in South Carolina. However, the existence of other economic models for farming among non-slaveholding whites would cause continual tension among the states until the Civil War, as well as afterwards in the Reconstruction and Redemption battles over civil rights and citizenship.[2]

On May 15, 1750, in New Kent County, Virginia, the very wealthy 39-year-old Daniel Parke Custis married 18-year-old Martha Dandridge.[3] Daniel's wealth was derived from the family's extensive real property holdings as well as an inheritance of "nearly 300 enslaved blacks."[4] Daniel and Martha had four children, including a son, John Parke Custis. Martha Dandridge is reported in some accounts to have had a half-sister, Ann Dandridge Costin, born enslaved to a mother who was half–Cherokee and half-black. That line of "illegitimate" heirs reached back in all directions.[5]

On July 8, 1757, Martha was widowed and left to raise her two surviving small children. Her dower estate comprised nearly 18,000 acres of land, valued at about "£30,000, of which about £9,000 represented the value of his enslaved in addition to about £10,000 in British accounts."[6] Martha Custis' bereavement and her considerable slaved-based fortune were "well known in the upper echelon of Virginia society." She was attracting new suitors; among those suitors would be the first president of the new country:

> The time and place of George and Martha's first meeting has thoroughly been debated by historians: did Washington deliberately seek out the widow Custis for her fortune, or did he happen to cross paths with her and receive, unbidden, Cupid's arrow? ... The bare fact is that Washington's first mention of Martha occurs in his daily record of expenses: he noted how much he tipped her servants on a visit in March 1758.[7]

On January 6, 1759, George and Martha were wed in grand style at the Pamunkey River plantation. Martha's shoes from that wedding day are on display at Mount Vernon, an early example in our narrative of historical artifacts. In 1778, Martha's 24-year-old son, John Parke Custis, known as "Jacky," purchased 1,100 acres on the Potomac River that he named "Arlington."[8] While serving in the Revolutionary War at Yorktown as an aide-de-camp to his stepfather General Washington, Jacky contracted typhus, or what was referred to as "camp fever," characterized by headaches, high fever, delirium and severe muscle pains. Jacky is just the first in our tale to die from infection while in time of war. On November 5, 1781, the 27-year-old died, leaving a young widow and two small children, who were sent to be raised by their grandmother

The Washington Family, painting by Edward Savage, 1789. U.S. President George Washington and First Lady Martha Custis Washington seated with an enslaved man standing in the rear. The picture also includes Martha's grandchildren, George Washington Parke Custis and his sister Eleanor Parke Custis (National Gallery of Art).

Martha at Mount Vernon.[9] The eldest son, George Washington Parke Custis (G.W.P. Custis) became the adopted son of General George Washington and the "designated heir to the Arlington plantation from his biological father."[10] The adopted father-son relationship was a close one, as illustrated in the Edward Savage painting that depicts G.W.P. Custis standing beside his adoptive father, who is leaning on the young man's shoulder.

During the hot summer of 1787, General Washington served as a Virginia delegate to the Constitutional Convention in Philadelphia, Pennsylvania. He was selected to be president of the convention as a sign of respect from his fellow delegates and due to his command of the Army. Washington had become "first in peace" after having been "first in war," in the immortal words of his close friend, Henry "Light Horse" Lee (father of Robert E. Lee). Henry Lee coined this description of Washington in 1799 when he gave the main oration at the President's funeral.[11]

At the conclusion of the convention, and with the ratification of all the newly decreed thirteen states, the United States Constitution was enacted.

Receiving all of the Electoral College votes, on April 30, 1789, General George Washington was inaugurated as the first president of the United States. The constitution would be ratified with the fateful Article 1, Section 1, and Clause 3 on enumeration for representation:

> Representatives and direct Taxes shall be apportioned among the several States which may be included within this Union, according to their respective Numbers, which shall be determined by adding to the whole Number of free Persons, including those bound to Service for a Term of Years, and excluding Indians not taxed, *three fifths of all other Persons.*[12] [Italics added]

The nation would from its beginning ratify that all voters did not have equal representation. This was an infamous compromise where the southern states would be over-represented as a result of their continuing the enslavement of African Americans. Virginia was at the forefront as the largest holder and trader of enslaved. The economic, labor and moral consequences of enslavement would be returned to throughout the next decades and eventually be resolved in a Civil War.

In 1799, at the age of eighteen, G.W.P. Custis lost the only man he knew as a "father figure," when George Washington passed. Three years later, when his grandmother, Martha Washington passed away, G.W.P. Custis inherited his biological father's 1,100 acres of land along the Potomac River, as well as his grandmother's enslaved from Mount Vernon.

Arlington (Gloucestershire County), England, is the ancestral home of the Custis family. Arlington Row is a set of feudal cottages in Bibury, England, that gave the Arlington estates their name, and is today a major tourist destination. Arlington National Cemetery has inherited a similar role as a destination with more than four million visitors walking the grounds annually. In addition to the cemetery's critical national role providing the location and backdrop to our memorializing those who have fought for American ideals and freedom; Arlington, Virginia, is a tourist destination, attracting large numbers of visitors finding their authentic linkage to American history.

G.W.P. Custis took control of Arlington and began to make plans to build a large home on the land known as Arlington Heights. This portion of Arlington commanded a view of the new federal capital city, newly named after his beloved adoptive father, President George Washington. He cleared the forest to improve the view of the swamp across the river that was the frontage to the White House, whose first occupants arrived in 1800. Custis developed the Arlington Plantation to serve not only as his private residence but also as a display space for his collection of George Washington memorabilia. The Plantation was intended to stand as a monument to the "father of the nation":

> Custis engaged the English architect-builder George Hatfield to design and oversee construction of the edifice. Hatfield, who had supervised construction of the U.S. Capi-

tol building between 1795 and 1798, sketched plans for a sixty-foot-wide central block with a twenty-five-foot-deep portico supported by six front and two side columns with Doric capitals, flanked by forty-foot wings on each side. Construction began with the North Wing in 1802, followed by the South Wing in 1804, and then by the central block, which was completed in 1818. Loggias were added to the rear of the house between 1818 and 1820. The structure then stood much as it looks today....[13]

The heavily wooded landscape was cleared primarily by G.W.P. Custis' slaves, who also provided the labor to build the Greek revival style plantation, "inspired in part by the Temple of Hephaestus in Athens."[14] The structural materials "were from bricks made on the estate, and timbers from its forest."[15]

The estate was divided by the Alexandria Georgetown Turnpike, the main thoroughfare from the District to the main commercial and slave-trading center at the start of the nineteenth century. The plantation agriculture was on the western half of the turnpike, while the southeastern and lower half of the property closer to the Potomac River became the cabins for the enslaved, cultivated gardens and a slave cemetery. G.W.P. Custis would administer his plantation for many years from the original log cabin he erected among the enslaved people's cabins prior to the building of the mansion. Later this area, the Arlington Springs, would become a popular tourist picnic destination. In the 1850s special cruisers would cross the Potomac and 50 to 200 people would disembark to purchase refreshments on an eight-acre site neighboring the slave huts.[16] Contemporary accounts describe how the picnics were a regular part of the social calendar, often attended by G.W.P. Custis: "Among the incidents of a Sunday school picnic at Arlington recently, was the christening of a little boy by a minister, who pronounced the name of the child to be Clarence Arlington. G.W.P. Custis was present at the celebration of the ordinance."[17]

At the time of original purchase, Arlington House was located in Alexandria County and was a part of the new federal District of Columbia. Once the home was completed its view of the developing capital across the Potomac River was unrivaled, as it was in the Civil War and remains to this day. The National Park Service has been able to ensure the view remains part of the grandeur of the current Arlington, even as it was pinned in by the Pentagon to the south and the towers of Rosslyn to the north. Protecting, cultivating and managing Arlington's trees was a constant theme among visitors for years before and after the Civil War. When the Marquis de Lafayette visited in 1825 he reportedly called the view from the portico the "finest in the world" and said, "Cherish these forest trees around your mansion. Recollect, my dear, how much easier it is to cut a tree down than to make one grow."[18]

The panoramic view did not pay the bills for G.W.P. Custis, who kept a detailed account of his financial transactions, a trait he learned from his adoptive father. Throughout 1813, G.W.P. had tried to sell a tract of forested land. Failing in that task, he leased timber rights for 10-acre lots. Economic pressure included the disruption that came from the continuing wars in Europe, blockades by the British, and the end of the importation of slaves, all of which placed a financial strain on the family's coffers. Not for the last time Arlington debts were covered by selling the estate's prized assets: its "slaves, with G.W.P., pledging to find them local homes so as to not break up families by distance."[19]

During the War of 1812, the construction of the Custis family's permanent home was delayed as a result of needing building materials for the war effort. On August 24, 1814, from the high grounds of the property, residents of the Arlington Plantation, white and black, could see the embers flying high over the city in the aftermath of the British torching many of the government buildings in Washington, including the White House and the Capitol Building. As the city burned, the residents at Arlington could only watch in shock and horror as buildings that symbolized American democracy and victorious independence were burned.

The wrath of the British army upon the city ended with the fury of an "epic" summer storm, akin to a hurricane. The storm brought pouring rain and put out the fires, the thunder clapping louder than the military explosions. The intensity of the winds did additional damage, ripping the roof from the Patent Office and destroying homes.[20]

The completion of Arlington House was further delayed until 1818, when G.W.P. Custis moved into the estate with his wife and child, Mary Anna Randolph Custis. With the move, the Custis family brought with them family heirlooms and their enslaved property. Many of the enslaved descended from blended families originally kept at the Custis and Washington plantations along the James River.

Mount Vernon, the Washington family home, was an early destination for travelers seeking witness to history and the "father of the nation." G.W.P. carried forward this tradition as the curator of the artifacts from the Washington estate. G.W.P. would be noted, and sometimes mocked, for trying too hard to associate himself with President Washington.[21] As this was an era before the treasures of public officials were considered national property, G.W.P. also saw fit to give artifacts away. One of Martha Washington's "States" cup-and-saucer sets was given to the Marquis de Lafayette during his 1824-5 return to the United States.[22] As late as 1893 it was normal to hold auctions of relics belonging to the Washington family.[23]

The tents used by General Washington in the Revolutionary campaign were used at the Arlington sheep shearings, his annual agricultural fair of plowing contests and animal exhibitions. The tents provided shelter from the elements for the banquet and dance that followed. These hardy tents are still providing service today: the general's headquarters tent is now the "heart and soul"[24] of the Museum of the American Revolution in Philadelphia, which opened in April 2017. The museum has developed an extended audiovisual introduction to the tents that ends with a spectacular "reveal" of the erected tent, now encased in a temperature and light-managed glass case.

The tents were bought for $5,000 by the Reverend W. Herbert Burk from Mary Custis Lee, daughter of Robert E. Lee, on behalf of the Valley Forge Museum of American History but had been out of public display for decades following Burk's death in 1933. Mary Custis Lee's sale to Burk was part of her fundraising effort for a Confederate widow's home.

G.W.P. Custis had a wide variety of interests and was frequently a leading voice and pillar in the community. He joined and led many civic organizations, including the Masons, who were lent the Washington tents for a display. In the early years of the republic, he was devoted to ensuring American independence, particularly its agriculture. He innovated farming practices at Arlington and advocated for "homespun" wool outfits and a domestic industry to avoid dependence on foreign (British) cotton clothing.[25] He introduced and bred his own Arlington improved sheep as a local source of wool for the clothing of the local militia unit he led in the War of 1812.[26]

G.W.P. Custis would also be an early advocate for the American Colonization Society, which supported the relocation of the enslaved to Africa. His wife's cousin was the first recruiter hired for the organization.[27] One biographer relates the state of agriculture in the 1810s forced G.W.P. Custis to assume this position regarding the disposition of his enslaved, while another notes that his "opposition to the institutions [of slavery] in theory" did not prevent him from selling the enslaved when he "became strapped for money."[28] His support for the American Colonization Society perpetuated the institution and yet proposed an eventual racial separation:

> In fact, so serious was his plight, he even had to sell some of his slaves. He abhorred selling slaves, and in no case would allow them to be taken out of the neighborhood. Had he been able to sell the Washington Mill, the black miller and an assistant would have been included in the sale; and when he did sell a slave and her two children, early in 1814, it was to a family in Alexandria. At a time when slavery was becoming ever more unprofitable in his section, the problem of what to do with the slaves for whom he had no use was to his way of thinking insoluble, for when freed, they usually drifted into the slums of Washington or some other Northern city.[29]

The Colonization Society would support the transport of more than 15,000 freed blacks to the African west coast. Their efforts would lead to the establishment of the nation of Liberia.

In 1831, G.W.P.'s daughter, Mary Custis, married her third cousin, U.S. Army officer Robert E. Lee, as two more prominent Virginians wed each other. Lee was born in 1807, at the Stratford Hall, a plantation passed down through family lines and marriages. The prestige of Stratford and its six generations of family history and legacy were diminished by Lee's father, Henry Lee III and his half-brother Henry Lee IV. At the time of their marriage, Lee had no inherited wealth of land or slaves. Although his family name would suggest social status and privilege, his family's impoverished status would follow him throughout his life. His lack of assets even after his death would have a crucial role in the status of his wife's Arlington Plantation and the status of his children's inheritance.

During the American Revolution, while in service to the Continental Army, Robert E. Lee's father, Henry Lee III, brought dishonor to the family. They suffered financially due to his poor management of the family estate and capital assets, as well as from Lee III's land speculation. He would serve more than a year in a debtors' prison and was later left disabled because of a riot in Baltimore while defending the editor of a newspaper opposed to the 1812 War.

Henry Lee III was nicknamed "Light Horse Harry," a tribute to his equestrian abilities in the Revolutionary War, where he commanded the cavalry of the Continental Army under a longstanding family friend, General George Washington. After retiring from military service in 1791, he served one term as the ninth governor of Virginia. In 1794, while still serving as Governor, Lee was commanded by General George Washington to suppress the Whiskey Rebellion, a revolt caused by the new federal tax on the whiskey made by Westerners.[30] After suppressing the rebellion, and a brief hiatus as a gentlemen farmer, Henry Lee III was elected by the Virginia House of Burgesses to represent Virginia's 19th district in the U.S. House of Representatives from 1799–1801.

While governor, Henry Lee's first wife and first cousin, Matilda Lee, died, leaving her inheritance to her children and leaving Stratford Hall Plantation to her oldest son, Henry Lee IV (known as Black Horse Harry). The 37-year-old widower and governor of Virginia, Henry Lee, then married his second wife, 20-year-old Ann Carter, the daughter of Charles Carter, one of the wealthiest men in the Tidewater area of Virginia. The wedding took place at the Carter plantation in 1793, and for many in attendance it "was the nearest to a royal occasion that could be provided in the nation newly formed from the thirteen colonies."[31]

The Virginia families liked to invoke their racial and monarchal connections to their English ancestors, even maintaining Tory sympathies. Amid the pomp and circumstance, the bride's family, steeped in tradition with strong ties to England, did not embrace the American Revolution, unlike the Lee family. Beyond differences in politics, Charles Carter was apprehensive of his new son-in-law and his financial acumen and prospects.

Henry Lee III and his wife Ann continued to live at his first wife's Stratford Hall Plantation, where they had five children, including their fourth child, Robert E. Lee. Upon leaving Congress, "Light Horse Harry" began to speculate in real estate with disastrous results. When Robert E. Lee was only two years old, disaster fell upon the family. In April 1809, Henry Lee "was imprisoned in the jail of the county he had represented (by birth right) in the state assembly. Being jailed for debts was not as disgraceful as criminal imprisonment [but] … it was undeniably a blot on the reputation" of the family.[32] The events that led up to Henry Lee's imprisonment left the family without wealth and prestige and had a profound impact on Robert E. Lee, his station in life, and subsequent decisions he would make relative to his immediate family years later during the Civil War.

When Henry Lee's oldest son, Henry Lee IV "Black Horse Harry," reached the age of maturity, he took control of the Stratford Hall Plantation he inherited from his mother, forcing his father, step-mother and his half-siblings out of the family home. The impoverished Henry Lee III left behind the gentile life of the planter society and moved his family to a town home in the city of Alexandria, Virginia, where Robert lived until he went to West Point at the age of eighteen.

Robert E. Lee and his bride were from the Virginia elite, and their wedding was an important social occasion, described in florid terms:

> The wedding of Mary Anna Randolph Custis and Robert E. Lee was the grandest event ever at Arlington House. June 30, 1831, was chosen as the date, and the house was decorated to reflect the magnificence of the occasion. Flowers from Mrs. Custis' famed gardens bedecked the halls. Friends and neighbors from all over Virginia and the Potomac Valley made their way up the hill to Arlington House. It was a grand day for the Custises and the Lees. Even the steady rain that fell in the afternoon could not dampen the spirits of those who had gathered to witness the ceremony. It was in this idyllic setting that Robert E. Lee realized he had married not only Mary Anna Custis, but Arlington House as well. And although his military career would lead them away from Arlington, it was on this estate that his life would be rooted for the next 30 years.[33]

In 1846 the Arlington Plantation was a part of the land the government retroceded to Virginia from the original 100 square miles of the Federal City. Slavery was, as ever, the abiding reason for the political shift. Retrocession would enable Alexandria to remain a major slave-trading port in anticipation that the practice would be stopped by the federal authorities in the city of Washington. The slave markets were not compatible with the avowed freedoms represented in and by the capital city and were not welcomed by an increasingly large freed black community across the river. During his life, G.W.P. Custis enjoyed the surroundings of his plantation. Along with his daughter, son-in-law Robert E. Lee, and his grandchildren, he served as the host to many grand parties and social activities on the plantation in the custom and style of southern Virginia gentry. According to the firsthand account of former slave James Parks, who grew up on the Arlington Plantation, Major Custis, as he referred to him, built "dancing pavilions and kitchens" for summertime picnickers—who paid to visit his property in the summer—in his grove down by the riverfront. According to Parks, Major Custis:

> Hired musicians to play for them; … on special occasions Major Custis would come down from the mansion house on the hill to watch the children play and to see if everyone was having a good time. All were welcome, except on Sunday, and the only restriction was that intoxicating liquor should not be brought on the place. At times … Custis would appear among the picnic merrymakers with his own fiddle tucked under his arm and would take his place among the musicians and himself help make music for the dancers.[34]

On October 10, 1857, when George Washington Parke Custis, the stepgrandson and adopted son of President George Washington, passed away, his entire estate went to his daughter, Mary Custis Lee, and her heirs. The *Port Tobacco Times* printed his obituary on Monday, October 12, 1857, including this excerpt:

> The venerable Mr. Custis, of Arlington, died at his residence in Alexandria county, Va., on Saturday last. The whole country knew him, and his patriotism will long be remembered. Closely allied to the Washington family, fond of calling himself the child of Mount Vernon, he was never so much in his element as when he was talking or writing of the great chief and the men and times of the revolution. He had been fondled on the knee of the Father of his Country, and received from him the kindness of a parent. He repaid that care and affection with filial devotion, and to the day of his death all the recollections of his life centred around or radiated from the time he was one of Washington's family. He lived to a good old age (seventy-seven years,) retaining his mental faculties to the last.[35]

One local paper, *The Evening Star*, while paying its respects, also chose to focus on future access to and disposition of Arlington Springs in announcing G.W.P.'s death. The paper notes his importance to the popular picnic spot:

> The news of the death of the venerable G.W.P. Custis, of Arlington, was received on Saturday with very general regret by our citizens, especially by those who have heretofore been in the habit of visiting Arlington Springs for the purpose of seeking recreation and amusement. Notwithstanding, it may be possible, from what we have gathered of Mr. Custis' intentions in relation to the property, he may have provided in his will, if he left one, for the citizens of the three cities using it as heretofore. Still the absence of the venerable former owner will tend in no small degree to lessen the pleasures of those who may hereafter visit this very popular place.[36]

In providing insights as to the man, his accomplishments and how others viewed him, a rival newspaper, the *Weekly National Intelligencer*, combined its focus on the pleasant picnic grounds with a positive benediction on his stewardship:

> Thousands from this country and from foreign lands who have visited Arlington to commune with our departed friend, and look upon the touching memorials there treasured

up with care of him who was first in the hearts of his countrymen, will not forget the charm thrown over all by the ease, grace, interest, and vivacity of the manners and conversation of him whose voice alas! is silent now. The multitudes of our fellow-citizens accustomed, in the heat of summer, to resort to the shades of Arlington will hereafter miss that old man eloquent, who ever extended to them a warm-hearted welcome and became partaker of their joy.[37]

According to James Parks, when G.W.P. Custis passed away, "[Parks] was a young man of 15 or 16 years of age at the time. He was present at the burial ... standing with the other black folks, when they laid Mr. Custis beneath his own trees not far from the great house, that stands today overlooking the Potomac and the Capital City."[38]

The *Evening Star*, moving on from its concern about picnic privileges, described how the water, long bridge, and aqueduct routes to Arlington were "fully occupied" with carriages carrying "all classes."[39] The *Weekly National Intelligencer* newspaper noted that "the least affecting incident of the day is the sorrow evinced by the colored people, who, at the expense of a long and painful walk, have started in numbers to be present at the funeral of one who was to them always the kindest of friends."[40] This is consistent with the first-hand account of James Parks; he and other Custis family slaves had respect for Major Custis. However, the death of any slaveholder created turmoil within the slave community. As chattel property, would they be treated only as simple property? Would they be set free, as some had come to understand, or would they be sold to pay off his debts or to enrich his family members?

Having executed his will in 1855, G.W.P.'s enslaved were well aware of the provisions that his "daughter was to have a life inheritance" and upon "her death, the property was to go to his oldest grandson, George Washington Custis Lee."[41] Upon his death, the executor of his estate, Robert E. Lee, listed as part of his father-in-law's personal property at Arlington House: "10 mules, 38 cattle, 44 sheep and 50 hogs; 5 double ploughs, 6 single ploughs, 1 wagon, 1 tumbie cart, 2 ox carts; and 196 enslaved to be emancipated within five years of his death."[42]

Nine months later, during a September 11, 1858, inventory of the enslaved at Arlington House, only sixty-three enslaved appear on the ledger, indicating that the net difference of 133 had been sold or hired out by his executor, Robert E. Lee, to pay off debts that the estate had at the time of G.W.P.'s death.[43] Upon visiting the property following Union occupation in 1861, John Nicolay, President Lincoln's secretary, described it as a faded glory, consistent with the state of Virginia and its moral standing:

> The house looks quite old ... evidently in its days it was a grand affair; and its arrangement, furniture, pictures, &c. at once carry one back to the good old "first family" days of Virginia before her social decay ... had bred political and moral corruption. In those days plantation glory atoned somewhat for their assumptions of family pride.[44]

Lee was responsible for the disposition of all of the plantation estates, including the "White House" on the Pamunkey River, where George and Martha Washington were married, and Romancoke. By the time Union troops came through the White House plantation during the Peninsula Campaign of 1862, conditions at Romancoke were dire, and, as observed by approaching Union troops, "the enslaved community's living conditions on the Lee plantation were disgusting." According to a Union soldier, "the more I see of slavery, the more I think it should be abolished." Another described the "long rows of 'quarters'" containing "log huts with no windows ... holes in the walls, and only a mud floor." A New York officer was even blunter: "Their quarters look like a village of pigsties."[45]

Lee, at the end of the line of enslavers, spent considerable time ensuring that he projected a benevolent image as an enslaver. On December 27, 1856, he wrote to Mary, his wife, "There are few I believe, but what will acknowledge, that slavery as an institution is a moral & political evil in any Country." Nonetheless, Lee never spoke out against slavery, nor spurned the wealth and opportunity it afforded him.[46] In 1858 he exchanged a series of letters with the *New York Times* describing his commitment to the manumission of the enslaved of Arlington.

On October 19, 1859, Robert E. Lee was issued an insurance policy on Arlington House to be insured for $5,000 based on the home's $20,000 valuation. He also insured the barn for $800 based on a $1,200 valuation with the Hartford Fire Insurance Company of Hartford, Connecticut. The property was described as a:

> Dwelling of Brick, main building, two stories high, and wings one story. In Alexandria County, Virginia, built about the year 1820. All occupied by the applicant. The Barn is of brick, one story high, with a stone basement. The main building of the Mansion House is covered with slate and the wings with gravel. The Barn is covered with gravel. The gutters are metal.[47]

For the "Five Thousand, Eight Hundred dollars on the property specified," Lee paid forty cents a year for the insurance policy.[48] Robert E. Lee would soon have other issues to engage in deciding the legal status of all enslaved persons in the nation, not just those at Arlington. Lee would use the five years he had to pay down G.W.P. Custis' accumulated debt by making as "much money from each slave's labors as possible." He petitioned the court to tie the enslaved individuals' terms of subjugation to the repayment of the debt and "no enslaved family at Arlington was spared a temporary or permanent separation."[49]

Chapter 4

Enslavement at Arlington

MANY OF THE ENSLAVED who resided at Arlington had descended from enslaved families who had been with the Custis and Washington families for generations. Some of the freed blacks living nearby at Mount Vernon or Arlington House were also descendants of the Custis' line, notably the Syphax family. The Custis, Lee and Washington families were prominent and influential leaders in their respective communities and helped define the system of slavery across generations in Virginia and, based on Virginia's importance in establishing legal rulings, by extension all across the South. A variety of historical records have described numerous and changing opinions about slavery and how different family members treated their enslaved.

At the time of G.W.P. Custis' death in October 1857, slavery and the control of its expansion into new territories was central to national politics. Six months before, on March 6, 1857, the Supreme Court passed down the Dred Scott decision, holding that any "negro, whose ancestors were imported into [the United States], and sold as slaves" had no standing before the federal courts. The ruling further reduced black futures, and ensured they were seen as property to be disposed of by their enslavers. Attitudes in the North supporting abolition hardened, and the split in the nation was more apparent in all political discourse. Rhetoric became harsher and even more personal. The already well-rehearsed contradictions of a country that had revoked monarchy and was founded on liberty and dedicated to the pursuit of happiness, yet was generating massive new wealth through violent denial of individual freedom were on open display.

The Dred Scott decision highlighted a core difference in the 1858 Senate race in Illinois, won by the sitting Senator Stephen A. Douglas over former Congressman and attorney Abraham Lincoln. The rhetoric was venomous across the dividing lines in the nation, a warm-up to the harsh judgments made in the press throughout the nation's Civil War. There was a bigger and deeper divide that ultimately would be a challenge to reconcile. The same unresolved challenges regarding race and the segregation of the races were carried forward during the period of Reconstruction after the Civil War, during the Jim Crow era, and the twentieth-century civil rights movement.[1]

The former congressman (1847–49) Abraham Lincoln was drawn back into politics by the passing of the Kansas-Nebraska Act in 1854, which ended the Missouri Compromise. Stephen Douglas played an instrumental managerial role in the Senate's passage of "Kansas-Nebraska." Lincoln was opposed to expanding slavery to any other states to the west, the degradation of the Union, and the ownership of people. Harold Holzer quotes from an October 16, 1855, speech Lincoln gives in Peoria:

> I hate [slavery's westward expansion] because of the monstrous injustice of slavery itself. I hate it because it deprives our republican example of its just influence in the world—enables the enemies of free institutions, with plausibility, to taunt us as hypocrites—causes the real friends of freedom to doubt our sincerity, and especially because it forces so many really good men amongst ourselves into an open war with the very fundamental principles of civil liberty—criticizing the Declaration of Independence, and insisting that there is no right principle of action but self-interest.[2]

The southern press saw the Dred Scott decision as a return to the rule of law that needed to be defended. The anti-abolitionist newspaper the *Southern Monitor* stated that it:

> ... will defend the decision and opinions of the Supreme Court of the United States in the Dred Scott case; and it will advocate the Constitution and the Union on the terms and stipulations agreed by our forefathers.... Its mission will be to combat Black Republicanism, and to repel assaults on Southern rights and Southern institutions.[3]

Many of the arguments in the northern press were based on the legality of a ruling that overturned established states' rights to extend the franchise and benefits of citizenship to African Americans in the North. The decision was the last straw for abolitionists who refused to allow themselves and their states to be complicit in enslaving people as property.

The press was partisan and had its own economic interest in division, scandal and ritual repetition. The northern press was full of coverage of the Dred Scott decision describing the burden being placed on the states to administer the system of slavery they had outlawed. The front page of the *Richmond Enquirer* would have both advertisements for a land sale that would include "most of the negroes," and an editorial directed at abolitionists on their misinterpretation of the decision:

> The Dred Scott decision has been so often held up to the ridicule and scorn and execration of those pious people, that it has ceased to command more than an occasional curse even from the most patriotic and philanthropic of their public journals. Uncle Tom's Cabin has been read by parents and rehearsed to the children, until its calumnies have become common-place, and its horrors to tedious to talk about.[4]

Lincoln, in a speech in the Illinois House of Representatives, lamented that the prospect of freedom for the enslaved had "never appeared so hopeless as in the last three or four years." In opposing the Dred Scott decision he attacked his electoral opponent Stephen Douglas:

> There is a natural disgust in the minds of nearly all white people, to the idea of an indiscriminate amalgamation of the white and black races; and Judge Douglas evidently is basing his chief hope upon the chances of being able to appropriate the benefit of this disgust to himself. If he can, by much drumming and repeating, fasten the odium of that idea upon his adversaries, he thinks he can struggle through the storm. He therefore clings to this hope, as a drowning man to the last plank. He makes an occasion for lugging it in from the opposition to the Dred Scott decision. He [Douglas] finds Republicans insisting that the Declaration of Independence includes ALL men, black as well as white; and forthwith he boldly denies that it includes negroes at all, and proceeds to argue gravely that all who contend it does, do so only because they want to vote, and eat, and sleep, and marry with negroes! He will have it that they cannot be consistent else. Now I protest against that counterfeit logic which concludes that, because I do not want a black woman for a *slave* I must necessarily want her for a *wife*. I need not have her for either; I can just leave her alone. In some respects she is certainly not my equal; but in her natural right to eat the bread she earns with her own hands, without asking leave of any one, she is my equal, and the equal of all others.[5]

The words are important, as are the actions, and the subsequent interpretations of the North and South. Yet without a doubt, at the dawn of the Civil War, the Lees, the Custises and their extended family members were direct beneficiaries of the system of buying and selling enslaved humans. Whatever their views, the institution of slavery was as integral as ever to the family's wealth and financial survival. The price of slaves in 1860 was at its apex, particularly in northern Virginia, and the value of an able-bodied enslaved man who was able to work for 20–30 years translates to $150,000 in 2016 currency.[6] In addition, the March 6 Supreme Court decision had a direct impact on the estate of the late G.W.P. Custis and how his executor, Robert E. Lee, handled the affairs of the estate.

The transfer of inherited wealth in the South was grounded in the institution of treating the enslaved as chattel property and commercial assets. The institution of slavery provided tremendous wealth to slave owners who were able to borrow money against their enslaved and use them as collateral in the purchase of land. The wealth of the Custis family was based on land throughout Virginia, but it was supported, managed and maintained by the slavery system. With each generation the family increased their ownership of land and the number of enslaved that they owned as new African Americans were born to enslaved parents. The close-knit marital relations of the planter elite meant this wealth moved through to the next generations.

The increase of enslaved on the Custis family plantations was not limited to just the purchase of additional enslaved, it was also a result of Custis men sexually coercing and assaulting the enslaved women. According to the family historian, Elizabeth Brown Pryor, over the years and generations the "Custis family had a reputation for interracial dalliances, and many of their mulatto servants had clearly descended from illicit ties" with the enslaved on the various plantations.[7]

The family patriarch John Custis served on the Virginia Colony's Governor's Council from 1727 for more than twenty years until he was stricken with ill health. He married Frances Parke, one of the wealthiest heiresses in British North America; Frances died before John Custis. Many years after his wife's death, in a highly unusual move for a man of his position, Custis took certain actions acknowledging an interracial son:

> In 1744 John Custis took the extraordinary step of petitioning the governor and the council, where he sat himself, to set a slave child free. The petition stated the boy was "Christened John but commonly called Jack, born of the body of his Negro wench, Alice." Though Jack was only about five years old, Custis had already bestowed property on him; now he wished that the boy be made free and specified that all of Jack's descendants would be free people. The implication of this petition would have been quite clear to Custis' co-councilors; he did not ruffle the serenity of the council chamber with a bald statement that the little John was his own son.[8]

During his life, John Custis used his affection for his multi-racial son "Jackie" over his "legitimate" son and heir apparent Daniel Custis. Frustrated by his son's determination to marry Martha Dandridge, John Curtis threatened Daniel with disinheritance in 1748. He swore that he would leave his estate to Jack, his mixed-race child by "young Alice," one of his enslaved women. This little boy, who was about 10 years old and recently freed, was one of the very few people the irascible old man cared about. To his father's surprise Daniel stood firm in his desire to marry Martha.

Upon the death of John Custis in 1749, his mixed-race child went to live with his half-brother Daniel and his new bride Martha Dandridge. But before Jack Custis could benefit from his substantial inheritance, he died of an infectious disease, likely meningococcal meningitis, at just sixteen years old in 1751.[9] Six years later, his half-brother and guardian, Daniel Custis also passed away. By fate of life and death, the land inherited and known as Arlington might have passed to a freed mulatto; certainly John Custis' petition could have intended that. Instead, through the second marriage of the widowed Martha Custis, it eventually came into the control of the first President of the United States, George Washington.

The Custis family was the personification of Virginia's slave-holding aristocracy. These familial relationships endured from one generation to another and became part of the story and history of Arlington House and of those who would eventually be buried on the grounds of the plantation. Slave children were often named after their slave owners and the owners' family members. As young adults, these enslaved toiled in the fields, worked in the house, and went to market, but some became embroiled in interracial relationships.

4. *Enslavement at Arlington*

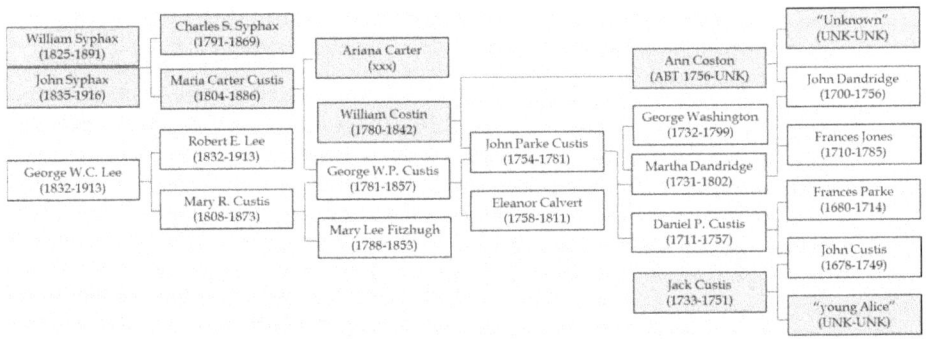

Figure 1. Enslaved Within the Family

The familial relationships between slaveholders and their mixed-race children were complicated; some family members were acknowledged, others ignored. Martha Dandridge Custis Washington's half-sister, Ann Coston (Dandridge), was kept as an enslaved woman at Mount Vernon and produced a child by her nephew—Martha's son John Parke Custis.[10] Continuing the family's sexual relations across racial lines, Martha Custis Washington's grandson, George Washington Parke Custis, also had a child by an enslaved woman, Ariana Carter. The daughter of this union, Maria Carter, married Carter Syphax, the son of a free black man and an enslaved woman. Highly respected and liked by G.W.P. Custis, Syphax oversaw the dining room in the main house and held a position of authority among the Arlington House enslaved.[11]

In 1826, Maria Carter Syphax was acknowledged by her white father, G.W.P. Custis, when he freed her, along with her 10 children. Custis then provided Maria and her family with 17 acres of land on his Arlington Plantation. According to the Alexandria County, Virginia, *Free Negro Registers*: Registration Number 416 (circa) August 3, 1847, Maria Syphax "…about 35 years old, 5 feet 4½ inches tall, with no visible marks … was born free … as evidenced by William Stabler."[12]

According to Arlington Cemetery historian, Robert Poole:

> Maria Syphax was, in the terms of those times, a mulatto with strong Caucasian features; unlike most other slaves, she had been raised in the Custis mansion, playing with Mary Custis (later Mrs. Robert E. Lee); she had been singled out for preferential treatment by George Washington Custis, who freed her and her children three decades before arranging to free his other slaves. He had given property to no other slaves, and for years had allowed the Syphax family to use their corner of Arlington as if they owned it. Within the Syphax clan, it was understood that Maria had been not only a slave of George Washington Custis—she was also his daughter, from a union with a household servant of Martha Washington's named Airrianna Carter.[13]

G.W.P. Custis gave Maria Syphax seventeen acres of land at the far western end of his plantation. The original plot line is still visible today, as a cutout by the pronounced turn the wall takes at the current entrance to Fort Myer. Although the land was given to her by G.W.P., it was never recorded with a land deed and was not confirmed until after the war and by an act of the United States Congress in 1866.[14]

The living conditions of Maria Syphax and her family differed dramatically from those of the other enslaved on the plantation, reflecting her elevated status within the enslaved community and within the Custis-Lee family. When Maria married Charles Syphax, they were honored and married in the living room of the Custis estate, followed by celebratory activities on the plantation.[15]

These family entanglements between the Custis family and their enslaved family members became part of the interwoven history of Arlington House and the Arlington Plantation. In 1857, when G.W.P. died, his daughter, Mary Custis Lee, "inherited the life interest in her father's estate, along with 196 enslaved people in a portfolio of scattered Virginia properties."[16]

G.W.P.'s views on slavery and freedom changed over his life and had the familiar contradictions of the planter class, holding to the egalitarian instincts of the American Revolution while firmly believing in their supremacy as whites and aristocrats. His adoptive father's nephew, Bushrod Washington, was president of the American Colonization Society (A.C.S), and G.W.P. Custis was a founding member of the local chapter. The religious group the Quakers formed the A.C.S in 1816. In 1821, they established the colony of Liberia in Africa as a new home for the repatriated enslaved.[17] John Liebertz, associate planner with the Arlington County's Historic Preservation Program, in *A Guide to the African American Heritage of Arlington County, Virginia*, wrote that while the Custis family "largely maintained slave families and manumitted several women and children," they were also "proponents of the Colonization Movement, [and] Custis relocated an enslaved family to Liberia."[18]

His evolution of thought may also explain why G.W.P., a leader of the A.C.S, paid for some of his enslaved to move to Liberia. It may also explain his reasoning in part for freeing his mixed-race daughter, Maria, and her children, and then giving her a portion of his land on the plantation. This may also explain why she was not forced to leave the state of Virginia within six months of her "freedom day" as required by the state's manumission laws.

G.W.P.'s views on slavery and freedom were captured in the firsthand account of James Parks, the formerly enslaved man born on the plantation. His parents, Lawrence Parks and his wife Patsy Clark, were some of the many enslaved people owned by G.W.P. Custis. The Parks family consisted of four girls—Amanda, Martha, Matilda and Leanna—and five boys—George, Perry,

4. Enslavement at Arlington

Living Room of the Custis-Lee Mansion. Lieutenant Colonel Robert E. Lee and Mary Randolph Custis were married in the living room at the Custis Arlington Plantation, as were her half-sister Maria Carter and Charles Syphax. The replica of the original room has an oversized Aubusson rug. On the room's walls are portraits of George Washington, as a colonel with the insignia of Cincinnati on his neck, and his young bride Martha Custis Washington. On the opposite wall is a portrait of French General Gilbert du Motier, Marquis de Lafayette, a guest of the household (courtesy National Park Service, Arlington House).

Robert, Lawrence, and James. The entire family was born on the Arlington Plantation as slaves of the Custis family. According to James Parks, his maternal grandfather George Clark once lived at Mount Vernon, the plantation of President George Washington and his wife Martha Custis Washington. In a 1928 interview in the *Washington Sunday Star*, Parks stated that his enslaved grandfather "was a gift from [President] George Washington to Mr. Custis, and was the family cook before the big house on the hill was [even] built."[19]

Having lived at the Arlington Plantation for almost 85 of his 90 years of life, James Parks provided direct insight into G.W.P., the man once called the "son of the Father of a Nation." Parks recalls that as a young boy "many a time he 'knelt down to dig up a gourd of water' for his slaveholder, Mr. Custis, whose log-cabin office was down by the cold-water spring that fed into the

Potomac River." As a teenager, Parks was responsible for ensuring that there was a "wood fire in the cabin on cool mornings before Mr. Custis arrived and then [made] himself generally useful" as directed by the slaveholder.[20]

Parks' remembrances included stories about the diverse activities on that portion of the Custis property that abutted the shoreline along the Potomac River, where "the steamboat wharf had been" and buildings that housed "the ice house, blacksmith shop, and the pavilions and kitchens which Mr. Custis had built for the comfort of his picnic guests."[21] Parks' remembrance of his former slaveholder was favorable and described an old man who was lenient towards the enslaved people on his plantation; Parks remembered a man who welcomed strangers to his property to enjoy the natural beauty of the landscape and who built accommodations for their enjoyment. Parks also described G.W.P. as a man who thought about the institution of slavery, vowed to free his enslaved after his death, and in small ways wanted them to have their own money, enabling them to gradually become self-sufficient. According to Parks:

> Major Custis had never farmed at Arlington plantation to any considerable extent, and that except for an adequate vegetable garden for his own table, there was no extensive cultivation. The slave families were allowed to cultivate their own designated acres, and were even allowed to sell their produce in Washington. Most of the acres allotted to the slave families for their own use and profit were down toward the river shore, east of the old road that runs through the place and connects Georgetown and Alexandria.[22]

Parks' remembrance of his former slaveholder is informed by the controversy that erupted upon G.W.P.'s death on October 10, 1857, and the narrative that Custis on his death bed gave freedom to his enslaved.

At the time of his death, Custis' son-in-law Robert E. Lee was the acting commander of the 2nd Cavalry regiment in San Antonio, Texas, where he had been promoted in 1855 as lieutenant colonel. Upon hearing of G.W.P.'s death, Lee returned to Arlington to be with his wife and family. Lee was named as the executor of the estate and began the lengthy process of probating his father-in-law's will.[23] When he arrived at Arlington, the burden of being executor became apparent. Lee soon learned the complexity of his father-in-law's financial portfolio and accumulated debts. Arlington Plantation was near financial ruin. Custis' evolving political beliefs on slavery tempered his ability to maximize profits from the enslaved on his property at Arlington Plantation. Further, there were problems from within the enslaved community, as many believed that at the time of G.W.P.'s death they were free.

Dissension was building in the slave quarters, and all the enslaved now expected to be set free quickly by the executor of the estate. When the enslaved were not set free, northern agitators seized the moment by highlighting the duplicity of slaveholders denying the rights of their enslaved,

4. *Enslavement at Arlington* 43

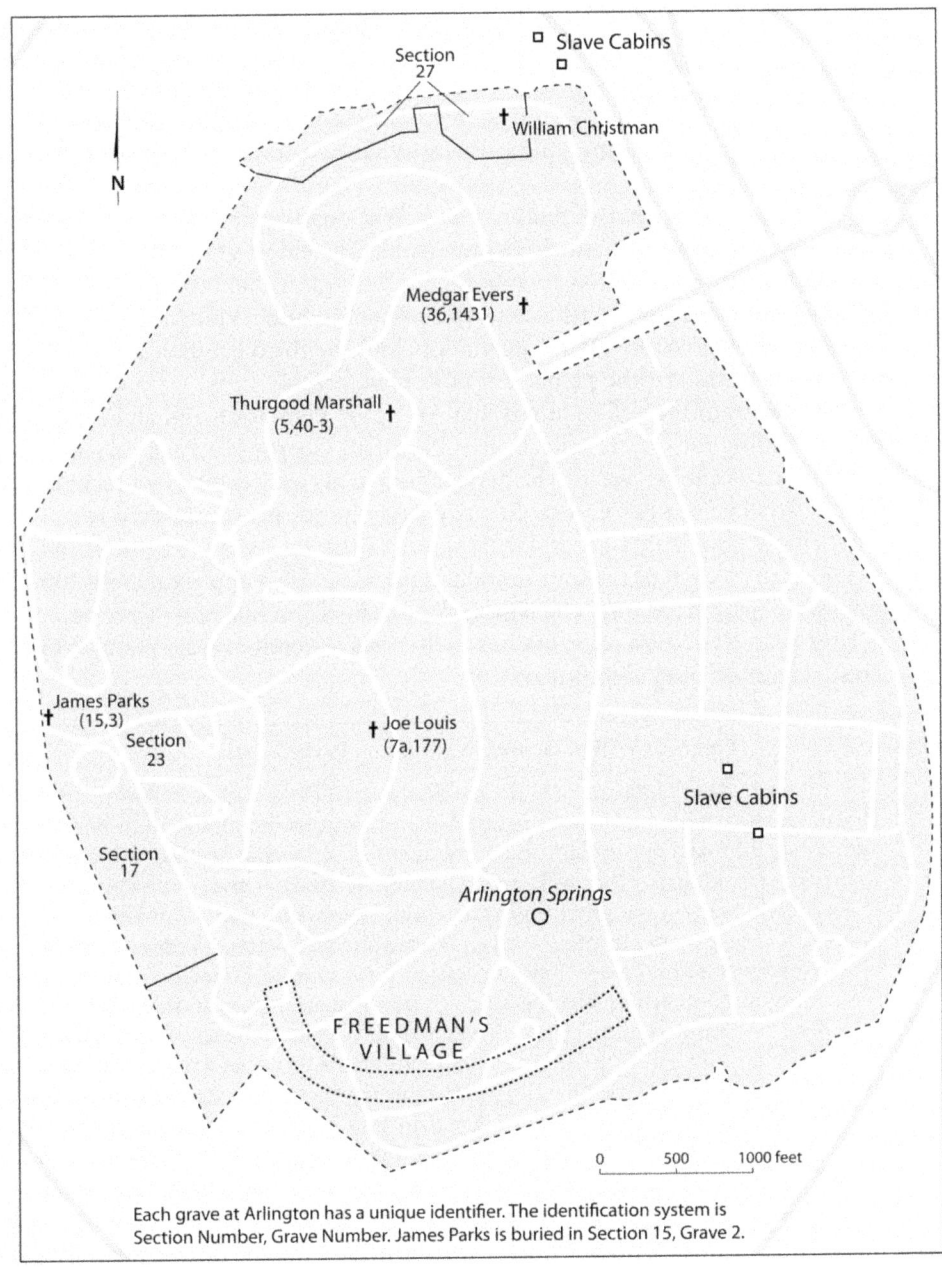

Arlington National Cemetery grounds, indicating location of Section 27, Freedman's Village, slave cabins and notable grave sites.

including the heirs of President George Washington. Intentional or not, the enslaved owned by G.W.P. Custis, as listed in his "Will and Inventory," would now come to play critical and historic roles during the days leading up to the American Civil War. They would eventually help to shape the land uses of the plantation and the emerging cemetery that in a few short years would follow.

The Custis will was not public. The G.W.P Custis' estate included three plantations to be given to his three grandsons. The eldest grandson, George Washington Custis Lee, was to inherit the Arlington Plantation upon the death of his mother Mary Custis Lee; his brother Fitzhugh, known as Rooney, was to inherit the White House plantation; and the third brother, Robert E. Lee, Jr., was to inherit the plantation of Romancoke.

The terms of the will required that Arlington plantation and all its contents, including the Custis collection of President George Washington's artifacts and memorabilia, were to be bequeathed to his only rightful white heir, Mary Custis Lee, for her natural life, and upon her death would then revert to his eldest grandson George Washington Custis Lee. G.W.P. bequeathed $10,000 cash to each of his four granddaughters, and his approximately 200 slaves were to be freed once the legacies and debts from his estate were paid, no later than five years after his death. In a slave economy the plantation debts were often paid with humans.

Figure 2: Will of George Washington Parke Custis[24]

In the name of God, amen. I, George Washington Parke Custis, of Arlington House, in the county of Alexandria and State of Virginia, being sound in body and mind, do make and ordain this instrument of writing as my last will and testament, revoking all other wills and testament whatever. I give and bequeath to my dearly beloved daughter and only child, Mary Ann Randolph Lee, my Arlington House estate, in the county of Alexandria and State of Virginia, containing eleven hundred acres, more or less, and my mill on Four-Mile Run, in the county of Alexandria, and the lands of mine adjacent to said mill, in the counties of Alexandria and Fairfax, in the State of Virginia, the use and benefit of all just mentioned during the term of her natural life, together with my horses and carriages, furniture, pictures, and plate, during the term of her natural life.

On the death of my daughter, Mary Ann Randolph Lee, all the property left to her during the term of her natural life I give and bequeath to my eldest grandson, George Washington Custis Lee, to him and his heirs forever, he, my said eldest grandson, taking my name and arms.

I leave and bequeath to my four granddaughters, Mary, Ann, Agnes, and Mildred Lee, to each ten thousand dollars. I give and bequeath to my second grandson, William Henry Fitzhugh Lee, when he shall be of age, my estate, called the White House, in the county of New Kent and the State of Virginia, containing four thousand acres, more or less, to him and his heirs forever.

I give and bequeath to my third and youngest grandson, Robert Edward Lee, when he is of age, my estate in the county of King William and State of Virginia, called Romancock, containing four thousand acres, more or less, to him and his heirs forever.

My estate of Smith's Island, at the capes of Virginia, and in the county of Northampton, I leave to be sold to assist in paying my granddaughters' legacies, to be sold in such manner as may be deemed by my executors most expedient.

Any and all lands that I may possess in the counties of Stafford, Richmond, and Westmoreland, I leave to be sold to aid in paying my granddaughters' legacies.

I give and bequeath my lot and square No. 21, Washington city to my son-in-law, Lieut. Col. Robert E. Lee, to him and his heirs forever. My daughter, Mary A. R. Lee, has the privilege, by this will, of dividing my family plate among my grandchildren, but the Mt. Vernon altogether, and every article I possess relating to Washington and that came from Mt. Vernon is to remain with my daughter at Arlington House during said daughter's life, and at her death to go to my eldest grandson, George Washington Custis Lee, and to descend from him entire and unchanged to my last posterity.

My estate of the White House, in the county of New Kent, and Romancock, in the county of King William, both being in the state of Virginia, together with Smith's Island, and the lands I may possess in the counties of Stafford, Richmond, and Westmoreland counties are charged with the payment of the legacies of my granddaughters.

Smith's Island and the aforesaid lands in Strafford, Richmond, and Westmoreland only are to be sold, the lands of the White House and Romancock to be worked to raise the aforesaid legacies to my four granddaughters.

And upon the legacies to my four granddaughters being paid, and my estates that are required to pay the said legacies being clear of debts, then I give freedom to my slaves, the said slaves to be emancipated by my executors in such manner as to my executors may seem most expedient and proper, the said emancipation to be accomplished in not exceeding five years from the time of my decease.

And I do constitute and appoint as my executor Lieut. Col. Robert Edward Lee, Robert Lee Randolph, of Eaton View, Rt. Rev. Bishop Meade, and George Washington Peter.

This will, written by my hand, is signed, sealed, and executed the twenty-sixth day of March, eighteen hundred and fifty-five.

      George Washington Parke Custis (Seal)

      Witnesses:
      Martha Custis Williams
      M. Eugene Webster

At the time of G.W.P. Custis' death, there did not appear to be competing claims or controversy surrounding the will relative to the distribution of his land holdings, the financial bequeaths to his heirs, or the execution of those assets. Yet much attention was paid to the freeing of his slaves. The manner in which the terms of Custis' desire to emancipate his enslaved, and the family's apparent lack of transparency, caused confusion, resentment, and in short order became a political albatross for Robert E. Lee.

Abolitionists in and around Washington, D.C., claimed a cover-up when the Custis will was not released publicly, particularly as they became aware the enslaved were to be freed.[25] There were stories of Custis himself summoning his enslaved to his bedside and freeing them while on his deathbed. Other rumors circulated that enslaved family units were separated and that family members were being sent south for profit. The enslaved on the plantation took whatever measures they could to keep pressure on the Custis-Lee family to expedite their day of freedom.

Ten weeks after the death of G.W.P., the Washington news bureau of the *Boston Traveler* on Thursday, December 24, 1857, wrote an article titled "The Slaves of Mr. Custis," addressing what it believed were the conditions at Arlington Plantation.

Figure 3: Washington Bureau, *Boston Traveler* Newspaper[26]

THE SLAVES OF MR. CUSTIS

The emancipation of the slaves left by the late Geo. W. P. Custis, of Arlington, will, it is feared, be much retarded, if not wholly prevented, by the heirs, chief among whom stands John Washington, Esp., the man who cuts down the old ancestral oaks of Mount Vernon to sell for canes, and who charges visitors fifty cents a head for the privilege of visiting the tomb of Washington, and who has turned the home of the Father of his country into a slaveholding pen. All attempts to see the will of Mr. Custis have proved abortive. After much inquiry, it has been admitted by the heirs that the slaves are to be set free in five years. The poor darkies tell a different story. They of Arlington House, say that they were called into the room, and stood by the deathbed of their master, and that after having taken leave of each of them personally, he told them that he had left them, and all of his servants, their freedom. At Arlington there were about one hundred negroes. Mr. Custis owned two plantations about sixty miles below Richmond, on which were about 250 more slaves. According to the statement of those who were about him at the time of his death, he died in full possession of his senses. Besides, it is well known that the old gentleman always said that he intended to free his slaves at his death. I have frequently heard him say as much, though not in exact terms. Unfortunately, when his declaration was made to the house servants of Arlington, no white man was in the room, and the testimony of negroes will not be taken in Court. It is already whispered about town that foul play is in process in regard to those negroes on the Virginia plantations; that they are now being sold South; and that all of them will be consigned to hopeless Slavery unless something is done. Unless the will is produced,

> nothing can be done. And that there is a will, and that the will contains something in regard to the emancipation of the negroes, has been publicly admitted by the heirs. It would be awful if the last remaining member of the household of WASHINGTON should not be allowed, should be prevented by fraud, from carrying out those precepts which he had learned, standing by the knee, and hearing from the lips, of that immortal Sage!

The Custis-Lee family was not happy with the attention given to them after the passing of the family patriarch. Reporters talking to the enslaved did not sit well with the family and caused further tension between white and black on the plantation. Family members and business associates were approached by reporters for insight as to the contents of the Custis will and the happenings at the three plantations owned by G.W.P. Based on the line of questions being raised by the reporters, Robert E. Lee knew that as a commander in the U.S. Army, he needed to prepare a response once articles were released against his family with speculation about G.W.P.'s will.

In a response to the accusations, on January 4, 1858, while on leave from the military to attend to the affairs of his wife's estate, Robert E. Lee wrote a response to the *New York Times* clarifying what he knew to be false information in the *Boston Traveler* article (note that Lee put "1857," the incorrect year on this letter).

Figure 4: *New York Times*, "The Will of Mr. Custis"[27]

Arlington, Monday, Jan 4, 1857 [sic]

My attention has been called to an article from the *Boston Traveler*, dated Washington, 24th December, republished in the *New York Times* of the 30th, under the caption of "The Slaves of Mr. Custis.

It is there charged that the emancipation of the slaves will be much retarded, if not wholly prevented by his heirs; that all attempts to see the will of Mr. Custis have proved abortive; that it is whispered about Washington that foul play is in progress in regard to the negroes on his plantation in Virginia; that they are now being sold South; that all of them will be consigned to hopeless Slavery unless something is done; and that nothing can be done unless the will is produced, &c.

As it is also stated that Mr. Washington, of Mount Vernon, is chief among the heirs who have conspired to suppress the will of Mr. Custis and to defraud the negroes of their rights, I think it proper to state that Mr. Washington is not one of the heirs, has no interest in Mr. Custis' estate, and so far as my knowledge extends, is ignorant of the provisions of his will. Mr. Custis left his property to his daughter and only child, and her children. His will was submitted to the Alexandria County Court for probate on the first day of its session (7th December) after the arrival of the executor at Arlington, and is there on record in his own handwriting, open to inspection.

> There is no desire on the part of the heirs to prevent the execution of its provision in reference to the slaves, nor is there any truth or the least foundations for the assertion that they are being sold South.
>
> What Mr. Custis is said to have stated to the Washington correspondent of the *Boston Traveler*, or to his assembled slaves, on his death bed, is not known to any member of his family. But it is well known that during the brief days of his last illness, he was constantly attended by his daughter, grand-daughter and niece, and faithfully visited by his physician and pastor. So rapid was the progress of his disease, after its symptoms became alarming, that there was no assembly of his servants, and he took leave of but one, who was present when he bade farewell to his family.
>
> R.E. LEE. Executor

Lee's direct public response served its purpose. The white residents of Arlington Plantation, who were members of the Lee family, were to be believed, and the enslaved people who lived on the same land were not to be believed. Yet the terms of the G.W.P. will and the financial conditions of the estate created a technical conflict; though Lee was legally bound to meet all the terms of the will, the desire of an old man to emancipate all his slaves was at odds with paying off the family debts. G.W.P. Custis "…in his grandiose thinking, while neglecting his properties … left no cash to be bequeathed—and that was not the worst, the estate was $10,000 in debt and non–self-sustaining Arlington was physically run down." The will allowed portions of the land to be sold from the inheritors to his grandsons to give his four granddaughters their $10,000 bequeaths each.[28] Lee, who had grown up poor, stripped of family riches and inherited wealth, had to make decisions to protect his own children's inheritance. The challenge "was how to pay off creditors from operations that were then losing money and raise the $40,000 cash for his daughters' legacies *within the five years* allotted by Custis's will for the emancipation of the slaves."[29]

With military precision, Lee began the task of generating the necessary funds by putting all of the enslaved to work. In short order, Lee developed observations and strong convictions of the enslaved at Arlington. According to Lee's biographer, Clifford Dowdey, Lee soon believed:

> … that Custis's Negroes had neither the habit nor the expectations of working. He resolved this with cold pragmatism: the prime field hands were hired out for cash to small planters and to the railroads. After one day three of the first eleven out returned to Arlington with plaints that the work was too hard. Lee sent them back.... For the less demanding work of rehabilitating Arlington, Lee used the younger and the older slaves. They helped him in rebuilding roads and fences, repairing leaks in the manor house roof and the stable roof, and making general repairs on the manor house and outbuildings.[30]

Historians have debated and will continue to do so whether Lee was in favor of or against slavery. The reality for Lee was that his wife and children had now become "land rich and cash poor," and he needed his father-in-law's slaves to bring the family's land to solvency, particularly the property at Arlington. As executor of the estate, Robert E. Lee was fully grounded in the planter's claimed rights to treat slaves as chattel property and as he saw fit. The Dred Scott decision had further validated this in the southern imagination, that enslaved people had no legal rights. This was tested by two separate but related incidents at the Arlington Plantation, both grounded in the desire for freedom from enslavement.

> **Figure 5: Letter from R.E. Lee:**
> **"[T]wo women belonging to the Estate of G.W.P. Custis"**[31]
>
> Arlington, near Alex^a Va.
> 24 April 1858
> Mr. A. E. L. Keese—
>
> There were two women belonging to the Estate of G.W.P. Custis, now in Washington, where they have been since 1 Jany last. One, black, about 35 years old, named Caroline Bingham with a child about 6 mos: old, has been seen frequently in the centre market, going & returning by N. 7th st. The other, mulatto, about 23 years old, named Catharine Burke, with a nearly white child about 2 years old, has also been seen in the centre market. Last Saturday evening she was seen in Mr. Bryans Grocers store near 7th St. with Austin Syphax, a freedman from this place. They report themselves at service with my consent—I have offered $10 for the apprehension of each of these women, upon their delivery in the Jail at Alex^a & the expenses of transporting them there.
>
> A robbery or some articles of jewelry has recently been discovered in this house, in which it is believed that one or both of these women are concerned either as principals or accorsorys. You will find an account of it in the Baltimore Sun for the week ending this day—I have offered a reward of $50 for the recovery of the articles & apprehension of the thief.
>
> A mulatto girl of about 14 years old, named Agnes Burke sister to the above Catharine Burke, who was hired in Jany last to Mr. I.W. Atkinson, Blksmith in Alex^a has recently left her place & is believed to be in Washington, where she has an Aunt Louisa Burke, & Cousin Hilliard Burke Carpenter in the 1st Ward, with other relatives. I will give $10.00 for her apprehension & delivery to Mr. Atkinson in Alex^a.
>
> Austin Bingham, brother to the foregoing named Caroline Bingham, a black boy about 19 years old, hired by Mr. Edw^a B. Powell in Jany last, & who resides on Four Mile Run, just above the old Factory, between this Place & Alex^a—left his place yesterday. I will give $10.00 for his apprehension & delivery to Mr. Powell—
>
> All these people are well known in Washington by any of the negroes residing

> there. I am told a Mrs Fleming Huckster in Centre Market, knows the two women first named & has seen them there. The people from this place, who frequent that market, meet them there.
>
> Very resp^y
>
> RE Lee Ex^r of G.W.P.C

The external pressures caused by abolitionists and reporters, and the desire for freedom, particularly for the young, of enslaved people at Arlington, conflicted with the militaristic management style of Lee. These pressures came to a head when he needed to hire out those same young enslaved to glean as much profit as possible. The enslaved Caroline and Catherine Burke, along with Austin Syphax, slipped away to work and live in the District as freed people. Lee issued a bounty for their capture and added that he suspected they were responsible for some missing articles.

The bounty for the two women and the young man had its desired effect: they were captured and brought back to the plantation. Their capture resulted in a melee where the sons of the enslaved family, Austin and Louisa Bingham, confronted Lee and refused to accept work assignments where the jobs were far from the Arlington plantation, and where they felt that they were being overworked for profits not benefiting them.

The incident was exacerbated when Reuben Bingham informed Lee that he and his brothers—Henry, Edward and Austin—were free men and were not going to do any more work off the plantation grounds. A disturbance erupted during which the Alexandria police were summoned to the plantation. The brothers were arrested and taken to the Alexandria city jail, where they were held until arrangements could be made to employ them in Richmond.[32]

When cooler heads prevailed, Mr. Lee was advised that he best refer the terms of G.W.P.'s will to the Alexandria Probate Court for resolution, before he ran into further problems with the other enslaved on the plantation.[33] As is often in the case with wills, the desire of the testator may conflict with the intent of the will, which could lead to different interpretations. Robert E. Lee believed that while his father-in-law may have wanted his enslaved to be freed immediately, it appeared to conflict with his desire to pay his legacies, who could only be paid by the hard labor of his enslaved.

To resolve this conflict, General Lee applied to the circuit court of Alexandria for an interpretation of the will provisions and for an order specifying the point in time when the will's provision regarding emancipation must be executed.

In 1859, a chancery case was ruled upon in the Superior Court of Law and Chancery, providing clarity on the G.W.P. will.[34] The plaintiff was Mary Ann Randolph (Custis) Lee and the defendant was her husband and the estate executor, Robert E. Lee. Mary was suing her father's estate and its executor Robert E. Lee on behalf of her children (the beneficiaries of the estate) and G.W.P.'s enslaved who wanted their freedom from the estate. The surnames of the enslaved family units (as identified in the January 1, 1858, *Inventory of Slaves Located at the Arlington Plantation*), including the Bingham, Branham, Burke, Check, Clark, Crump, Custis, Derricks, Dotson, Grey, Lancaster, Lee, Meredith, Norris, Parks, Patterson, Richardson, Syphax, and Taylor families, were each listed as co-defendants.[35]

Eventually, the Court ruled that Lee was legally empowered to hold the enslaved in service to the estate until the legacies were satisfied. Notwithstanding this, the enslaved had to be freed no later than five years from the date of Custis' death, or by October 10, 1862.[36]

While the Alexandria Court was reviewing Lee's request for interpretation, a second incident tested Robert E. Lee's treatment of the Custis enslaved, his beliefs about slavery, and his use of the enslaved to increase his wealth. In 1859, the siblings Wesley and Mary Norris, along with a cousin, decided to escape from the Arlington Plantation. They had assumed they would be freed upon G.W.P.'s death in 1857. They were captured in Maryland just before they reached the Pennsylvania border and returned in shackles back to Arlington House.[37] There are contradictory reports of how the returned enslaved were treated by Lee. Later, these contradictions would serve as key support of the different understandings of Lee as a man of high honor, an accidental secessionist or a traitor, and the political claims made on and with his memory.

According to Wesley Norris, when interviewed in 1866 about his sense of his freedom:

> ... it was the general impression among the slaves of Mr. Custis that on his death they should be forever free; in fact this statement had been made to them by Mr. C. years before; at his death we were informed by Gen. Lee that by the conditions of the will we must remain slaves for five years; I remained with Gen. Lee for about seventeen months, when my sister Mary, a cousin of ours, and I determined to run away, which we did in the year 1859; we had already reached Westminster, in Maryland, on our way to the North, when we were apprehended and thrown into prison, and Gen. Lee notified of our arrest; we remained in prison fifteen days, when we were sent back to Arlington....[38]

Wesley Norris' and other accounts state that the enslaved were whipped in Lee's presence and their wounds salted, to inflict as much pain as possible.[39]

> ... we were immediately taken before Gen. Lee, who demanded the reason why we ran away; we frankly told him that we considered ourselves free; he then told us he would teach us a lesson we never would forget; he then ordered us to the barn, where, in his presence, we were tied firmly to posts by a Mr. Gwin, our overseer, who was ordered by Gen. Lee to strip us to the waist and give us fifty lashes each, excepting my sister, who received but twenty; we were accordingly stripped to the skin by the overseer, who, however, had sufficient humanity to decline whipping us; accordingly Dick Williams, a county constable, was called in, who gave us the number of lashes ordered;

Gen. Lee, in the meantime, stood by, and frequently enjoined Williams to "lay it on well," an injunction which he did not fail to heed; not satisfied with simply lacerating our naked flesh, Gen. Lee then ordered the overseer to thoroughly wash our backs with brine, which was done.[40]

Norris and his sister Mary were hired to work on the "Orange and Alexander" railroad before being sold south to Alabama and then on to Richmond, Virginia. Eventually they escaped through rebel territory to the freedom of the Union lines at Arlington. Wesley Norris clearly expected his narrative to be challenged because of the contested nature of their enslavement and status of their new master:

I have nothing further to say; what I have stated is true in every particular, and I can at any time bring at least a dozen witnesses, both white and black, to substantiate my statements: I am at present employed by the Government; and am at work in the National Cemetery on Arlington Heights, where I can be found by those who desire further particulars; my sister referred to is at present employed by the French Minister at Washington, and will confirm my statement.[41]

Because other records are lost to history, it's unclear if the other enslaved people on the plantation were forced to bear witness during the horrific treatment of the Norris cousins. Nonetheless, Lee's intentions were clear; he needed to set an example to the remaining enslaved on the property. Any enslaved who dared to run away would receive the harshest of physical punishments when caught. He also wanted the three runaways to remember their lashings; rubbing salt in their lacerated wounds would ensure that they would suffer such excruciating pain so as not to forget "their crime" against the Custis-Lee family.

Shortly after the whipping of Wesley and Mary Norris, a series of articles appeared in the New York newspapers captivating the national press on the conditions at Arlington House. The intent of an anonymous 1859 letter written to the editor of the *New York Tribune*, Horace Greeley, a key abolitionist voice, was to show the role of the Custis-Washington-Lee families on the issue of slavery. The quest for equality, liberty and freedom for the planter-aristocracy class in Virginia was limited and not available for the enslaved who lived among them.

Figure 6: Letter on the Treatment of the Enslaved at Arlington House[42]

SOME FACTS THAT SHOULD COME TO LIGHT.

To the Editor of the N. Y. Tribune.

SIR: It is known that the venerable George Washington Parke Custis died some two years ago; and the same papers that announced his death announced also the fact that on his deathbed he liberated his slaves. The will, for some reason, was never allowed any publicity, and the slaves themselves were cajoled along with the idea that some slight necessary arrangements were to be made, when they would all have their free papers. Finally they were told *five years* must elapse before they could go. Meantime they have been deprived of all means of making a little now and then for themselves, as they were allowed to do during Mr. Custis's life, have been kept harder at work than ever, and part of the time have been cut down to half a peck of unsifted meal a week for each person, without even their fish allowance. Three old women, who have seen nearly their century each, are kept sewing, making clothes for the field hands, from daylight till dark, with nothing but the half-peck of meal to eat; no tea or coffee—nothing that old people crave—and no time given them to earn these little rarities, as formerly. One old man, eighty years old, bent with age, and whom Mr. Custis had long since told "had *done enough*," and might go home and "smoke his pipe in peace," is now turned out as a regular field hand. A year ago, for some trifling offense, three were sent to jail, and a few months later three more, for simply going down to the river to get themselves some fish, when they were literally starved.

Some three or four weeks ago, three, more courageous than the rest, thinking their five years would never come to an end, came to the conclusion to leave for the North. They were most valuable servants, but they were never advertised, and there was no effort made to regain them, which looks exceedingly as though Mr. Lee, the present proprietor, knew he had no lawful claim to them. They had not proceeded far before their progress was intercepted by some brute in human form, who suspected them to be fugitives, and probably wished a reward. They were lodged in jail, and frightened into telling where they had started from. Mr. Lee was forthwith acquainted with their whereabouts, when they were transported back, taken into a barn, stripped, and the men received thirty and nine lashes each, from the hands of the slave-whipper, when he refused to whip the girl, and Mr. Lee himself administered the thirty and nine lashes to her. They were then sent to Richmond jail, where they are now lodged.

Next to Mount Vernon, we associate "the Custis place" with the "Father of this free country." Shall "Washington's body guard" be thus tampered with, and never a voice raised for such utter helplessness?

A.

Washington, June 21, 1859.

The published letter was intended to further discredit the family and its hypocrisy of "liberty and freedom for all," embarrassing Robert E. Lee. Another anonymous 1859 letter written to the "Editor of the New York Tribune" was used by abolitionists to highlight the hypocrisy of slavery on southern plantations, and what better plantation to demonstrate this than the estate of President George Washington's own namesake and adopted son, George Washington Parke Custis' Arlington House? The reference in the letter to the editor that Custis had fifteen children with his slave woman may be a reference to his own mixed-race daughter, Maria Carter Syphax and her ten children.

However, G.W.P. may have had more unacknowledged mixed children or grandchildren on the property.

> **Figure 7: The Hypocrisy of Enslavement at Arlington House**[43]
>
> To the Editor of the N. Y. Tribune.
>
> Sir: I live one mile from the plantation of George Washington P. Custis, now Col. Lee's, as Custis willed it to Lee. All the slaves on this estate, as I understand, were set free at the death of Custis, but are now held in bondage by Lee. I have inquired concerning the will, but can get no satisfaction. Custis had fifteen children by his slave women. I see his grandchildren every day; they are of a dark yellow. Last week three of the slaves ran away; an officer was sent after them, overtook them nine miles this side of Pennsylvania, and brought them back. Col. Lee ordered them whipped. They were two men and one woman. The officer whipped the two men, and said he would not whip the woman, and Col. Lee stripped her and whipped her himself. These are facts as I learn from near relatives of the men whipped. After being whipped, he sent them to Richmond and hired them out as good farm hands.
>
> Yours,
A CITIZEN.

Some of the enslaved on the Arlington Plantation, angered by the Norris cousins' flogging, were more than happy to quietly talk to willing abolitionists around Washington, D.C., about their treatment by Robert E. Lee and his overseer and their belief that they were to be immediately set free by the terms of G.W.P.'s will. As family members were separated and sent south for profit, the enslaved on the plantation used whatever means necessary to expedite their day of freedom.

The clandestine meetings at the farmers' markets in Washington, D.C, and late nights with reporters perhaps had unintended effects. With the public pressure and media attention on Lee, he may have hesitated to sell the more difficult and sullen enslaved to the slavers in the Deep South. He certainly could have raised the required cash to meet the terms of the G.W.P. will quickly by selling at auction the healthiest of the young men to the highest bidders at the Franklin and Armfield slave pen on Alexandria's waterfront, but for fear of public reprisals he chose not to do so.

The Franklin and Armfield slave pen was one of the largest slave pens in the South and served as the primary slave pen transferring the enslaved. In addition, the slavers kidnapped freed and free people from Virginia, Maryland, and other points north, sending them to the backbreaking jobs on the cotton fields of the Gulf States. Young healthy enslaved men and women knew that they could "fetch a good price" and planned to escape before they were sold.

This was a period when one man believed he had the right and the duty to own another, simply because he was white and privileged; while black individuals such as Wesley and Mary Norris felt they had the right to be free. At the time of their escape, capture, and violent punishment, the Norris cousins were living in a nation that once fought for its own independence and was on the brink of a war that would test the founding principles of its constitutional beliefs. The account of Wesley Norris, like so many others, helps to explain the raw emotions of the period that led a nation to civil war.

The states would divide and secede, and within them would be further divisions. New York's mayor would support southern secession and the Virginian Know-Nothing Winfield Scott would organize the Union defense of Washington, D.C., before President Lincoln was inaugurated.[44] Brother would fight brother, great new fortunes would be made, and the Union Army would develop laws and regulations that would lead to emancipation. The nation would fight a hand-to-hand war with industrial weaponry, photograph its dead for the first time on the battlefield, and telegraph news, rumor and other preconceptions to an eager audience. More than 10 percent of the male population would be armed, but almost a quarter of them would die in the conflict. Approximately 185,000 formerly enslaved would fight for the Union, dying at a rate twice that of their white comrades. The great emancipator President Lincoln would be assassinated.

The nation would never be the same. The Civil War would change the economy and culture profoundly and end legal slavery through a series of amendments to the Constitution. Racial equality, civil rights and the free provision of labor would still cause conflict into the twenty-first century, but the war fundamentally changed the nation.[45] The men and women, white and black, who lived at Arlington and owned the land and defined how it would be used, would all be subject to these changes, and more.

Chapter 5

Civil War

In 1860 slavery was at its apex; the number of enslaved represented their greatest exchangeable value for the enslavers. The value of an enslaved person was at an all-time peak, worth more than $150,000 apiece by 2017 standards. Cotton production was strong in 1860—the price was high and stable, and demand was growing, particularly in Europe, which was enjoying a long period of relative peace.

With the November 6, 1860, election of Abraham Lincoln as president, southern states threatened to secede from the Union if their rights to own enslaved property were compromised. Between the time of Lincoln's election as president and his inauguration in March 1861, seven states seceded from the Union and formed their own nation of Confederate States. Virginia called a legislative session on February 3, 1861, to consider secession and by the time of the inauguration had passed its conditions for remaining in the Union.

Before Christmas 1860, South Carolina seceded. Violence erupted over Fort Sumter, South Carolina, on December 26, 1860, when rebel militia started shelling the federal fort. For the remainder of December, the United States made several unsuccessful attempts to provide the fort with food and supplies, while South Carolina demanded that Union forces abandon the fort, also without success. The secession of South Carolina and the hostile act of a southern state taking up arms against a federal installation amplified the echo chamber of the partisan press.[1] A southern democrat and leader in the secession movement, Treasury Secretary Howell Cobb, said in a resignation address that the North was not to be trusted:

> The Union formed by our fathers was one of equality, justice and fraternity. On the fourth of March it will be supplanted by a Union of sectionalism and hatred.... Is there no other remedy for this state of things but immediate secession? ... They have trampled upon the Constitution of Washington and Madison, and will prove equally faithless to their own pledges. You ought not—cannot, trust them. It is not the Constitution and the laws of the United States which need amendments, but *the hearts* of the northern people.[2]

The sectional, partisan press was equally sure the South and their apologist President Buchanan could not be trusted, and that measures to protect the federal arsenals were needed:

> Everybody here feels, as the people everywhere do, that the Government is in the hands of traitors. It is not long since a Southern State was supplied with twenty thousand muskets out of the Springfield arsenal, under the form of a sale, at a nominal price. If Fort Moultrie is captured by the nullifiers Mr. Buchanan will never show his face in Pennsylvania.[3]

The secessionist's actions at Fort Sumter prompted federal forces to take steps to protect their assets in Washington, deploying troops to defend the southern entrance to the District:

> In the District of Columbia the new year brought a flurry of military activity. Rumors of insurrection filled the newspapers and streets. The War Department, worried over the safety of the capital, decided to bolster its defenses. Early in January 1861, a company of United States Marines, sailed eleven miles downriver to Fort Washington. There they garrisoned the old stone structure on the Maryland shore. For years the fort had been unoccupied, and Federal authorities feared that lawbreakers might rally at this citadel.[4]

During his conciliatory inaugural address, Lincoln attempted to bridge the national divide, but it had no effect on the South. Despite the president's attempt to reconcile differences, the southern states, led by South Carolina, began to commission an army to defend their Confederation of States rebellion. On March 11, 1861, the Constitution of the Confederate States of America was signed in its then-capital, Montgomery, Alabama. Alexander Stephens, former (and future) senator from Georgia and vice president of the Confederacy, gave his widely distributed Cornerstone Address, at the Athenaeum in Savannah, Georgia, on March 21, 1861, where he proclaimed: "Our new government is founded upon exactly the opposite idea; its foundations are laid, its cornerstone rests, upon the great truth that the negro is not equal to the white man; that slavery subordination to the superior race is his natural and normal condition."[5]

Still, Virginia, on April 4, 1861, at a statewide convention voted not to secede. Six days later the states that comprised the "newly constituted government of the Confederate States began battering the walls" of Fort Sumter.[6] The Civil War had begun. Two days later, the Union troops were forced to evacuate the fort due to lack of supplies. President Lincoln, in response to the attack on Fort Sumter, called for the states to provide 70,000 troops; Virginia was included in the request. Thus, on April 17, 1861, the Virginia legislature reversed its previous decision and voted to secede, if a majority of Virginia voters agreed in a plebiscite.

The plebiscite would take the state of Virginia a few weeks to organize; in the meantime the sides were gathering arms and attitudes were hardening.

Robert E. Lee, a colonel in the U.S. Army, was torn between his allegiance to the Union he served, as had his and his wife's families long before the Civil War, and his allegiance to his home state of Virginia. On April 20, 1861, Colonel Lee sided with Virginia and resigned his 30-year commission only a day after President Lincoln had offered him command of the Union army.

John Nicolay and John Hay were Lincoln's secretaries throughout the war and were a party to the most intimate administrative details of the war. Nicolay and Hay claimed Lee was a "traitor," who had renounced his U.S. army commission even though President Lincoln had made clear in 1861 to the "Virginia commissioners on the 13th [of April], that he intended no war, no invasion, no subjugation—nothing but defense of the Government."[7] The secretaries further note that Lee's first acts were to exploit the knowledge he had gained while a trusted colonel in the Union army. Lee encouraged Jefferson Davis' plan to invade Washington, D.C., while rioting prevented the Union army from moving troops safely through Baltimore on April 19.

In the 1880s, Nicolay and Hay produced a bestselling biography of Lincoln and his conduct of the war. By that time, 20 years after the end of the war, the recovery of Lee's image was fully underway among the adherents to the Lost Cause. Nicolay and Hay's publisher, Century, did not want the authors' opinion that Lee "could or should have been shot for treason" to make it to print. The publisher made sure the "secretaries did not enjoy full leeway in hacking down the idols of Confederate mythology. They were being paid handsomely for their efforts and could not ignore the Century's concerns."[8]

Nicolas and Hay wrote their biography of Lincoln and the events they witnessed beginning with their hiring in Springfield, Illinois, after the 1860 election and ending with Lincoln's assassination in April 1865. They had no illusions about how the Virginia class of planters, with their airs and graces, played a significant role in articulating the war's cause, nor about their devotion and dependence on continuing enslavement in the state of Virginia:

> CIVIL war, though possible, did not at the moment seem imminent or necessary: Lincoln had declared in his inaugural that he would not begin it; Jefferson Davis had written in his instructions to the commissioners that he did not desire it. This threw the immediate contest back upon the secondary question—the control and adhesion of the border slave–States; and of these Virginia was the chief subject of solicitude. The condition of Virginia had become anomalous; it was little understood by the North, and still less by her own citizens. She retained all the ideal sentiment growing out of her early devotion to and sacrifices for the Union; but it was warped by her coarser and stronger material interest in slavery. She still deemed she was the mother of presidents; whereas she had degenerated into being, like other border States, the mother of slave-breeders and of an annual crop of black-skinned human chattels to be sold to the cotton, rice, and sugar planters of her neighboring commonwealths. She thought herself the leader of the South; whereas she was only a dependent of the Gulf States.[9]

Left: R.E. Lee's wife, Mary Custis Lee, daughter of George Washington Parke Custis (courtesy National Park Service). *Right*: Robert E. Lee, 1864 (Library of Congress).

On the morning of April 22, leaving his wife and family behind, Lee departed for Richmond, where he accepted a commission in the Army of the United States of the Confederacy and took command of Virginia's military and naval forces. Lee took with him several enslaved people from Arlington, including "George Parks as his cook and Perry Parks as his valet," the older brothers of James Parks.[10]

Colonel Lee was educated at the U.S. Military Academy at West Point, where he trained as an engineer. He understood the strategic advantage of Arlington House in the overall defenses of Washington. He needed to convince his wife to leave the plantation immediately. Lee knew that the property:

> ... climbed more than two hundred feet above the surrounding countryside. Any artillerist occupying that position could easily harass troopships plying the Potomac River, blow up the capital's bridge crossings, and lob shells at the most tempting target of all—the White House, its roof peeking from the green fridge of trees just across the river. There was no way that war planners in Washington were going to cede the high ground of Arlington to enemy forces, and within days of her husband's departure, Mary Custis Lee received notice of the Federals' intent.[11]

Mary Custis Lee proceeded with securing her plantation estate and the collection of her father's Washington artifacts, a task undertaken by women all across the South who were abandoned by husbands, fathers and sons off to war. She summoned her trusted enslaved servants and pulled together her most valuable possessions. She was now the Washington-Custis-Lee family archivist. She had her grandfather President George Washington's papers loaded onto wagons. Other family valuables were thought to be protected by burying them throughout the property.

After receiving several additional letters from her husband in Richmond insisting that she leave Arlington House for her safety, on May 15 Mrs. Lee took the ride down the winding road from the plantation, with the caravan of wagons in tow; she and the enslaved at Arlington House could have realized that none of the Custis-Lee family might ever return to the estate and the Custis-Lee wealth, bound to enslaving African Americans, might be greatly diminished. Recognizing changed economic circumstances of the Custis-Lees in the Confederacy, the city of Richmond resolved "that the sum of sixty thousand dollars be appropriated for the purchase of a house and lot to be tendered to General R.E. Lee and family, free of rent."[12]

Mrs. Lee abandoned the plantation and "decamped with 12 wagons of household goods, eventually settling in Richmond."[13] The wagon train was not large enough; and "unable to remove all of the Washington artifacts from the house, Mary Custis Lee left the household keys with Selena Gray, a personal maid." For six months Gray actively protected the relics from pilfering soldiers. In December 1861, when Mrs. Gray noticed that the cellar door to the room where the relics were stored was broken into and exposed, she requested that General McDowell safeguard the collection. McDowell "subsequently removed the items to the patent office" in Washington, D.C., for safekeeping.[14] "The relics were put on display in January 1862 in an exhibit titled Captured from Arlington, where they remained until they were deposited in the Smithsonian."[15]

McDowell drew praise from the northern press for this act, but Selena Gray's role was not acknowledged. Later, popular neo–Confederate histories do acknowledge Selena's role, giving her the title "keeper of the keys." Selena Gray is written back into the narrative, but as an example of loyal slavery. These histories:

> ... aim to recover and celebrate Selena Gray's contributions to the preservation of a national heritage that is necessarily biracial and mutually affectionate. They look to dispel racism and forge reconciliation by claiming an integrated past grounded in notions of loyalty and faithful slavery.[16]

These histories are consistent with the preservation of the Arlington Mansion as a relic of the antebellum South as opposed to other eras. Preserving the Arlington Mansion of 1857, rather than the 1864 Arlington when it is occupied by Union troops, is a *choice* made by preservationists, a choice that elevates the relationships between the slavers and the enslaved. The choice elevates one epoch or owner over another. Both of those times at Arlington have important, yet different, lessons for current tourists. Ironically, the preservationist's choice is possible only through the work of the enslaved Selena Gray who lived with both realities.

Mrs. Gray, a second-generation enslaved woman born on Arlington Plantation, was the aunt to Wesley and Mary Norris, who attempted to escape Arlington and reported they were whipped by Colonel Lee, and then were rented out in Richmond to prevent any further agitation on the property and raise additional revenue for the estate.

Mrs. Selena Gray, enslaved woman at Arlington Plantation at Arlington Heights (courtesy National Park Service Arlington House).

She became the guardian of some of the most revered artifacts of the country's first president, as well as the mansion. Selena Gray and her husband Thornton would take advantage of being newly in charge of the estate and expand their house. They connected the entire "South Dependency" duplex into one living space in 1863 by knocking out the common wall. Their expansion of their living was plastered over in the 1929 designation of the national monument.[17] Mrs. Gray, in the sanctioned and official histories, reportedly worked to maintain the normalcy of the plantation culture as Mrs. Lee left: "For almost a fortnight everything went on much as usual at Arlington. Overseer McGuire saw to it that work went on at the farm, and the housekeeper, Selena, kept the other slaves at their customary tasks. Almost it seemed as if the family had only gone off on a visit and might return at any moment."[18]

Selena Gray's role in protecting and documenting the artifacts would not end with the war. Mrs. Lee sent Mrs. Gray many letters after the war, and Mrs. Gray provided information about the state of the property. One four-page response from Mrs. Gray in 1872 to yet another request from Mrs. Lee is described as "Selena Gray's declaration of emancipation and self-possession." She writes, "…I was hoping to see you once more at Arlington it is a most lovely place now everywhere around it looks beautiful there is not a tree to be seen except in the cemetery the whole of it is rented to the freemen they have little huts all over that beautiful place...."[19]

The home high above the Potomac River had a bird's eye view of the city of Washington, and would, if captured by rebel militia, threaten all parts of the capital. The majority of voters in the Arlington section of Alexandria County opposed secession, just as they had opposed retrocession in the 1840s. The city of Alexandria's voters were in favor of both retrocession and secession; enslavement and trade in African American lives were, after all, key to the city of Alexandria. The land and house would undergo another change of hands and usage before the end of May:

> On May 23, Virginians voted overwhelmingly in a referendum to affirm the state's secession. Within hours, in one of the first major actions of the Civil War, 14,000 union soldiers crossed the Potomac to capture Alexandria and to occupy the high grounds above the river. Within a week three New York regiments were camped on the Arlington estate, felling trees and dismantling rail fences for firewood. The house soon served as a headquarters for Brigadier General Irvin McDowell.[20]

By noon on May 24, 1861, the Union army crossed the river and captured the port of Alexandria. In the same reinforcing maneuvers, the army took control of Arlington Plantation and took steps to transform the property into a military compound. Temporary tents were pitched until barracks could be built for the soldiers. Much of the 400 acres of virgin oak forest on the prop-

Union soldiers at Arlington at the start of the Civil War (courtesy National Park Service).

erty was harvested as the soldiers built corrals for the animals. These were the same trees Marquis de Lafayette had directed Custis to cherish in 1825, now cut down out of military necessity. Later James Parks would head an effort to replant Arlington, giving us the magnificent flora we associate with the property today.[21]

The Union soldiers were supported by the plantation's enslaved who remained on the property, as they built trenches around the property and cleared additional trees to enhance sightlines in all directions in the event of a Confederate attack. Fort Whipple and Fort Cass, as well as the uncompleted Fort McPherson, were constructed on the property. Fort Albany was constructed just to the south, commanding the Columbia Pike and defending the approach to the Long Bridge. These forts comprised part of the sixty-eight forts built around the city as part of the defense system.[22]

As the Union Army took measures to protect the capital city, the President and many in Congress began to prepare for a longer war. A volunteer force would need to be supplemented and supported by regular troops. Montgomery C. Meigs was elevated to quartermaster general of the army on "June 13, 1861, with the rank of brigadier general dating from May 14, and began the development of the systems to support an expanded force."[23] The extent of the reliance on an African American labor force of teamsters, cooks, and nurses remains underappreciated and was overlooked in the later histories of reconciliation.

On July 4, 1861, President Lincoln addressed Congress and requested the formal enlistment of a Union army. The United States Congress authorized 500,000 men for war. Generals were recruited from West Point, strategic maps were drawn, soldiers trained, supplies commissioned, all to prepare the Union for battle. Once the Union army crossed the Potomac, both armies began to solidify their positions. On July 21, 1861, the Union army marched to take control of the railroad at the town of Manassas Junction, Virginia, in an attempt to sever the Confederate supply line to its new capital, Richmond. The Union assumption was there would be a quick victory for a superior force. The Confederate army moved resources northward via railcar, an innovation in war, and won the first major engagement, known as the Battle of Bull Run.[24] The necessity of the fortification on the Arlington Heights was underscored, as the Union army had to retreat to behind the defenses for the security in Washington. The fate of Arlington would again be bound to the District of Columbia, just 15 years after it had been retroceded to the state of Virginia, parts of which were now seeking further separation through secession.

To raise funds for the war effort, on February 6, 1863, Congress passed a direct property tax in the secessionist states. The Custis-Lee property fell within the scope of the law.[25] The federal government acquired the plantation at a tax condemnation hearing:

In 1862 the U.S. government levied a tax on the Arlington property, about which Mrs. Lee was informed in 1864. Confined to a wheelchair, she sent representatives with the payment of $92.07, but the tax commissioner refused to accept the payment, insisting the tax had to be paid in person by the owner. The property was soon seized, auctioned off, and purchased by the U.S. government for $26,800; the estate had been assessed the year before the war broke out at $34,100.[26]

In the early days of the war, the battles were near Washington. As war wounded came from area battlefields, the need for additional hospital space was increased. Alexandria churches, homes, schools and warehouses were converted into makeshift hospitals. Tents were pitched on the southern slope of the Arlington plantation to accommodate the overflow patients from Washington-area hospitals and makeshift medical facilities.

The first fallen soldiers who died in combat near the Union capital city of Washington were buried at the United States Soldiers' Cemetery in the capital and the nearby Alexandria Cemetery in Alexandria, Virginia. By autumn 1863 the two cemeteries had reached capacity. At this point, however, the only graves at Arlington were the graves of slaves, the formerly enslaved, G.W.P. Custis and his immediate family. The slopes of Arlington Heights were also filling with camps of former enslaved who walked north or came with the Union forces as support personnel as the Union exerted control over southern and eastern Virginia.

Chapter 6

Washington's Contraband

ABRAHAM LINCOLN WAS FIERCELY DETERMINED to keep the union of the states and not let it divide over slavery. He campaigned to keep slavery from spreading to the territories but not for emancipation or for the ending of enslavement in southern states, even as he insisted "slavery is wrong" in his Cooper Union address.[1] He restated his message of maintenance of the Union on the night of his election; on his speaking tour from Springfield to Washington via the northern state capitals and other municipalities in Indiana, Ohio, New York, New Jersey and Pennsylvania (but not Maryland); and at his inauguration on March 4 1861.[2]

Lincoln never once declared himself an abolitionist, but regularly declared his belief in the insoluble union.[3] President Lincoln communicated to the secession states that he continued to consider them part of the United States: "no State, upon its mere notion, can lawfully get out of the Union."[4] He proclaimed that the secessionist desire to extend slavery into the new territories was in opposition to his understanding of self-government for and by the people. Lincoln believed that slavery:

> ... threatened the virtue necessary to sustain a republic. It threatened the proper balance between God, government, society, the family, and the individual. And no matter which side of the divide a Civil War soldier stood on, he knew that the heart of the matter, and the reason that the war came, was the other side's stance on slavery. From first to last, slavery defined the soldiers' war among both Union and Confederate troops....[5]

At the time of Lincoln's election, Virginia's landed gentry had an outsized influence, sense of their leadership role, and economic power resulting from being the center of the enslaving ideology. Virginia was the most socially rigid of the original colonies, having been deliberately made in the image of the landed English gentry class.[6] The institution of slavery was the economic foundation for the southern state's economies, and permeated all aspects of living.

In late 1860 and early 1861 greater control over the enslaved was exerted in anticipation of the coming war. Robert E. Lee's actions were in line with his fellow slavers as he increased his hiring out of the enslaved. At the outbreak of the war these controls broke down as men headed to enlist.[7] There were now more opportunities to escape to freedom, and on May 24, 1861, Major-General Benjamin Butler learned that three slaves (Frank Baker, James Townsend and Sheppard Mallory) had come into his camps at Fort Monroe, Virginia. These three each were enslaved by the commander of the local Virginia troops and sought refuge to avoid being sent further south. Fearing they would never come north or see their families again, the enslaved men had left wives (one a freewoman) and numerous children in the vicinity.[8]

Their enslaver sent a flag of truce, demanding the return of the enslaved men under the Fugitive Slave Law. General Butler refused to comply on the ground that slaves belonging to insurgents employed in military service would consequently become *contraband of war*. General Butler submitted his action to the consideration of the Secretary of War, who responded:

> SIR—Your action in respect to the negroes who came within your lines, from the service of the rebels, is approved. The Department is sensible of the embarrassments which must surround officers conducting military operations in a State, by the laws of which slavery is sanctioned.[9]

Secretary of the Navy Gideon Welles further instructed Butler to put the freed enslaved men to work, account for the value of their time, and not return them to their "alleged" slaveholders. Butler's contraband declaration was seen as strengthening the Union capacity by applying the might of the black labor force:

> And when the novel, but very sensible doctrine with which that singular demand was met, that slaves are to be regarded as articles contraband of war, chattels capable of a military use, a kind of locomotive gun-carriages and intrenching-tools, and as such to be taken and confiscated when found belonging to armed rebels, shall have been practically applied for a time, with its natural and obvious result, it may be that even the Palmetto State will exhibit some general symptoms of returning reason.[10]

Anti-slavery pragmatism and principles fused into a growing commitment to emancipation; treating the enslaved as a military asset also satisfied conservatives in the North not yet ready for emancipation. Just as the power of black labor might change the minds of the most hardened secessionists from the state of South Carolina, it also impressed on the white Union troops their relief from the menial tasks they loathed. As one commander stated: "I have 11 Negroes in my company now. They do every particle of the dirty work. Two women among them do the washing for the company."[11]

The enslaved also served another valuable purpose—reconnaissance. Union leaders at times lacked the basic understanding of where they were fighting or the topography of the land. The arriving enslaved brought with them current information on the movement of the enemy combatants and

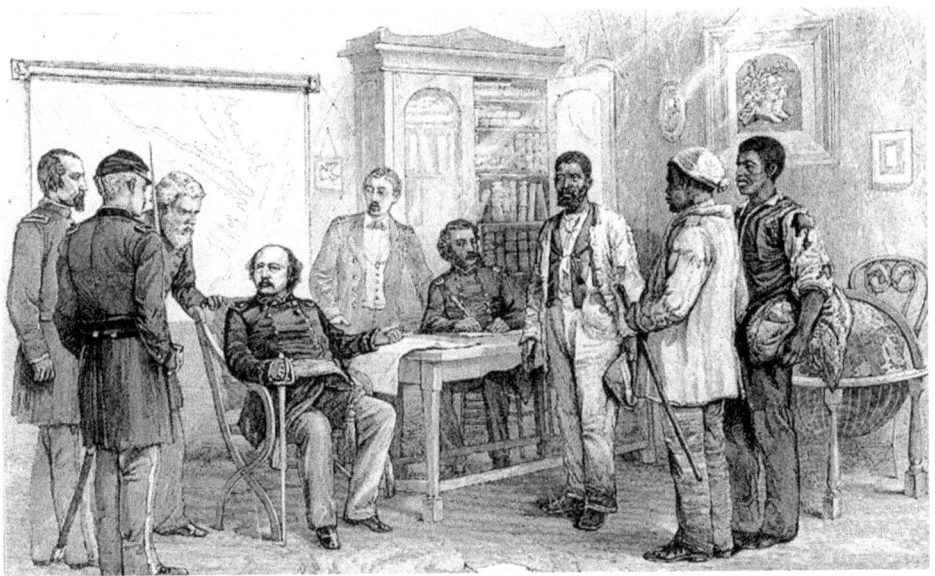

Major-General Benjamin Butler contemplating the fate of the enslaved men Frank Baker, James Townsend and Sheppard Mallory (courtesy New York Public Library, Wallach Division Picture Collection).

local knowledge of the terrain, troop strength and resources in the area. This information was prized by the likes of General Butler who was unfamiliar with the southern states. The need for local knowledge was a constant throughout the war; Butler was in need of a map to be sent to him from Baltimore as late as 1864 as he planned to assault Richmond.[12]

The contradictions of liberating slaves from their plantations only to then apply their labor to the Union's military ends are manifold. The restrictions and discipline of the military grated and were antithetical to the enslaveds' desire for freedom. The assumptions of how to fight the war were continually debated. Frederick Douglass criticized General Butler for putting down a slave rebellion in Maryland on his march from Annapolis to Fort Monroe in March 1861.[13] In his famous essay calling for a war on slavery, Douglass was forthright about the contradictions in Butler's operation:

> To our mind, there is but one easy, short and effectual way to suppress and put down the desolating war which the slaveholders and their rebel minions are now waging against the American Government and its loyal citizens. Fire must be met with water, darkness with light, and war for the destruction of liberty must be met with war for the destruction of slavery.... We are ready and would go, counting ourselves happy in being permitted to serve and suffer for the cause of freedom and free institutions. But you won't let us go. Read the heart-rending account we publish elsewhere of the treatment received by the brave fellows, who broke away from their chains and went through

marvelous suffering to defend Fort Pickens against the rebels.—They were instantly seized and put in irons and returned to their guilty masters to be whipped to death! Witness Gen. Butler's offer to put down the slave insurrection in the State of Maryland.[14]

Douglass directly connects Butler's demeanor and behavior to that of southern slavers. General Butler himself reports to his senior officer that troop health is good, and he has run into no "disasters, except the great influx of the slaves."[15] For the enslaved, the status of being defined as "contraband" was a means to an end; for them, this tool of war was an interim state, and hopefully one final step before their full emancipation. The protection provided by the regiments at Fort Monroe (recast by the enslaved as "Fortress Freedom") sent out a powerful message to other African Americans:

> The three pioneer negroes were not long to be isolated from their race. There was no known channel of communication between them and their old comrades, and yet those comrades knew, or believed with the certainty of knowledge, how they had been received. If inquired of whether more were coming, their reply was, that, if they were not sent back, others would understand they were among friends.... Proclaim an edict of emancipation in the hearing of a single slave on the Potomac, and in a few days it will be known by his brethren on the Gulf.[16]

Denying slaveholders the opportunity to sell them south for much needed cash meant thousands of escaped enslaved sought protection and refuge with the Union army. Many of those would eventually work their way to Washington, D.C., a comparative refuge and location of opportunity given the number and concentration of Union forces. As the migration of runaway slaves moved north the very basis of the plantation economies were walking away. By July 6, 1861, Congress had passed legislation forfeiting any rebel claims on the enslaved used in fighting the Union.

More than 900 enslaved had reached the regiments under General Butler's command by July 1861. The flow was constant, as was the need for supplies and clothing:

> CONTRABANDS ON A WAR FOOTING—A Massachusetts firm, engaged in the manufacture of shoes, is now filling an order for three thousand pair of brogans, to be forwarded to Fortress Monroe for the use of the contrabands at that station. The sizes of the men range from eleven to sixteen, and in one instance, a special order was given for a pair of twenties.[17]

Throughout the war, and afterwards, Benjamin Butler played a major role in the redefinition of African Americans in support of the Union. Despite his early complaints about the burden the contraband put on his military resources, Butler was instrumental in ensuring that African American soldiers participated in actual combat and not just support tasks away from the front. In addition, once black soldiers were able to "fight for freedom" in combat,

Stampede of slaves to Fortress Monroe (courtesy of Library of Congress, Prints and Photographs Division, LC-DIG-ppmsca-35556).

Butler cast a medal at his own expense to honor their bravery. The medal remains the only one cast specifically for black troops in U.S. history.

The enslaved were primarily field hands without education and with little knowledge of the world outside of the plantation they were forced to live.[18] Their resilience was evident, having endured massive labor demands and physical violence, but their experiences and learning had been deliberately limited. Union commanders welcomed their labor; but they often assumed the former enslaved had more capacity to work than white counterparts, further stressing the refugees' health.[19] The former enslaveds' behavior was also positively contrasted to the crudity of some soldiers who offended the gentlemanly sensibility of the officer class:

> There was one striking feature in the contrabands which must not be omitted. I did not hear a profane or vulgar word spoken by them during my superintendence, a remark which it will be difficult to make of any sixty-four white men taken together anywhere in our army. Indeed, the greatest discomfort of a soldier, who desires to remain a gentleman in the camp, is the perpetual reiteration of language which no decent lips would utter in a sister's presence. But the negroes, so dogmatically pronounced unfit for freedom, were in this respect models for those who make high boasts of civility of manners and Christian culture. Out of the sixty-four who worked for us, all but half a dozen were members of the Church, generally the Baptist. Although

without a pastor, they held religious meetings on the Sundays which we passed in Hampton, which were attended by about sixty colored persons and three hundred soldiers. The devotions were decorously conducted....[20]

The enslaved traveled north in search of freedom and opportunities denied to them on their plantations. As they traveled at night for fear of being recaptured, they initially kept away from the burning fires of the soldiers, not sure what camps were close by. During the daytime, Confederate and Union armies crisscrossed northern and eastern Virginia; gun shots and cannon fire were always close. The chaos of war created tremendous anxiety in the farmlands and communities surrounding the battlefields. As dead bodies and human remains were scattered throughout the fields of northern Virginia, the enslaved took every opportunity to plot their strategy for escape.

In order not to be bogged down with hungry, weak and often sick refugees who wanted to go north while the military went south, the Union military helped many of the refugees reach Washington by boat, including some 360 transported from Suffolk, Virginia, in October 1862.[21] The District of Columbia was rapidly becoming the refuge of choice for the runaways from the slaveholding states, particularly for those from Maryland and Virginia. They would often arrive in poor shape:

> Some 25 or 30 contrabands came across the Potomac and through Georgetown to the city yesterday. Most of them were women and children, and the sight was one to excite the sympathy of lookers-on at their apparent helpless condition.[22]

For the contraband the District of Columbia became a haven. The capital city had a high proportion of freed black people and many federal troops for their protection and safety from their slaveholders. It also promoted itself as a location for work with pay, enabling the "contraband of war" the ability to start fresh.

> After the second Battle of Bull Run (Second Manassas) late in August ... some four hundred slaves arrived in the capital over a two day span. Although most came on foot, the *Washington Evening Star* reported the arrival of a group of twenty-seven in a wagon drawn by six fine oxen. Simultaneously, another one hundred contrabands disembarked from military transport ships resupplying troops at Fredericksburg.[23]

For many the journey would be long and hard, and for some, fatal. Most left in small multi-generational family units; and while hunger and thirst often led to frustration and bickering, the ultimate goal of freedom helped them persevere. They and the animals that brought them to the city were malnourished, sick and on the verge of death. Living on remote plantations, the fugitives had little natural immunity to protect them in the seething urban camps where infectious diseases were rampant and reliably clean water sources nonexistent.

The war placed tremendous burdens on local governments across the nation, but no city was more burdened than the city of Washington. Governments at all levels and in all regions of the nation had resisted developing such a system of care for the runaways, afraid that a system of dependency would erode existing government services and break down systems of authority. Once Congress provided emancipation to the enslaved in the District of Columbia in April 1862, the federal government intervened to develop a support system. For the black refugees, Washington was a beacon of hope, and they kept coming to seek protection. The region was inundated with refugees and "during the summer of 1863, Camp Barker averaged twenty-five deaths per week."[24] As the city suffered under the weight of dying fugitives and as the carcasses of their dead animals lay in the street, benevolent societies and abolitionist groups were sought by the government to assist in the public health crisis.

The challenges the enslaved faced in order to reach freedom were enormous; the challenges of staying alive in the city were equally profound. For the contraband there was no path to a stable income or to secure the basic necessities of life. The public health conditions in the city, the continuing black laws (restricting movement and setting curfews), the commonly held and expressed racism, and continued restrictions on their labor made freedom less than easy. The documentation of these civilian challenges has been less understood than conditions among the enlisted; it is a tale of overcoming adversity, of walking sick in freedom:

> The experience of sick freedpeople was often pushed aside in favor of a liberation narrative that heroically described the abolition of slavery, or it was chalked up as a natural outcome of the war, which caused massive carnage and produced an enormous death toll among the soldiers. Consequently, agents of the federal government did not tell the stories of the tens of thousands of emancipated salves who suffered and died.... The names and experiences of these freedpeople were too politically problematic to be recorded.[25]

As the city of Washington struggled to manage the complex changes of civil war and as the contraband moved into the city, it was apparent to all that the city's infrastructure could not handle the diverse challenges brought by the refugees. A *Boston Herald* correspondent painted a "sad picture of the liberated and fugitive slaves in and about the Federal capital," a city it called "Lincoln's Bastille":

> The small-pox is raging fearfully among them, as high as twenty dying in one day.... Besides, the strongest pro-slavery people here will not hire negroes, and will have nothing to do with them unless they are slaves, which is now impossible. A large number of the advocates of the abolition of slavery here trusted that it would soon cause the disappearance of the colored population, but the reverse has been the case.... White labor in families is daily being substituted, and the demand and price are large in consequence.

The result of this idleness is, of course, crime, and for a month past two-thirds of the police records have involved the negro. They dare not beg, and therefore steal. As for the contraband camp, such a motley assemblage was never seen before.... The questions of labor and society are seriously involved, and he who devises human means for the relief of forty thousand contrabands now in our lines and the thousands yet to come will be a wise man. Do you want them North?[26]

The contraband arrived while the city was absorbing another population: sick, wounded, maimed and dying soldiers from the battlefields. The city had no existing system in place to absorb this large influx of people in need, whether white or black, civilian or military, sick or even able-bodied. There was only one contraband hospital in the original camp Duff Green's Row on Capitol Hill; it reformed at Camp Barker and morphed into Freedman Hospital, but it was always "small compared to the need ... conditions were poor and supplies low."[27]

The city of Washington was the hub for military strategic discussions, as well as political debates on the tactics for fighting the war and winning the peace. Washington was also a city confronted with human suffering. The city had now become the epicenter of the raw debate over slavery, race and class. At the core was the widespread assumption that no whites wanted to live close to blacks, to potentially have to support them, or perhaps to compete with them for the manual labor contracts. Challenged by abolitionists, thought leaders were coming to the realization that the current migration of present contraband to the city would eventually be followed by large numbers of freed people coming north to seek shelter, services, and, potentially, employment.

For many northern politicians with little to no experience with poor, itinerant black field hands, they feared what they did not know. In contrast, African American abolitionist Frederick Douglass expressed no fear of African Americans being lazy or drifting at emancipation, but, rather, confidence in their application and understanding of natural law:

> What shall be done with the Negro if emancipated? Deal justly with him. He is a human being, capable of judging between good and evil, right and wrong, liberty and slavery, and is as much a subject of law and any other man; therefore, deal justly with him. He is, like other men, sensible of the motives of reward and punishment. Give him wages for his work, and let hunger pinch him if he don't work.... "But will he work?" Why should he not? He is used to it. His hands are already hardened by toil, and he has no dreams of ever getting a living by any other means than by hard work.[28]

Douglass had his own experience as a refugee from slavery to draw on. *The Narrative of the Life of Frederick Douglass*, written and compiled ten years after his escape to New York, is full of stories of malnourishment, deliberate starvation, and a need for well-honed survival skills in the face of daily violence.

Conditions in the city were an unhealthy mix of infectious disease, a degraded environment polluting the water supply, and a high concentration of military-only hospitals. Hospitals and medicine were segregated, reflecting the Union army's segregated regiments. The city lacked a government support system for the black refugees. Nevertheless, the city continued to become for many a sanctuary from enslavement and the plantation.

At 2 a.m. the night after Virginia formally announced secession, General Heintzelman led troops out of the District to the heights across the Potomac. Three and half hours later, Colonel Willcox reported he had secured the City of Alexandria.[29] By the afternoon of May 24, 1861, work had started on the forts that would circle Arlington—they would be named Forts Runyon, Ellsworth, Corcoran, Albany, Haggerty, and Bennett. Once the city was under control, the rebel Confederate flags were removed from all buildings. Colonel Elmer Ellsworth was shot and killed by the proprietor of the Marshall Hotel in Alexandria following the removal of the rebel flag from the building. Ellsworth, just 24 years old, yet already an admired military tactician and recruiter, had led his volunteers across the Long Bridge on the first day Union troops moved into Virginia:

> The murder of Colonel Ellsworth yesterday morning at Alexandria, occasioned a grief and indignation among the soldiers and citizens here, from which they were not perceptibly diverted by the excitement of the attending military events.... His conduct in going into the Marshall House in person, to haul down the offensive flag flying over it, although an evidence of the energy and impulsiveness of his age and temperament, can hardly be said to have been an imprudence.[30]

Colonel Ellsworth's death impacted the president personally. Ellsworth had accompanied Lincoln to vote in Springfield, Illinois, and was part of the traveling party from Springfield to Washington for the inauguration. Lincoln is described as having "shed tears freely."[31] Ellsworth would be laid out to rest in the White House, before being returned via New York City to his upstate home, as was customary for those with sufficient funds. Flags were set at half-staff, and the body was accompanied by a black-shrouded flag from the New York Fire Department, the core of the Zouave regiment he had raised.[32]

The spring campaign of 1862 provided the enslaved with opportunities to escape to Union lines and for black labor to support the war effort. The fugitives arrived in large numbers, not just in Washington but in the series of military camps and fortifications around the city:

> Between one hundred and two hundred contrabands are at work in setting things in order upon the Arlington estate. Numbers are employed by the government elsewhere, but the cry is still they come. Duff Green's row in Washington is full of them, and many of them decline to work for private parties.[33]

The camps were composed primarily of canvas tents, and they, too, became overcrowded. As soon as one group was found shelter, more space needed to be identified. When James S. Wadsworth became the military governor, he tried to improve living conditions for some of the fugitive enslaved by moving them to Duff Green's Row, in the old capital prison.[34]

In short order, the area and the tenements at Duff Green's Row (now the site of the Library of Congress) could not absorb the influx; the area was soon transferred by the military to the National Freedman's Relief Association. The lack of adequate sanitary conditions led to a smallpox epidemic killing many of the refugees. In May 1862, the District appropriated $1580 to reimburse the "wars physicians for vaccinating persons" during the epidemic.[35] The Duff Green prison buildings were converted and annexed to the adjacent military prison, and "the occupants were moved to Camp Barker, a tent enclave,"[36] and to vacated army barracks and stables near the current Logan Circle.

Former enslaved were registered and given their "free papers" and provisions. The camp processed nearly 5,000 former enslaved men, women and children in less than eight months, with 1,400 arriving in September 1862 alone.[37] President Lincoln visited the contraband camp on his way to the Soldier's Home north of the city limits. He was greeted by African American children singing in the newly established Freedman's Village School, as captured by Civil War photographer, Mathew Brady.

Between June 1862 and June 1864, the death rate at Camp Barker approached one in seven, as an extraordinary 700 of the approximately 5,000

Freedman's Village School in Washington, D.C. (courtesy National Archives, Records of the Department of State, G 94).

residents passed away.[38] As conditions in these mini–tent cities deteriorated and "a high rate of death due to disease resulted, it was decided to relocate some of the contraband outside of the city."[39] Washington was also receiving an increasing number of sick, injured and dying soldiers. By the spring of 1863, "more than 10,000 persons seeking asylum were living in Washington."[40]

The city was now experiencing a public health emergency: the combined lack of infrastructure and waste disposal systems, clean water supplies, heat, and inadequate understanding of disease transmission were proving deadly. In the aftermath of Antietam, the military medical system had been radically realigned and an ambulance system ensured that soldiers were being triaged and treated on the battlefield. An elaborate network of hospitals connected by rail brought soldiers into enormous hospitals in the Union cities.[41]

In contrast, the formerly enslaved who reached the city had few resources and social systems to aid them in adapting to freedom. For contraband camps across the country, widescale reports of a lack of basic necessities were numerous in the northern newspapers. Conditions on the Tennessee-Mississippi border were typical: "At Pine Bluffs, below Memphis, are seventeen hundred [contrabands], who are without food, clothing or shoes to an alarming extent, and many are dying at that point for want of food, clothing and medicines."[42]

As part of an appeal for private charitable donations to supplement governmental funds, General Grant sent his chaplain and superintendent of contrabands to present to the people of Washington the "destitute condition of the 'contrabands,' and to solicit means to provide for the comfort of the wives and children."[43]

By 1864, during a smallpox outbreak, the open, healthy heights of Arlington were suggested to Secretary of War Edward Stanton as an appropriate relief location for the contraband.[44] This decision would lead to the model Freedman's Village, the most permanent solution to relocating the enslaved to be established in the Washington area. A public health emergency, defined by social and political conditions in flux, was driving a change in Arlington. The Civil War was a time of violent social change, liberation of the enslaved, explosions in medical knowledge and great changes in attitudes towards death and the value of life.

Chapter 7

Health and Medical Care

THE PHYSICAL, EMOTIONAL, AND PSYCHOLOGICAL CONDITIONS of the enslaved that arrived in Washington not only placed a tremendous strain on the city's resources, but also predicted the enslaved's success once they arrived. The death rate for the new arrivals was extremely high and reflected years of illiteracy, malnutrition, physical and psychological abuse, and long hours working in the fields, each a predictor of premature death. The first burials at Arlington National Cemetery and its Section 27 resulted from the horrific health conditions in the federal city of Washington during the Civil War. This war was bloodier than any other in American history and forced the migration of hundreds of thousands of enslaved across the South to the safety of contraband camps, bringing to light the horrific conditions in which they lived and their compromised health conditions once they arrived.

America's enslaved population was largely illiterate, particularly in the South, because of laws prohibiting the education of the enslaved. As much as slaveholders and their overseers took great pains to ensure an illiterate underclass, most enslaved understood the importance of being self-taught and often connected literacy with independence. Literacy or lack thereof impacted the overall health of most enslaved. Poor prenatal care for mother and child often placed tremendous strain on mothers and their unborn, as the women were forced to work long hours in the field until their infant was born, often expected to return within hours of giving birth.

For the enslaved, the family structure was tenuous at best. It depended on the economy of the plantations they served—particularly in Virginia before the war—and the desires of the men on the plantation. As with any society, the wish to have a close-knit family and the ability to protect the family's honor and reputation was important to enslaved families, but these ties were so often broken to satisfy legal debts and obligations or to fulfill insatiable personal appetites. Enslavers were also cruel to their enslaved men, viciously punishing them for speaking out or trying to protect the women, and leaving them with physical and emotional scars that had a profound psychosocial effect on the victim as much as those around him.

The enslaved were unhealthy; the repeated physical violence and stress from being overworked, instances of communicable and non-communicable diseases, and poor dietary options and malnutrition—all treated with only homemade remedies and little to no formal medical attention—contributed to high mortality rates and premature deaths on most plantations across the South.

But the Civil War now provided over 470,000 enslaved persons throughout the South the first opportunity to escape and change the conditions of their lives forever, as well as the ability to be paid for the work they did. The actual number of enslaved who escaped to freedom is unknown. However, the closest estimate is based on the number of former enslaved and free blacks who entered into various work programs:

> By the spring of 1865, at least 474,000 former slaves and free blacks had taken part in some form of federally sponsored free labor in the Union-occupied South—as soldiers, military laborers, residents of contraband camps, urban workers, or agricultural laborers on government-supervised plantations and farms.... [Other] former slaves, whose numbers are also impossible to estimate, had left the South to become free workers in the North, some of them under the auspices of official relocation and employment programs, others on their own or with the assistance of individual army officers.[1]

As the war raged on, primarily on the battlefields of northern Virginia, whites moved south behind the safety of Confederate lines below Richmond, while the enslaved escaped to the safety and protection of Union troops, then on to Washington. For the enslaved, psychological terror was the vehicle used to control every aspect of their daily lives. The battles of northern Virginia now provided not only a physical but a psychological escape to safety behind the Union army lines, then hopefully on to freedom.

Contraband camps were found throughout the South, wherever the Union army had a large enough presence to provide protection. At the campsites of the Union army, the arrival of refugees created a strain on already limited resources. A military camp usually only had enough food for its men, scant medical resources and an allotment of tents only for the soldiers. Upon arriving in a camp, the contraband never quite knew how they would be received. Some soldiers and military camps were more receptive than others. Some soldiers entered the war for altruistic reasons; while others were recruited and perhaps blamed the refugees for the horrific conditions of their surroundings, despite seeing the vulnerable people they were there to fight for arriving at camp.

The first wave of arrivals was initially sent to the contraband camp at Duff Green's Row (current site of the Library of Congress). The site was selected as a means to purposely provide the necessary support to the new arrivals, but also to be able to restrict the movements of the contraband to other parts of the city.

With President Lincoln's January 1, 1863, Emancipation Proclamation, freeing the enslaved in the Confederate States, came the first real opportunity for an enslaved man or woman to make a permanent change in their lives. According to an article in the January 16, 1863, *Chicago Tribu*ne, the enslaved in Northern Virginia were on the move:

> The northern neck of Virginia, the heart of aristocratic and wealthy slavery, is alive with a vast hegira of bondmen and bondwomen, traveling under President Lincoln's pass. The proclamation is depopulating the whole region between the Rappahannock and the Potomac. In farm wagons, in coaches, on horseback, afoot and in buggies with valuable property, in every case, this second movement from Egypt to the promised land fills the highways and the woods.[2]

In due time the contraband camps in the Washington area became overpopulated hubs with poor sanitation, inadequate housing and medical facilities, and disease-carrying mosquitos and other vermin—the perfect breeding grounds for bacterial and viral illnesses. Each day, the camps saw new arrivals, with torn and tattered clothing, hungry from long travel without adequate food or water. During the winter months, the refugees arrived cold and shivering from the winter elements, often with colds, the flu, and other winter respiratory ailments. During the spring and summer months, the arrivals were subjected to sleeping out in low-lying mosquito-infested swamp areas, often arriving sick with whooping cough, measles and yellow fever.

Slavery was outlawed in the District of Columbia by the Compromise of 1850. In 1860 the total population in the District of Columbia was 75,080, and by 1870, the population nearly doubled to 131,682. During the same period, the black population in the city exploded from 14,346 in 1860 to over 43,400 in 1870.

Table 1: 1800 to 1870 District of Columbia Ten-Year Population Growth[3]

Absolute Population					Rate of Increase				
Census	White	Free Col.	Slave	Total	Census	White	Free Col.	Slave	Total
1800	10,066	783	3,244	14,093	1800	—	—	—	—
1810	16,079	2,549	5,395	24,023	1810	59.73	225.54	66.30	70.46
1820	22,614	4,048	6,377	33,039	1820	40.64	58.80	18.20	37.53
1830	27,563	6,152	6,119	39,834	1830	21.88	51.97	4.04	20.57
1840	30,657	8,361	4,694	43,712	1840	11.22	35.90	23.28	9.74
1850	37,941	10,059	3,687	51,687	1850	23.75	20.30	21.45	18.24
1860	60,788	11,107	3,181	75,076	1860	60.22	10.41	13.72	45.25
1870	88,278	43,404	0	131,682	1870	—	—	—	—

7. Health and Medical Care

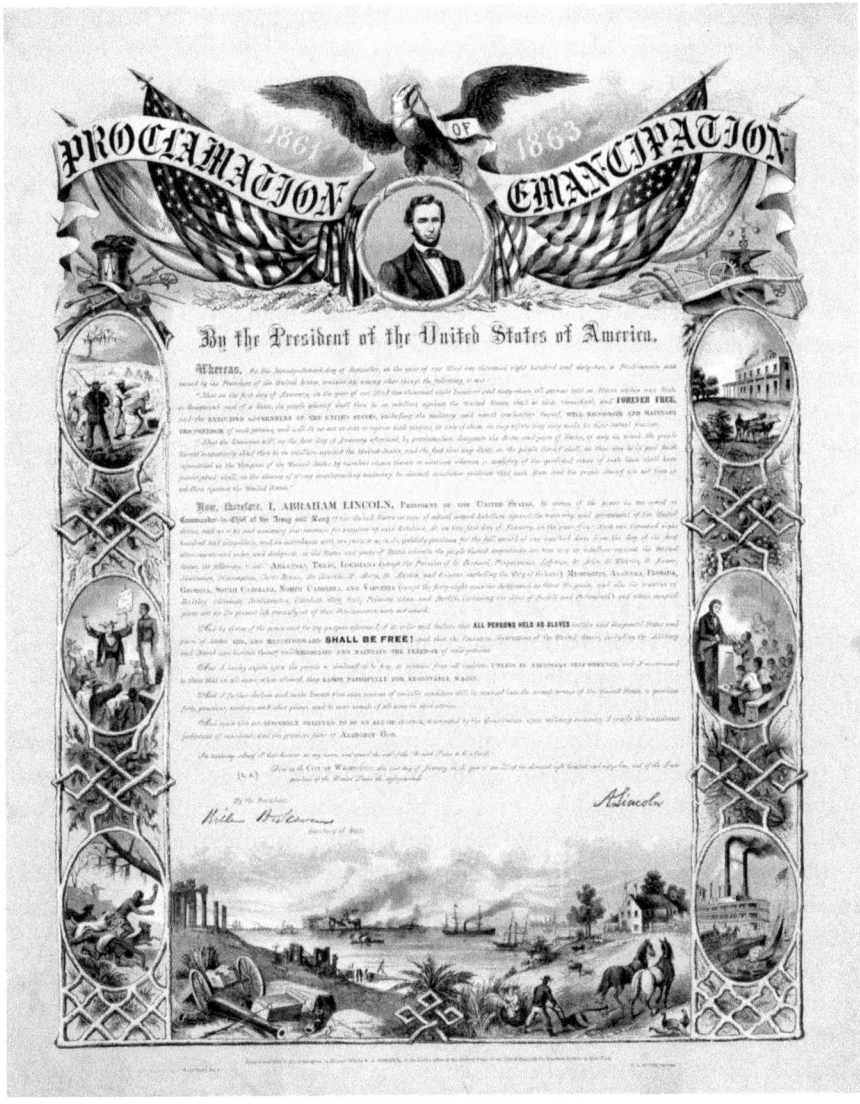

President Lincoln's Emancipation Proclamation (Library of Congress).

Washington's proximity to the slave states of Virginia and Maryland was encouraging to the enslaved seeking the promises of freedom found in the words of Abraham Lincoln's Proclamation. Their eager search for freedom left them unconcerned that the city lacked housing, sanitation and infrastructure to support new residents, particularly those with compromised immune systems.

For thousands of contraband, their ultimate success in reaching the safety of the contraband camps in Washington also facilitated their own premature deaths. For many, their compromised immune systems were not strong enough to endure the diseases they encountered once they arrived. Infectious diseases such as diphtheria, measles and typhoid fever were rampant in overcrowded camps. In some camps, the dreaded and highly contagious smallpox spread, causing fear and panic; there was an overall fear that the isolated outbreaks would eventually spread and overtake the city.

Despite hundreds of years of observation and writings on disease, by 1861, doctors still lacked a scientific understanding of many of the viruses and bacteria that caused whooping cough, typhus, meningitis, influenza, and measles outbreaks suffered throughout the war. The differences between bacteria and viruses, as well as fundamental transmission routes between animals and humans were still to be discovered. However, there were some things that medical professionals knew and public health measures could address. The contraband deaths, in those cases, had less to do with scientific knowledge than with the fundamental differences in care between black and white patients at the time.

The vaccine for smallpox,[4] for instance, had been developed by Edward Jenner in 1796, after he demonstrated in 1794 England that milkmaids were conferred immunity to smallpox due to their exposure to the biologically similar cowpox virus. Jenner inferred that controlled exposure to smallpox could tame the disease. Prior to this, Cotton Mather, educated and supported by the slave Onesimus, deployed inoculation in the 1721 Boston smallpox outbreak.[5] Benjamin Rush lectured on the disease and inoculation in 1781 in Philadelphia. The virus was not isolated nor its transmission fully comprehended until 1931, yet smallpox was controllable at the time of the Civil War and had been controlled by the armies. In 1860, smallpox was the only infectious disease that had a proven prevention strategy.

One population that was invariably not inoculated was the enslaved people in the Southern states. The tens of thousands who innocently sought freedom in Washington arrived only to experience the squalor of the contraband camps, leading to their deaths caused by the smallpox virus and other infectious diseases.

As population shifts occurred, particularly in the early days of the war, disease threatened everyone's health, as the *Washington Evening Star* made clear in its article "ANOTHER SMALL-POX CASE" on the January 21, 1862:

> Last night, a colored man, named Cornelius Newman, was arrested and taken to the Central station by patrolman McDevitt, for an assault and battery on a man named Kelly. This morning being brought into the trial room for a hearing, his face and hands were noticed by the officers generally, it being perceived that the pustules were not fairly healed from the small-pox, and in some places the flesh was apparent.... He seemed

perfectly indifferent as to what would be done with him, or the consequences of his mingling with the people on public places.⁶

Unsuspecting victims of outbreaks of smallpox and other diseases were also victims of a public outcry blaming them for the spread of disease, particularly during the smallpox outbreak that occurred in early 1862. A January 16, 1862, *Evening Star* editorial praises control actions in Cincinnati and proposes a $50 fine or 30 days imprisonment for anyone "willfully disobeying a proclamation" to stay in their house when convalescing from smallpox. Public health police powers were called for:

> The metropolitan police requested that the army remove the bodies of former slaves who died of smallpox and were left on the city streets. As the virus spread throughout city, military and municipal officials, as well as city residents and newspaper reports, blamed the virus on the arrival of freed people to the area.... Brigade Surgeon Stewart informed his subordinate, B.B. French, that in every case in which "smallpox had come under his notice it originated among Negroes." He then ordered that former slaves "should be removed to some place where they can be kept apart from the respectable white people, and where, if possible constant employment can be given them."⁷

Government-mandated vaccination, quarantine and exercise of police powers were controversial in civilian populations. The use of these powers challenged the essence of newly achieved freedoms, and the conditions in the hospitals were more akin to imprisonment. Among the former enslaved there were well-developed traditions of caring for their own and self-inoculation practices handed down across generations.

The spread of smallpox and other diseases was often associated with morality and work ethic (or perceived lack thereof) among the former enslaved. Widespread belief in black mental and physical inferiority reinforced that disease was random, an act of God, or related to poor habits. At emancipation, this noxious stew of ideas served to link freedom with disease, as if it was a consequence rather than an artifact of the social and political turmoil of the Civil War.⁸

Knowing how to deal with smallpox was insufficient, and did not mean inoculation protections were systematically extended to places where the contraband and freed people lived. Caleb Horner, as Chief of the Medical Division for the Freedman's Bureau, is reported to have "...failed to perceive smallpox as a problem that demanded immediate action," and "despite issuing orders on numerous other medical issues" ... neglected to inform Bureau physicians of the protocol to respond to the smallpox epidemic.⁹

Neither was disease bound by race; isolation of large numbers of African Americans on plantations might have contributed to their lack of immunity when they moved north to freedom. The isolation and identification of viruses and bacteria in laboratories to enable specific interventions would not be feasible until later in the century. For lack of a scientific public health system experience, intuition, culture and military authority would inform care.[10] In Washington the diseases of war mixed with diseases of population concentration, lack of sanitation, poor diet and lack of access to clean water:

> Due to the fact that the war had ultimately freed them from the institution of slavery, it became almost linguistically impossible to articulate his family's suffering ... [authorities] did not classify freed slaves as casualties or count them among the soldiers who died, but defined them as "fugitives," "contraband," "refugees," and ultimately as "freedmen." Casualties referred only to white soldiers, whose deaths ... were described as the ultimate sacrifice for a greater political cause.[11]

According to the Freedmen and Southern Society Project, during the war approximately "40,000 lived in the District of Columbia, in Alexandria, Virginia, and in the contraband camps on the Virginia side of the Potomac River" at Arlington.[12] The true number of contraband who ultimately arrived in the city has now been lost to history, and the number who died on their way will probably never be known.

Although medical tents were set up in an attempt to address the ever-growing challenges with the health conditions of the contraband, the challenges were just too great, and the number of deaths was overwhelming. Eventually, Arlington Heights would be dotted with hospitals associated with the military camps and forts that sprung up on the grounds of the former plantation during the war.[13] The Freedman's Village would notably have a hospital, as well as a church and school. The presence of hospitals would come to represent an advance in civic organization, when prior to the war they were places to avoid.

Despite the poor black former enslaved who crowded into the contraband camps and received substandard medical care, the Civil War was a time of great medical and surgical innovation; the conditions, the number of injuries and the demand on both sides necessitated that heroic soldiers be provided urgent care. The military's need to return men to battle became the mother of invention. Embalming of bodies was regularized, new surgical techniques were literally invented on the battlefield, the triage ambulance system for carrying the injured from the field was devised, and there was an explosion in the number and organization of hospitals.[14]

In the eighth United States Census, taken in 1860, more than 31 million Americans were enumerated, among them just under four million enslaved, 12.9 percent of the total. Current estimates put the number of *soldier* deaths in the four-year war at 750,000.[15] More than 2.5 percent of American men died having enlisted in the war, more than would die in all of the other wars fought by the United States combined—the Revolutionary War, the War of 1812, the Mexican War, the Spanish-American War, World War I, World War II, the Korean War, Vietnam and the Iraqi wars. The greatest number of deaths, more than two-thirds, were not from wounds, but from "considerable measure

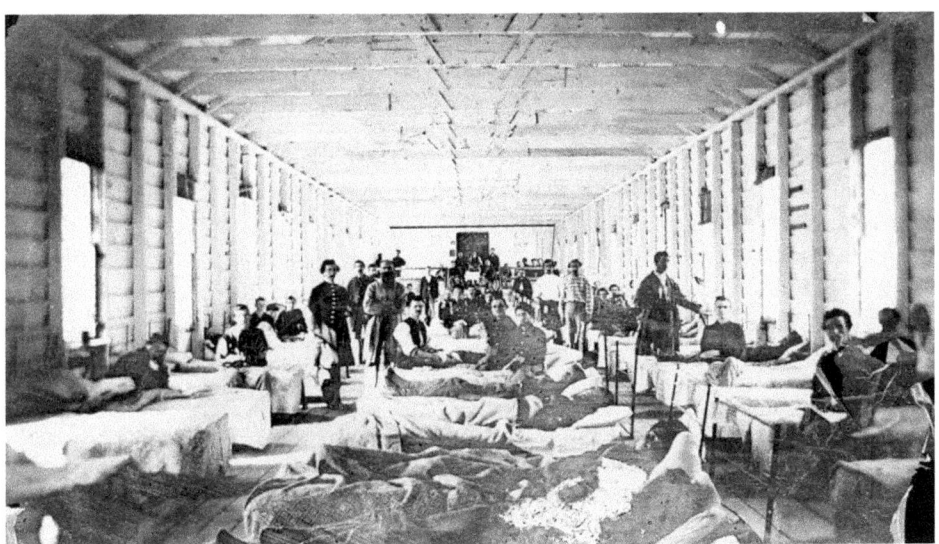

Camp Convalescent (Library of Congress Prints and Photographs Division).

of poor sanitation in an era that created mass armies that did not yet understand the transmission of infectious diseases like typhoid, typhus, and dysentery."[16] All of the advances in medicine were insufficient to overcome the parlous state of public health and interrupt infectious diseases.

Just as the battles taking place to the south of Washington had a profound effect on the city through relocation of former enslaved and wounded troops, so would the Arlington plantation be transformed during and after the war. Military hospitals were built, and hospitals were made out of the available buildings that surrounded the battlefields or towns close to large numbers of troops. In Alexandria, the Quaker Meetinghouse was converted to a hospital. South of Arlington, Camp Convalescent was established, nicknamed Camp Misery by Union troops; Union army nurse Clara Barton would describe the area as "a sort of pen—into which all who could limp, all deserters and stragglers, were driven promiscuously."[17]

Hospitals and doctors' practices were places feared by many people prior to the Civil War. They were known as places to die more than survive, but military necessity would profoundly change that perception and the reality. At the start of the Civil War, Dr. Jonathan Letterman was assigned to the army as the medical director of the Potomac and became known at the "father of battlefield medicine." In August 1862, Letterman had his "plan approved for the establishment of the Army Ambulance Corps.... This transferred the control of ambulances from the quartermaster to the Medical Director and permitted ambulances to carry medical supplies."[18] As medical director,

Letterman established medical triage procedures for on and off battlefield, including mobile field hospitals to be located at division and corps headquarters.

Dr. Letterman was also instrumental in the transformation of care in military hospitals and for civilian hospitals after the war. He implemented strategies that would have a profound effect on the District of Columbia. On December 15, 1862, during the bloody Battle of Fredericksburg, a truce was called "so that the wounded of both armies could be removed from the field, the Union army had suffered 12,700 casualties, with 6,000 of them dead."[19] In anticipation of heavy casualties, Dr. Letterman:

> ... took advantage of the delayed arrival of the pontoon bridges to be sure his arrangements for treating and evacuating battlefield casualties were in order. With a a storehouse of supplies at the nearby railroad depot at Aquia Creek, five hundred hospital tents, and almost a thousand ambulances.... In Washington, fifty-some miles away from the battlefield, the staff at Union Hospital anticipated the arrival of the wounded.[20]

The purpose of the military camps was to provide shelter for the men and to house equipment and the animals. The troops in the field needed to be prepared at a minute's notice to engage in combat, and many of the refugees created logistical problems when the troops needed to relocate or fight. The healthy refugee men were often recruited from the military campsites to volunteer for the United States Colored Troops, while the women, the elderly and the young children, along with the sick and infirmed, were advised to continue going north to contraband camps found in Alexandria, Virginia, and Washington, D.C.

As the war progressed and casualties increased, Lettermen was able to take advantage of the lessons learned from the military medical care provided to the British army in the Crimean War (1853–56). Secretary of War Jefferson Davis sent Captain (later General) George McClellan as one of three officers in a Military Commission in 1855 to study European tactics and logistics in the conflict. Crimea was considered the first industrial war that integrated advancing technologies into the war effort, such as the use of telegraph between nations; the transport of troops by rail to the front line; extensive coverage on the battlefield provided by the newspapers; and the first use of repeating rifles, with their destructive capacity to rip human flesh and bone apart.

The number of dead and the variety of injuries led to major advances in the field of surgery and the understanding of human anatomy. The sheer volume of dead led to a significant shift in the perception of how their bodies were to be treated, how they could be reunited with families, and how and where they should be buried.[21] For medical doctors on the battlefield, the most common Civil War surgery was amputation. Anatomy lessons for American physicians took place at the "margins of legality"[22] prior to the Civil War, when trafficking in dead bodies and grave robbing conducted by and for medical schools was common. Nearly 20 percent of U.S. physicians sought education in France to have better access to cadavers.[23] The use or abuse of the poor to meet the educational needs of elite physicians led to at least seventeen cases of "anatomy riots" from before the Revolutionary War until 1855.[24]

As guns were perfected, due in part to the introduction of the Minié ball bullet invented by Claude-Étienne Minié, they became weapons of mass carnage. The Minié bullet was designed to cause as much physical damage to its victim as possible. The unique design made the bullets enter the body with ease, seldom becoming lodged and instead exiting the body and causing tremendous pain and internal damage. Days and weeks after being shot, victims often died from the infections caused by the bullet wounds, rather than from the bullet itself. Soldiers and civilians in the Civil War would die in greater numbers from infectious diseases than injuries and combat wounds. The estimate is that twice as many died from infections:

> Infection was the curse of the wounded soldier. No matter how slight a wound, once the skin was broken the chances were good that a deadly bacterial infestation would lead to drastic therapies, multiple operations, amputations and frequently death. Hospitals were filled with patients slowly healing over months and then a secondary infection would take hold. These infections were particularly painful and deadly. What medical science did not know was the cause of these infections or how to adequately prevent or treat them. The Civil War was fought two decades before the germ theory of disease was elucidated and just a few years before Scottish Surgeon Joseph Lister (1827–1912) presented in 1867 his antiseptic principles of surgery and wound care.[25]

The deaths were normalized by belief systems; suffering came as an act of God, infections were the result of bad air and other science theories later refuted. The spread of infection was compounded by the surgeons (re)use of tools.[26] At the time of the civil war, all wounds were expected to get infected. The war and the companion knowledge derived from the doctors on both sides of the Crimean War did produce some innovations in cleaning wounds and antiseptic solutions. These innovations occurred without the science of bacteriology, and Joseph Lister would not offer his principles on surgery and wound care until two years after the Civil War.

Disease was even seen as a potential military advantage. The specter of disease among the Union army was welcomed by some secessionist newspapers as a bulwark against invasion. The first attack on Vicksburg failed due to the Union forces being depleted by disease. Disease spread was not restricted to the Union forces, southern doctors were concerned through the war that the northern blockade limited access to quinine to treat malaria.[27]

> The first test of this theory came in April 1862 in Shiloh, Tennessee, where Union General William T. Sherman's forces met the enemy in a bloody battle. Before and after the

fight, typhoid, diarrhea, scurvy, and the fevers associated with malarial diseases ravaged troops on both sides. One physician wrote, "The pestilential atmosphere of the country about Shiloh was producing an amount of sickness almost without parallel in the history of the war." In May, Sherman mustered only half of his 10,000 troops because the other half were sick.[28]

With the specter of war on the horizon, politicians on both sides knew the importance of having adequate medical care for soldiers to keep them ready for the fight. Just before the war broke out, in 1859, Virginia Governor Henry Wise encouraged two hundred University of Pennsylvania medical students to return to their southern homes and study in Richmond.[29]

The U.S. Army employed fewer than one hundred doctors at the outset of the war, none of them African Americans. As colored troops were introduced to combat roles, the need for black doctors became apparent. The ranks of nurses were even thinner. Prior to the Civil War there was no formal training for nurses in the United States.[30] Self-care and nursing was the daily task of women, based on observation and informal passage of knowledge from generation to generation.

The introduction and application of medical innovations would be applied and proscribed by social norms and racial attitudes. The National Civil War Medicine Museum provides the most comprehensive digest of all things medical in the war. They document that:

> At least 13 African Americans physicians served with the Union Army during the Civil War. Three men were commissioned officers and ten served as contract surgeons (acting assistant surgeon). Two of these men had attended medical school but had not yet graduated when they received their appointments as Acting Assistants Surgeons. All of these men served with the United States Colored Troops or in various Freedman Hospitals, working with African American patients, or were involved in recruiting of U. S. Colored Troops.[31]

African American doctors were hired to treat other African Americans in an Army that segregated its units based on race. Treatment of Union civilians, white and black, was secondary or overlooked, provided at the margins to the contraband working in support of the troops as teamsters and cooks. These physicians were the few African Americans in the officer class. Segregated care was a continuing reality for another hundred years, reinforced by a medical establishment that discussed physician and patient access to hospitals in terms of "privileges." Anderson Ruffin Abbott was the first black Canadian-born doctor. He applied for a commission in the Union army in February 1863; when rebuffed, he became a medical cadet to the USCT in June. Dr. Abbott was the son of free black wealthy "business and property investor" Wilson Ruffin Abbott and his wife Ellen (Toyer) Abbott. After leaving Alabama and relocating to Toronto, Canada, in 1835, "Wilson Abbott became one of the wealthiest Africans Canadians in Toronto."[32]

... became prominent in Chatham. He was appointed coroner for Kent County, Ontario in 1874 and by 1878 he was president of both the Chatham Medical Society and the Chatham Literary and Debating Society. As president of the Wilberforce Educational Institute between 1873 and 1880, he fought against racially segregated schools in Canada. Anderson Abbott returned to the United States in 1894 where he accepted a position as surgeon-in-chief at Provident Hospital in Chicago, Illinois, the first black-owned hospital in the United States. He remained at Provident for only one year, returning again to Canada to resume his practice in Toronto.[33]

As one of the thirteen African Americans commissioned as surgeons by the U.S. army during the Civil War, Dr. Abbott received his commission after writing directly to Secretary of War Stanton (note Canadian spelling conventions):

> I learn by our city papers that it is the intention of the government of the United States to raise 150,000 coloured troops. Being one of that class, I beg to make application for a commission as assistant surgeon. My qualifications are that I am 24 years of age; I have studied medicine five years; I am a licentiate of the college of Physicians and Surgeons of Upper Canada.... I am also a matriculant of the Toronto University where I intend to take my degree in the spring of Bachelor of Medicine.[34]

Abbott was a founder of the Freedman's Hospital when it opened on June 15, 1864. He served as a surgeon at the Freedman's Village before returning to Canada to secure his medical degree in 1866. His service and skill was highly commended by his commanding officer:

Left: Anderson R. Abbott, MD. *Right:* Alexander Thomas Augusta, MD (both photographs courtesy Toronto Ward Museum).

> I take great pleasure in bearing testimony to the good and faithful service rendered by assistant surgeon A.R. Abbott to sick and destitute freedmen…. My attention was directed to Dr. Abbott, then executive officer of the contraband camp and Freedman's Hospital, where his efficiency soon gained him the promotion to the position of surgeon in charge…. His resignation is accepted with regret.[35]

This letter from May 1866 is worth noting for how "contraband" remains a term for describing the formerly enslaved and their circumstances. Abbott was mentor to Alexander Thomas Augusta, MD, who was freeborn in Norfolk, Virginia, but had to go to Toronto, Canada, to receive a medical education. Augusta was the first African American to receive a commission as a surgeon (and therefore as an officer), putting him in charge of two white assistant surgeons.

After the war, Dr. Augusta would become the first African American faculty member at a medical school (at Howard University), and upon his death he was buried at Arlington (Section 1-124C).[36] Despite the fact that black doctors were deployed by the military, as with every other aspect of life, medicine and healthcare was also segregated. The care afforded to United States Colored Troops, while separate, was not always equal to that afforded to white soldiers.

Casualty statistics highlight the racism, segregated healthcare and military assignments in the use of black troops. The African American mortality rate was more than their white compatriots, as shown in figures compiled by Frederick H. Dyer in *A Compendium of the War of the Rebellion, Vol. 1*; a total of 36,847 black men died in Union service, or about one in five of the 178,975 that enlisted in the USCT. Yet 29,658 of these men died of disease rather than from combat-related causes, constituting more than 80 percent of all black deaths in the Union Army. While many white soldiers also died of disease, only about 60 percent of them did so compared to the aforementioned 80 percent of black soldiers.[37]

Little quarter was given to African American troops, or their white officers. When injured in battle, they would be executed or left on the field as at Fort Pillow and the Battle of Saltville.[38] There were instances of USCTs convalescing in their hospital beds, only be executed by Confederate soldiers. Infection and disease could be used as additional tools of terror in the war; a white officer (deemed equally dangerous in the rebel minds) was deliberately exposed to the blood and germs of dying black soldiers who were bleeding out:

> When these two black soldiers died, other severely wounded black soldiers were placed close enough to the officer so that the men's wounds could infect one another. This was contrary to standard practice, even under Civil War prison camp conditions.[39]

As the fatalities of the Civil War mounted, deciding what to do with the bodies and where to bury them became a challenge for the District of Columbia. Battlefield commanders sought to collect their dead, and rather than stop to bury them, they took steps to send them to Washington for final resolution. The arrival of war fatalities every day continued to strain city resources, and as medical procedures on the battlefield improved, men whose lives were saved by enhanced medical procedures such as amputation now added to the city's burdens. The city was overwhelmed not only by the war dead from the battlefields, but by soldiers in need of long-term medical care in area hospitals, as well as a number of sick and dying fugitive enslaved.

Documentation of civilian health conditions is scant. As within the military, it is difficult to capture the full complexity of racial attitudes, due to the wholesale lack of documentation of care, particularly for African Americans. However, it is not difficult to prove that African Americans died in similar or higher numbers than their civilian and military white counterparts, on and off of the battlefields. They died receiving little regard for their suffering and less respect for the disposition of their remains. Documented evidence of the attitudes to black health is filled with assumptions about racial inferiority, imagined genetic conditions of susceptibility, moral shortcomings and hygienic delinquency, and the assignment of blame for the introduction of infections. Segregated care was the norm, enforced and supported by existing racial dogma. Brigade Surgeon Stewart ordered sick African Americans to be segregated to avoid offending the "sensibilities" of sick Confederate prisoners in the same prison.[40]

Many cities and military commanders regularly inoculated their population. Casualties among the ranks in the Revolutionary War were also largely from disease as opposed to combat. George Washington, as commander of the Continental Army, faced the Redcoats during a smallpox outbreak, and is commended for his actions:

> When historians debate Washington's most consequential decisions as commander in chief, they are almost always arguing about specific battles. A compelling case can be made that his swift response to the smallpox epidemic and to a policy of inoculation was the most important strategic decision of his military career.[41]

The U.S. army and the Confederacy in 1861 rapidly instituted inoculation campaigns to keep their troops healthy for battle. However, these programs did not extend to contraband or other blacks who lived on isolated farms and plantations.

Army leaders looked across the Potomac and saw the wide expanse of Arlington. The land was unencumbered and free of burial pits, and it was well sloped and not subject to flooding. The land had historical associations with good living and was well known as a healthy respite and recreational escape valve for city residents. It would be ideal for those able to help the war effort by applying their labor to raising food on the land the military had cleared of trees. Food that was desperately needed for the growing population coming into the District of Columbia could be grown on the cleared ground by laborers used to these tasks.

The contraband's labor power as a tool of liberation and support for the Union cause was well understood by May 1863. Colonel Elias M. Greene, chief quartermaster of the Department of Washington, was commanded by General Heintzleman with:

> ... the control of all of the contrabands formerly quartered at the contraband camp north of Washington. The object of this transfer is to enable Col. Greene to cultivate the farms on the south side of the Potomac, in the vicinity of Washington, abandoned by the former owners. The dwelling houses and quarters on these farms, which have survived the fortunes of war, will be sufficient to accommodate the laborers, with but a small outlay for repairs and for additional buildings. It is proposed to plant corn and millet, and to cut and cure the grass (estimated to make more than 10,000 tons of hay), so as to partially supply with forage the public animals in the department; also, to establish a garden farm for vegetables on the Arlington estate. This garden to be worked by the younger contrabands, and the produce either sold or distributed to the troops as the Secretary of War may direct. Operations have been commenced already, and a considerable number of contrabands are now engaged at Arlington on the bottom just [west] of the Alexandria Canal.[42]

Similarly, the primary labor pool for the construction and support of hospitals was African Americans. This was as true for Confederate hospitals as Union. At the vast Chimbarazo hospital complex in Richmond, Virginia (150 buildings, 8,000 beds) the enslaved provided "much of the domestic labor."[43] Hospitals were a military necessity, helping to return men the battle. They did not address the full social and health burden experienced by civilians in the public health emergency.

The civil war would lead to a "carnival of crime" in the post-war years due to the massive changes in social and political relations. The emotional stress experienced both by the soldiers and civilians in the war was suppressed in order to keep the armies fighting.[44] The full expression of this trauma exploded after the war as violence, racial savagery, drunkenness and extensive expressions of mental health fatigue, civilian and combatant. The Ku Klux Klan was formed in 1868; the economy contracted for more than five years after 1873; a spiritual revival exploded; railway workers' wages were halved in the 1870s even as the railroads issued stock dividends; and the first race-based immigration laws passed to exclude Chinese in the west. These were only a few major developments in a decade of huge change. The era concluded with Republican Rutherford Hayes' election and the end of Reconstruction. The federal guarantee of civil rights was traded to ensure continued Republican hold over the executive branch.[45]

Before the war was concluded there was a search for new post-slavery relations and experiments in new freely organized communities. The grounds at Arlington would provide the location for one of the best-documented new communities. The Freedman's Village would occupy 20 acres of the southwest corner of the former plantation; it was a village that had a church and school, but no factories, no saloon and no deed of ownership given to the occupants of the houses. More than 100 years later the buildings have been cleared and the ground re-graded; the rows of graves betray no hint of the cottages that occupied this area.

CHAPTER 8

Freedman's Village

IN THE AFTERMATH of the Battle of Antietam on September 22, 1862, President Lincoln issued an executive order intended to free all slaves residing in any rebellious and secessionist Confederate state that did not return to the Union by January 1, 1863. When the New Year came and none of the Confederate states returned to the Union, Lincoln duly issued the Emancipation Proclamation.[1] Understanding that they were now freed, the former enslaved began the slow, arduous process of moving north to ensure their freedom.

There was one group of enslaved people who were freed by their slaveholder just days before Lincoln's proclamation was to take effect. On December 29, 1862, Confederate General Robert E. Lee, as executor of the estate of his father-in-law George Washington Parke Custis, emancipated all of the Custis enslaved people per the instructions in the will—though Lee's actions were, however, eighty-seven days late according to the terms of the will.

Lee papers were officially recorded on January 2, 1863, in Richmond at the Henrico County courthouse, Virginia. Apart from a few individuals who were inadvertently omitted on the Freedom Paper due to a clerical error, the paper lays out that all of the Custis enslaved from the three plantations were set free.

The conditions in Washington, D.C., were pressing on the military authorities, as was the need for a more stable food supply. By May 1863, the quartermaster of the Washington Military District, Colonel Elias M. Greene, recommended the resettlement of the contraband, now freedmen, in the "pure country area" of the Arlington Plantation.[2]

Initially the expectation was that the former slave cabins in the bottomland would be sufficient to house the contraband, as they transferred across the Potomac and began their cultivation of the Arlington fields for grain and vegetables to sell in Washington and to feed the troops in the field. The population at Camp Barker required a larger settlement. Greene reviewed the property for a more suitable location and focused on the elevated land west of Fort Cass, southwest of the Arlington House and just north of the Columbia

The emancipation of the Custis enslaved by R.E. Lee (courtesy of the Museum of the Confederacy, Richmond, Virginia, Robert E. Lee personal papers).

Pike. The area would also be adjacent to the 17 acres given in 1826 by G.W.P. Custis to his mixed-race daughter Maria Syphax.

By June 1863, within a month of the decision to resettle the contraband, 100 people were resident in a camp. They lived in temporary Sibley-military styled tents on the south side of the property near the springs until permanent structures could be built. The movable Sibley tents would be repurposed and moved across the property to support another community on Mason's (now

Roosevelt) Island to the northeast of the plantation. The expectation was that the contraband would increase the agricultural output, but not necessarily develop a new labor system. Once permanent structures were installed, the village became a planned community in every aspect, with the layout resembling period military-style housing. On December 4, 1863, a formal religious dedication opened the village[3]:

> According to a history of the village it consisted of approximately 100 [duplex] frame houses, each a story and a half high, with a bedroom on the second floor. The houses were neatly whitewashed and divided in the center so that two families could be accommodated. The houses each faced each other with a clean street dividing the rows. Each tenement was numbered, and a rent of $3 dollars a month was charge to all except those employed by the government. The wages of those employed by the government were regulated to include the rent. Wells were dug to provide a more adequate supply of water. There were workshops where the children and women could be trained in mechanical occupations.[4]

The rents paid by the residents of Freedman's Village were to reimburse the military for their care and aide. As more contraband filled the city of Washington, the growing numbers added to the financial burden of the city resources. All able-bodied persons were expected to work and defray all costs associated with their care and the care of others unable to contribute financially in the form of rent or tax. Washington's wartime economy provided for the first time an opportunity for the former enslaved to participate in a wage-based economy.

> The government hired thousands: carpenters and masons, teamsters and blacksmiths, nurses and orderlies, and laborers of every description to move supplies, chop wood, haul coal, tend animals, build roads, and dig fortifications. The government paid black employees at the same rate as whites—at times as much as $30 per month plus a daily ration—and accommodated them and their families in the contraband camps. To defray operating expenses of the camps, in September 1862 military authorities created a "Contraband Fund" by deducting $5 from the monthly wages of each black employee, regardless of status or residence. The tax continued until after the war.[5]

The growth of employment in Washington, D.C., from 1850 to 1870 was 438 percent, with many of the occupations during the war in the fields in which the unskilled former enslaved were trained. According to the Consolidated Statement of Contraband Tax from the residents of Freedman's Village, tax revenue— deducted (by order of the Secretary of War) from payments made to colored employees of the quartermaster's department—totaled over $50,000 for eleven months alone in 1863.

Another large group that was moved to Freedman's Village was involved in a failed repatriation scheme that recalled the earlier efforts of G.W.P. Custis and the American Colonization Society. Bernard Kock, a cotton speculator, had obtained a ten-year lease from the Haitian government for the timber

Table 2: Consolidated Statement of Contraband Tax[6]

Date	Month	Amounts	
		Dollars	Cent
1863	February	1,123	63
"	March	2,408	25
"	April	4,144	49
"	May	3,563	29
"	June	3,431	26
"	July	4,382	61
"	August	6,839	13
"	September	7,002	05
"	October	6,623	60
"	November	5,899	98
"	December	4,910	98
	Total Amount	$50,379	27

on Île-à-Vache.[7] He needed labor and was able to obtain support from President Lincoln. In numerous speeches before his presidency, Lincoln spoke in favor of state-sponsored resettlement of the enslaved to their "fatherland."[8] Once he was president, Lincoln's point of view drew suspicion from abolitionists and "nearly universal" opposition from African Americans.[9]

The contraband, mostly from eastern Virginia, numbered 453 when they left Fort Monroe on April 14, 1862, at a transport cost to the federal government of $50 per person. The colonization was an "unmitigated disaster" from the outset: some 25 would die of smallpox on the boat journey to Haiti, there were insufficient supplies, and they were denied food if they did not work. Lincoln's secretary, John Hay, was happy when the president "sloughed off that idea of colonization [as he had] always thought it a hideous & barbarous humbug." A federal vessel was sent to Haiti to bring them back.[10] The 368 survivors from the failed colonization scheme returned to be received at Freedman's Village.[11]

Each building was constructed in the same style, based on the military footprint of twenty-one feet in width and twenty-eight feet in length, with the placement of doors and windows offering plenty of ventilation. The entry doors were constructed in the front and back of each unit to be side by side, maximizing the internal floor plan for each duplex unit. The plan of the village included a pond. While there are no pictures or narrative accounts of it having ever been developed, the village had only one source of potable water, a well that was dug away from the swamp area.

Equally, the lush green lawn is nowhere documented; similar to contemporary photographs of the military camps, the once-forested grounds of

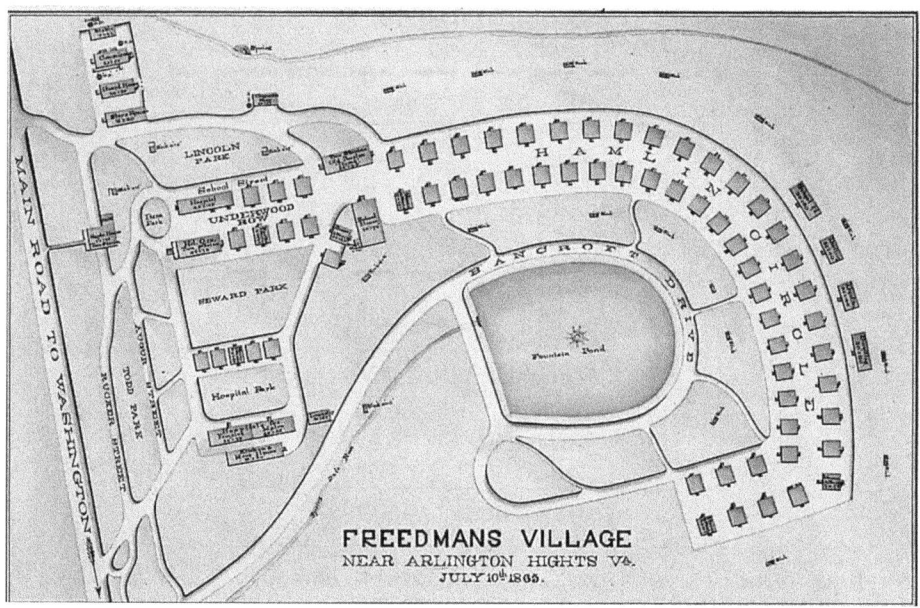

Proposed General Plan of Freedman's Village (courtesy National Park Service).

the plantation are stripped of trees, as the wood was used by many for warmth in the winter and fuel for stoves. The documentary evidence shows a landscape shorn of all grass, with an open sewer running past the front of the housing units. While the air was "cleaner and healthier" than that of the city of Washington, the residents were still plagued by flies and other pests associated with densely populated areas. As the diseases of war were never far away, the village suffered from its share of illnesses such as smallpox.

The village was initially run by a white civilian superintendent, D.B. Nichols, who was relieved of his duty due to "incapacity," (drunkenness) in January 1864. During Nichols' tenure there were also reports of abuse of villagers, as when Lucy Ellen Johnson described being "tied to a tree" by guards and subjected to "gross abuse."[12] Nichols was assigned to manage the contraband camp newly established at Mason's Island, Freedman's Village perhaps being too important an assignment given its nationally prominent role in the demonstration of freedom. Military commanders and special agents of the Treasury Department took over. The Bureau of Refugees, Freedmen and Abandoned Lands was established on March 3, 1865, and the Freedman's Village came under its jurisdiction.[13]

In accordance with military rules the residents were required to comply with established and narrowly defined regulations for positive cohabitation with the Union forces distributed about the property. Other partners involved

Freedman's Village Regulations (courtesy Boston Public Library, Rare Books and Manuscripts Department).

in administering the village were the American Missionary Association (AMA) and the American Tract Society (ATS), the relief agencies. These agencies brought their own flavor of moral discipline, temperance, and an expectation of having their orders followed. The relief agencies had a deep regard for the healing properties of hard work and were eager for the freed people to demonstrate their "free labor" credentials.[14]

To protect the inhabitants of Freedman's Village from white vigilante groups from outside of the compound, and to maintain law and order within the village, members from the 107th United States Colored Troops were assigned to the village. The village met many official goals and political needs; the village was promoted as a special place and as a national model community for freedmen as they transitioned from slavery to independence. The goal Colonel Greene had expressed was the plantation's "idle" lands could be aligned with unencumbering the government of the "dead weight of contraband," "employed to very great advantage."[15] Civil rights and abolitionist leaders from around the country came to observe the physical layout of the community and the amenities and training provided to teach and support life survival skills. Institutional structures were developed to help transition the enslaved into becoming self-sufficient and financially independent citizens.

> Within a year of its opening Colonel Greene viewed the village as successful because of the bountiful crops raised and the money earned by farming. There were over 1,000 acres of the estate alone and large amounts of vegetables and grains were raised there by the freedmen. They produced large quantities of buckwheat, corn fodder, potatoes and other vegetables. The freedmen raised 191 tons of corn fodder in one year. The corn was sold for $12.00 per ton and the buckwheat and potatoes were used to help supply the people in the local hospitals for freedmen.[16]

107th Regiment, United States Colored Troops (courtesy of the New York Public Library).

For many of the residents of Freedman's Village, unfamiliar as they were with military regulations, the village's movement restrictions chafed and undermined feelings of freedom. Some residents felt that life in the village was tantamount to living on the plantation, since they were living under the formal rule of military discipline, to them not very different from the rules of plantation life. One woman, when interviewed, reported "don't Freedman's feel as if I was free (ap)pears like there's nobody free here," despite appearing comfortable in her life at Freedman's Village.[17] United States Colored Troops were deployed to the property, including "two sergeants, four corporals, and twenty-nine privates."[18]

The village was designed to meet every challenge the former enslaved might experience, anticipating the transition to full citizenship. Schools were built to educate the young people, hospital facilities were provided to heal the sick, and lodging was made available for the elderly.

After meeting with President Lincoln, prominent abolitionist and preacher Sojourner Truth was appointed by the National Freedman's Relief Association (NFRA). The NFRA hired Truth as a counselor to solicit funds to recruit, hire and train educators suitable for instructing former enslaved in industrial and mechanical arts, and successfully making the transition to self-sufficiency.

Figure 8: Sojourner Truth Appointment[19]

NEW YORK, DEC 1, 1864.

This certifies that The National Freedman's Relief Association has appointed Sojourner Truth to be a counselor to the freed people at Arlington Heights, Va., and hereby commends her to the favor and confidence of the officers of government, and all persons who take an interest in relieving the condition of the freedmen, or in promoting their intellectual, moral, and religious instruction.

        F. G. Shaw President,
        Charles C. Leigh,
        Chairman of Home Com.

President Lincoln, in their initial meeting in November 1864, suggested Sojourner Truth visit the contraband camps in the city and tour Arlington Heights. She shared that "I have not language to tell you what rags and wretchedness and hunger and poverty I saw [in the camps]," where thousands "suffered with cold and hunger until death."[20]

A deeply religious woman, Sojourner Truth brought her tremendous credibility of experience to the villagers, particularly the women, through her religious convictions and abolitionist teachings. To combat the disheartening impact of slavery, religion played an important role in the lives of the African enslaved, as many "endured threats to their lives, their family stability, to the existence of their very community."[21] As a former slave, Sojourner's "heritage, race, gender, and servitude bonded her" with the women.[22] Many of the women's hands were calloused and rough as animal leather from having been field workers. They had little to no knowledge of basic domestic duties, managing household chores, or family budgeting. To the residents of Freedman's Village, Truth became friend, preacher and mentor, and insisted: "Be clean, be clean, for cleanliness is a part of godliness."[23]

Sojourner Truth not only counseled the villagers in domestic chores, but she also helped the unemployed find work and counseled the villagers in how to stand up for their rights as freed people.[24]

Built as an emergency response camp for the rising number of contraband, Freedman's Village became more than a temporary home for over 1,000 inhabitants.

Sojourner Truth (courtesy National Portrait Gallery, Smithsonian Gallery).

The people who lived there would be a disappointment to some in the federal government and civilian relief agencies who expected more rapid change. Some of the disappointment was in their lack of moral standing—Sojourner Truth said ministrations were rejected by "those who desire nothing higher than the lowest and the vilest of habits."[25]

The American Missionary Association would retreat from its support for the cause of African American liberation, deeming blacks "ungrateful" for the assistance of the AMA, and describe black suffrage and Reconstruction a failure.[26] Yet there were many times when the probity and progress of the village were cheered. John C. Underwood, an Alexandria district court judge, "writes the following letter to William Syphax (negro) of Washington," in July 1865 telling the story of residents undertaking construction improvements and "good conduct." William Syphax sent the letter to the *Alexandria Gazette* for republication:

> Their sobriety, industry, and economy have far exceeded my expectations....
> Within the last year, I have invested for a large number of individuals in Government Seven thirty bonds, amounting in the aggregate to nearly $8,000.

They have now twenty teachers employed in the education of their children, and I think are, in proportion to their numbers, giving more earnest and general attention to education than the white people of this city.[27]

Underwood remained a supporter of voting rights for African Americans and was instrumental along with other radical republicans in writing the Virginia Constitution of 1870, securing the state's return to the Union. The state constitution was nicknamed the "Underwood Constitution" by white conservative opponents.[28]

After the war, measures were taken by the government to try to close the village, but the residents successfully resisted. "The government then moved the inhabitants of the Abbott Hospital and Home for the Indigent to Freedmen's Hospital in Washington, D.C.," which would later become Howard University Hospital. In 1868, the residents of the village were allowed to "purchase their dwellings and rent approximately 600 acres of land in 10-acre lots" for farming. The purchased wooden structures had shingled roofs, brick flues, and were sheeted on the outside with the rough weather-board siding. They were not plastered or sealed inside. The price paid was from $35–$50 for each building.[29]

According to the Arlington County, Virginia, Department of Community Planning, Housing and Development:

> Most of the purchasers made improvements to the premises by re-flooring, by reroofing, by plastering or ceiling the rooms, and in several cases such improvements have been equal to twice or thrice the original cost of the building. [The buildings] ... are occupied by the builders, or by those who purchased from the builders. To these have been added small outbuildings, such as stables, sheds, chicken-houses, etc.[30]

The residents continued to live on the property for another 30 years and invest in the community. They believed that they would possess a claim to Arlington as implied by the government. Between 1868 and 1888, new homes were constructed, improvements were made to the purchased dwellings, and a brick church was built. The buildings at Freedman's Village were part of the landscape at Arlington for longer than Robert E. Lee lived at the plantation, yet there is no indication or memorial in the National Cemetery of where it stood, the public health emergency and deaths that required it to be developed, or the promise of freedom that it represented for the enslaved. Within a year of the Freedman's Village being established, a new use for the land came into being:

> The national cemetery, which today is synonymous with Arlington, was the last of the plantation's wartime uses and to some people seemed even its least. It was born of necessity and not a little vengeance on the part of its creator, United States Quartermaster General Montgomery C. Meigs, who sought to destroy the traitor Robert E. Lee by stripping his family of their plantation seat.[31]

At the founding of Freedman's Village, the public health emergency in Washington, D.C., raged on, and additional uses for Arlington's expansive landscape were being developed. The battles in the spring of 1864 would add to the death tolls. The Battle of Wilderness and the Overland Campaign led by General Grant to capture Richmond would create pressure for new burial grounds, as the cemeteries in the federal city were already full.

CHAPTER 9

National Cemeteries

BETWEEN APRIL 1861 AND 1864 the conduct of and beliefs about the war had changed radically. In July 1861, on a battlefield in northern Virginia, those at home and others around the world came to realize that the Civil War in America would not be short, but would be costly in terms of money and American lives. The soldiers' early hope that the war would be short and they would be released to go home and tend to their farms was a long-lost dream.

The First Battle of Bull Run was a Confederate victory. The noise and mayhem of these first encounters were such that a North Carolina soldier assigned to protect Fort Aquia in Stafford County, 30 miles south of Washington, would report:

> As I commenced your letter on yesterday and did not have any opportunity of finishing it, I have received some news of the battle near Washington City. I heard this morning that news was brought on the 12 o'clock train last night that General Beauregard had taken Arlington Heights with the loss of an immense number of men, perhaps 14 or 15000. The above is a mere report, and I am unwilling to vouch for the truth of the same though we are unable to give you the particulars, it is unnecessary to doubt that a tremendous battle has been fought for we heard the report of cannon a large part of the two days.[1]

The Confederate soldier illustrates that many men fought in a fog and reported both informed and uninformed opinions back to their loved ones. The first fully industrial war was also a war documented by an enormous number of letters, many still being digested and interpreted. No such encounter near Arlington nor such loss of life ever occurred. In fact, unlike Antietam, Gettysburg or any of the battlefields turned cemeteries, no one was killed at Arlington. The nearest fighting casualties that would come to Arlington would be the bodies that floated down the Potomac from the Battle of Ball's Bluff (thirty or more miles outside of Arlington) on October 22, 1861.[2]

At Bull Run, casualties on both sides were relatively even and, compared to later encounters, small. The Union Army had 460 killed, with 1,124 wounded and 1,312 missing, for a combined casualty list of 2,896. The Confederate Army reported 387 killed, 1,582 wounded, and 13 missing, for a combined total of 1,982.³

The Union wounded were sent to makeshift medical facilities and Washington-area hospitals. The Union war dead were also hastily sent to Washington for burial. The remains and body parts of Union and Confederate soldiers languished on the battlefield. The mismanagement of battle casualties caused a public outrage that challenged the justification for the war. The first newspaper accounts described the disrespect of the war dead:

> As might have been expected from the fiendish spirit manifested for some years past, by southern slaveholders towards northern men, the cruelties inflicted by the rebel soldiers on prisoners taken in battle are most atrocious. Not only did they wreak their cruel vengeance on the living who fell into their hands at Bull's Run, but even the bodies of the dead were mutilated in a manner to put to shame forever the boasted Southern chivalry.... Scarcely in the history of the world can we find the parallel of this atrocity.... The faces of dead soldiers beaten in with the but[t]s of muskets; the bayonets of the wounded driven through their hearts....⁴

In July 1861, the Army ordered its commanders to take responsibility for recording and verifying their war dead and ordered that land for battlefields be designated for their burial.⁵

The war was fought with numerous protocols, boundaries, logistics and duties. Historian Shelby Foote talks about the North fighting with "one hand behind its back," believing that the material advantages of its industrial economy would inevitably beat the Confederacy. There were other forces that limited the destruction:

> When army officers spoke of extermination in the case of the Indians they meant it and they thought they were capable of bringing it about.... The entire nation could be captured and put in a concentration camp. That could not be done to the Confederacy. The Confederacy could not actually be exterminated. When people in the North spoke of wars of extermination or scorched-earth campaigns waged against the Confederacy, they were not serious. They could not scorch the earth there, and they could not exterminate the Confederacy, a numerous people living in a vast region with plenty of rainfall and a vast commercial economy. Talk along those lines about the Confederacy was bluster indicative only of the intensity of national feeling in the North. It had nothing to do with realizable strategy and tactics.⁶

The starkest controls would emerge as the war changed the understanding of how to honor the dead. A civil war produces different sentiments, later requiring different needs for reconciliation and retribution. Differences in approach are distinct to this war, as it is the only war in which Americans count the dead on both sides.⁷ By counting the deaths in both armies, the magnitude of the conflict is increased in comparison to the other "total" wars, but this obscures the toll on civilians, particularly on African Americans. African

Americans, when no longer counted as chattel or collateral, found they were more relevant in the liberation cause but less documented. The protocol for engagement on the battlefield was frequently cited in describing the behavior of the officer corps in both armies.

In 1864 the extent of deaths in the prisons was so staggering that the U.S. Sanitary Commission reported more than half of the Union soldiers treated in Richmond (1396 of 2721) died. Breaches of the protocol became the fodder for journalists characterizing the moral standing of the combatants on each side. The *Columbus Enquirer* is reported to have encouraged swift prisoner swaps, because otherwise "the Confederacy will derive little benefit from it," so deadly were the camps at Andersonville and elsewhere. The *Soldiers' Journal* asked why the enemy "[fails] to provide for whom the fortunes of war have placed in their hands."[8]

Washington, D.C., was in many ways an anomaly, a capital behind enemy lines. This complicated the ability to leave the battlefield and bury the dead. Maryland did not secede but was a constant source of concern as a haven for rebel sympathizers. Washington was the Union city closest to six of the ten deadliest battles in the war; the other four were fought in Georgia, Tennessee and Mississippi. Approximately 280,830 men were killed in just these ten battles. Washington would bear the greatest responsibility for interring the Union fallen, unless they were fortunate enough to have families that could afford to bring them home.

The protocols for burying such large numbers of casualties had not been developed. Future Union and Confederate leaders had been sent to study the war in Crimea, but they did not return with a full set of new practices. Henry Dunant's work on the battlefields of Solferino on June 24, 1859, would lead to the Geneva Convention for the Amelioration of the Condition of the Wounded and Sick in Armies in the Field, but those protocols would not be ratified until 1864. During the early battles of the Civil War, the generals were quick to pull their regiments off the battlefields. They took their wounded but often left their war dead. Soldiers became gruesome nutrients for the soil, to the glee of one rebel observer:

> The capture of Hatteras and opening of the Pamlico Sound will finally result in feeding the fish and sharks of the Sound or manureing some if its sandy beaches with a large number of Yankee carcasses. Just think of Manassas plains! What fine wheat and tobacco they'll bring in a year or two.[9]

New systems would be developed to deal with the Union dead. On July 16, 1862, Congress passed legislation authorizing the U.S. federal government to purchase land for national cemeteries for the military dead and put the U.S. Army Quartermaster Brigadier General Montgomery C. Meigs in charge of the program.[10]

Carnage of the Battle of Antietam, the bloodiest one-day battle of the Civil War, near Sharpsburg, Md., was captured in this Sept. 17, 1862, photograph (National Archives, Records of the Department of State, G 94).

Swapping prisoners of war was another protocol in the war management system that would change as the ferocity of the conflict was fully understood and the rhetoric from the political parties soared. The protocols would change again when the Confederacy refused to treat U.S. Colored Troops by the same rules as other soldiers.

Approximately one in every four soldiers who went to war never returned home, dying from disease or combat wounds. After the Battle of Gettysburg, approximately 7,000 Union and Confederate Corps lay in the fields around the town. In the aftermath of the war, and with commanders leaving the dead on the battlefield, family members of dead or missing soldiers were forced to go to the battlefield to find their loved ones in the carnage.[11]

As the city of Washington became increasingly burdened with the bodies of the war dead arriving after each battle, its cemeteries were at or near full capacity. Arlington House, just across the Potomac River via the Aqueduct Bridge, with its fields cleared of trees, was an opportune site for burials.

Military leaders, particularly General Meigs, were angered by Colonel Lee turning his back on the Union by resigning his commission and considered him a traitor. Meigs' bitterness was more poignant since the two men had worked together and had a prior close relationship. Both were 1837 graduates of West Point. A year after graduating from college, Meigs worked under Lee in Ohio for the Corps of Engineers, making surveys and plans for improving the navigation of the Mississippi River.[12] They spent the summer together surveying the effects of the river on the Missouri and Illinois shorelines, and they developed solutions for making the river more navigable to the increasing number of steamboats and barges.

General Meigs had worked to provide Washington with its first water supply, managing the engineering work on the Chesapeake and Ohio Canal in 1853. The same system still provides water to the city today, via the two reservoirs at Dalecarlia and Georgetown, as well as to Arlington, Fort Myer, the Pentagon and large parts of Fairfax County to the west. Meigs was well acquainted with Arlington, as he had visited the property several times at the invitation of his friend and onetime mentor, Robert E. Lee.

After more than 25 years of friendship, Meigs felt a stinging betrayal once Lee joined the Confederacy. Now quartermaster general for the Union army, Meigs faced increasing pressure to find adequate space for burials for the ever-increasing numbers of Union dead. Meigs could now strike back at his one-time friend by burying bodies on the plantation fields that the Custis-Lee family profited from, denying the family access to an estate they treasured by possibly tainting the ground water supply.

The Battle of the Wilderness started on May 5, 1864, and lasted three days. This was the first engagement of General Ulysses S. Grant, commander of the Army of the Potomac, with General Robert E. Lee (CSA) in the Overland Campaign and the war of attrition that would eventually grind the Confederacy to submission. The battlefield is where Stonewall Jackson's arm was famously buried. The Union lost more than 2,200 men in the Virginia counties of Spotsylvania and Orange, some 70 miles south of Washington. The new spring campaign would mean new measures and new locations would be required to secure the memory of the Union's fallen heroes.

United States Colored Troop regiments participated in the Overland Campaign and were given no quarter, killed rather than taken prisoner, and hanged when found among the injured. The USCT would fight alongside Grant into Richmond and be at Appomattox to secure the victory. On May 13, 1864, President Lincoln requested that Quartermaster General Meigs accompany him on a buggy ride to Arlington. Historians are unsure whose idea it was to use the land at Arlington House as a national cemetery, but according to Lee biographer Elizabeth Brown Pryor:

> The Meigs family story stated that President Lincoln, who admired his quartermaster general, asked him what should be done with the property. It concerned Lincoln that Lee was still alive, and that no just outcome seemed clear. "Mr. President, why not make it a field of honor?" Meigs was said to have replied. "The ancients filled their enemies fields with salt and made them useless forever but we are a Christian nation, why not make it a field of honor." Lincoln reportedly adopted the idea immediately. In fact, interments had already begun, mostly near the cemetery at Freedman's Village. On June 15, 1864, Meigs wrote a memorandum to Secretary of War Edwin M. Stanton

... suggesting that "the land surrounding the Arlington Mansion, now understood to be property of the United States, be appropriated as National Military Cemetery." The grounds around the stately home, added Meigs, were "admirably adapted to such a case." Stanton approved the plan the same day, and the first official burials, both Union and Confederate, followed quickly. By the end of June, some 2,600 soldiers lay at Arlington.[13]

Prior to the meeting with President Lincoln, General Meigs had already taken steps to repurpose the home of the nation's greatest traitor by having war dead buried at the Arlington plantation in the low fields just above the Custis-Lee slave cemetery. Several of the enslaved men, including James Parks, began the process of assisting Meigs by digging the graves for the anticipated war dead. This would one day become Section 27.

As the Union army took control, James Parks was employed as a grave digger. Many of the earliest graves at the cemetery, specifically those in the area later named Section 27, were dug by Parks. According to the National Park Service:

> A major impetus for the development of the Arlington National Cemetery was the Wilderness Campaign, fought in central Virginia between May 4 and June 12, 1864, during which approximately 60,000 Union soldiers were killed. Existing space at the Soldiers Home National Cemetery in Washington D.C., and the Alexandria National Cemetery, which had been established in 1862, was filling quickly and new burial locations were needed immediately. By May 1864, there was a critical need for military burial space.[14]

Section 27 initially started out as a potter's field on the very land where the Custis-Lee enslaved once lived. Many of those who were set free under the terms of the G.W. P. Custis will immediately left the property to start new lives as free people of color. Once Freedman's Village was built, the slave cabins were torn down and the remaining enslaved moved over to Freedman's Village. The location of the former cabins is not currently marked within the grounds of the cemetery, as the outline of the village remains unmarked. The ground has been re-shaped and smoothed, yet the boundaries are well documented enough to warrant a National Park Service marker.

Secretary of War Edward M. Stanton did not sign the authorization to transform Arlington into a national cemetery until June 15, 1864. General Meigs did not wait on the formal approval. On May 13, 1864, presumably immediately after Meigs met with the president, the first soldier was buried at the cemetery, a 21-year-old man named Henry from the Pocono Lake region of Lehigh County, Pennsylvania.

Private William Henry Christman (Section 27:19)[15] enlisted in the U.S. Army on March 25, 1864, for a $60 cash bounty and a $240 promissory note from his government.[16] A little more than a month later he was hospitalized with the measles. He was, like many farm boys, highly susceptible to the different infectious diseases found in the capital city. Measles is a disease of community; as an airborne virus it needs population concentration to propagate. Shortly after Christman arrived in Washington, he was admitted to Lincoln General Hospital, a mile east of Washington, D.C. The measles virus and the hygienic environment present in the hospital weakened him and likely enabled bacteria to assault his system. In less than six weeks, on May 11, he died of peritonitis, a toxic inflammation of the membrane lining the abdominal cavity.[17]

At death, Christman joined the ranks of the deceased in Washington with no place to be buried. His family did not have the resources to return him to be buried alongside his kin. Indeed, he had signed up as a soldier to improve the economic circumstances of his family. Barges were coming up the Potomac River with bodies of those killed on the battlefields in Virginia, while fighting in the Wilderness and at Spotsylvania Courthouse was producing a new spring harvest of bodies. The ships also brought into the city soldiers seriously injured on the battlefield, and the local hospitals, in an attempt to preserve the lives of the injured, were also amputating body parts that needed to be respectfully handled. The day after Christman was buried, William H. McKinney (Section 27:98), became the first soldier who died in battle to be buried at Arlington.

On the day that the national cemetery became official, Quartermaster

Section 27 first burials (private collection of Ric Murphy).

General Montgomery C. Meigs toured and had engineers survey the grounds to accommodate as many bodies as possible. Upon his arrival, he was angered to see that the bodies were interred in the Lower Cemetery and not around the plantation as he had instructed. Before leaving the property, Meigs provided specific orders that burials were to take place around the Custis-Lee mansion.

In August, Meigs once again visited the property to inspect the progress of the cemetery and was dismayed to find that still none of the burials were around the mansion as ordered. The commanding officers who were residing in the Custis-Lee home didn't want to live near a graveyard and had reordered that all burials were to take place in the lower section of the property in what had become the potter's field. Angered by the disrespect of his order, Meigs ordered that coffins stored in Washington be sent directly to Arlington, and he oversaw their burial close to the mansion in Mrs. Lee's prized rose garden:

> On June 15, 1864, Meigs proposed to Stanton that Arlington House and two hundred acres around it be made a military cemetery, and, on the same day, Stanton approved. Burials near Arlington House began that day, or were directed to be made, and at Meigs' insistence, some graves were dug in Mrs. Lee's Rose Garden. When Meigs came out to Arlington in August ... he was furious. Instead of seeing the Lee house ringed with graves, he saw the mansion looking much as it always had.... Near the old slave quarters was a neat looking cemetery filled with all of the bodies Meigs had wanted placed near the house. Enraged, he ordered twenty-six more bodies brought over from Washington right away, and in the hot August sun.... Meigs ... stood by and personally supervised their burial in the rose garden just south of the house.[18]

Separated by military class and rank, privates continued to be buried in the Lower Cemetery. But once Meigs had his plans in place, "Mrs. Lee's garden began to fill with graves. Union captains and lieutenants joined the handful of officers already sleeping on the hilltop."[19]

The public, particularly as reported in the North, was pleased that the Custis-Lee property was going to be used as a military cemetery to honor the nation's war dead and serve as a home and tribute to American freedmen. In an article printed on July 15, 1864, *The Liberator* wrote:

> How appropriate that Lee's lands should be dedicated to two such noble purposes— the free living Black man whom Lee would enslave and the bodies of the dead soldiers who Lee has killed in a wicked cause. Let this record stand to the everlasting credit of Secretary Stanton. We cheerfully award it.[20]

To ensure that his orders were being followed, throughout the late summer, Meigs continued to be directly involved in the burials at the National Cemetery. Despite his hectic schedule, according to Meigs' biographer, David W. Miller:

Suddenly the world for Meigs took on a dreary cast. On the night of October 6th, Secretary of War Edwin Stanton came to the Meigs' home and asked that Montgomery come outside. His initial thought was that Stanton had bad tidings—maybe it was that Grant had fallen, or a dreadful fate had befallen the president. Alas, it was news that 22-year-old Lieutenant John Rodgers Meigs was dead.[21]

There are many different accounts of what happened to the younger Meigs that fateful evening. One account said that while on patrol with two others, John Meigs was captured and, upon discovery of who his father was, murdered. Another story was that while scouting out territory for troop advancement, the three Union soldiers were spotted by three Confederate soldiers and they each fired upon each other, leaving Meigs dead.

Whatever the truth, the elder Meigs was devastated in the wake of his son's death. Upon hearing of the news of Lee's surrender at Appomattox, Meigs furiously blamed the Confederates for his son's death:

> The rebels are all murderers of my son and the sons of hundreds of thousands.... Justice seems not satisfied [if] they escape judicial trial & execution ... by the government which they have betrayed attacked & whose people loyal & disloyal they have slaughtered.[22]

Quartermaster Meigs was determined that the Lee family would not return to a normal life at their beloved Arlington plantation. He took every step possible to bury more Union soldiers and many former enslaved on the property, making it un-farmable and thus politically and economically worthless due to the sheer number of the Union dead.

Initially the Lower Cemetery was segregated. White privates were separated from the United States Colored Troops, who were separated from those buried in the potter's field. The residents from the Freedman's Village were buried in their own graveyard in the southern section of the property fully a mile away, adjacent to the land owned by the free African American Syphax family.

The fight for equal treatment and opposition to segregation of black soldiers continued after the war, and at Arlington this was further complicated by the burial of Confederates in the first years of the national cemetery. Burial rights were extended to all of the citizen-soldiers honorably discharged from the Union Army, requiring a major expansion of federal cemeteries. At the 1871 Decoration Day ceremonies at Arlington, southern women were prevented from decorating Confederate graves with flowers by armed troops. The same graves had been painted with the word "Rebel."[23] At the same ceremony, Frederick Douglass' newspaper reported that black women were threatened as they tried to decorate the graves of their loved ones and had increasingly few white allies:

> The colored ladies of the committee, be it said to their praise, with all the slurs from the papers, and the strong influence of some of the opposition brought to bear to keep

them from joining the decoration, did not falter in the discharge of their duty, no more than their brothers and kindred did in the times that tried men's souls.... [A]nd the community saw that there were still some Union men and women left who dare discharge the responsibility they owe to their country....[24]

Douglass would lead a delegation to seek to move the USCT to the upper cemetery. Meigs denied the request, declaring in a letter to Secretary of War Belknap that he was opposed and "that the dead, *once decently buried*, should have rest."[25] However, in the same year Meigs did allow 89 Confederate graves to be moved to the Hollywood Cemetery in Richmond. Eventually all the rebel bodies would be collected at Arlington and made into an "honor guard" around the Confederate Monument.

CHAPTER 10

United States Colored Troops

ONCE PRESIDENT LINCOLN PAVED THE WAY for African American men to serve in the Civil War, they were prepared, no matter the cost, and were ready to take charge of their own destiny and the total abolition of slavery. On May 22, 1863, the United States War Department established the Bureau of Colored Troops. African American men from the North and the South enlisted into regiments that included cavalry, infantry, engineers, and light and heavy artillery units. They became known as the United States Colored Troops.

> The Bureau of Colored Troops recruited and organized over 185,000 blacks into the U.S. Colored Troops. Blacks accounted for about 9 to 10 percent of the Union Army and one-quarter of enlistments in the Navy. When black volunteers in independent and state units are included, it is estimated that close to 390,000 blacks served in the Civil War.[1]

But for members of the United States Colored Troops, who served in 163 military units, military service did not come easy. "More than 38,000 black soldiers lost their lives during the Civil War—a mortality rate almost 40 percent higher than that of white troops"; they made the supreme sacrifice to save the Union and, most importantly, end slavery.[2]

By official counts there are more than 16,000 Civil War soldiers buried at Arlington. The number of USCT is officially estimated at 1,500 in Section 27 and hundreds more in Section 23. By contrast, a complete enumeration of the Confederates buried at Arlington has been undertaken and fully described for more than one hundred years; records include: "Among the 482 persons buried there are 46 officers, 351 enlisted men, 58 wives, 15 southern civilians, and 12 unknowns."[3]

Many of the USCT were buried at Arlington National Cemetery during and after the war. Sergeant Frank Welch of Philadelphia, who served in the Massachusetts 54th Regiment and was a career serviceman, is buried in Section 1 of Arlington. Prior to the U.S. War Department enacting the Bureau of Colored Troops, the wealthy abolitionist community in Boston, Massachusetts, recruited African American men as soldiers of the Massachusetts 54th

United States Colored Troops recruiting poster (public domain).

and 55th Regiments, and the Massachusetts 5th Cavalry. Another prominent recruiter for the 54th was Orandatus Simon Bolivar Wall (buried in Arlington Cemetery in Section 1:124) of Oberlin, one of the first African Americans to be commissioned as a captain.

The Massachusetts 54th and 55th Regiments and the Massachusetts 5th Cavalry were organized at Camp Meigs near Readville, Massachusetts. At the time of their recruitment, black soldiers were told they would be treated and paid the same as their white counterparts. Once enlisted, the men found out that the Commonwealth of Massachusetts was paying them only $10 a month, with $3 being withheld for their uniforms, while their white counterparts were being paid $13 a month, with nothing withheld—a six dollar monthly difference. The men of the 54th and the 55th immediately began a protest and refused to accept any payment until the entire payroll matter was rectified. In 1864, Congress granted equal pay to the U.S. Colored Troops, to be paid retroactively.

On July 11, 1863, as part of the operations against the Defenses of Charles-

54th Regiment Massachusetts Volunteer Infantry assault on Fort Wagner (Library of Congress).

ton Campaign, the Union army attempted to take the beachhead fortification on Morris Island known as Fort Wagner in South Carolina. In the first unsuccessful attempt, the Union lost over three hundred soldiers, while the Confederate army defending the Fort lost only twelve men. On July 18, 1863, the gallant African American Massachusetts 54th attempted to overtake the strategic Fort Wagner that protected South Carolina's Charleston harbor.

While many whites questioned the skill, tenacity, and commitment of African American troops, the Massachusetts 54th proved them all wrong. Though the assault was unsuccessful, the Massachusetts 54th was later commended by their military superiors for their determination and valor. The unit suffered 272 casualties, including the death of young Colonel Robert Gould Shaw.[4] The heroic actions of the Massachusetts Regiments encouraged other African American men to join the military. After the brave assault on Fort Wagner, the men of the United States Colored Troops participated in every major campaign of the war, including key battles during the Richmond-Petersburg Campaign that helped bring the war to an end with the surrender of Confederate General Robert E. Lee.

The Confederate army, well aware of the tactical importance of the capitol city of Richmond, built permanent defenses around the city and the surrounding countryside. Confederate soldiers, supported by the enslaved, constructed a series of elaborate earthworks that consisted of extensive obstacles and trenches to deter a possible Union advancement or attack on the city. Before the city of Petersburg, part of the Richmond outer defense line, could be captured, Union General Ulysses S. Grant had to march southeastward towards the Confederate capital city of Richmond.[5]

General Grant suffered tremendous casualties in his initial effort to reach Richmond. On May 5, 1864, at the Battle of the Wilderness (Orange Turnpike), after three days of fighting, "the Union had staggering casualties of 17,500 men while the Confederates lost only 9,000."[6] Two weeks later, the two armies met again in one of the fiercest and bloodiest battles of the entire war, "where the Union lost 32,000 more soldiers."[7] Despite the casualties, Grant continued the campaign moving toward the capture of Richmond and the taking of Petersburg's railroad junction—the hub of the Confederate supply line.

General Grant tried to end the stalemate around Richmond and Petersburg, but the first attempt by the Union forces to take Petersburg on June 8, 1864, ended badly. The Union lost "7,000 men in less than twelve hours, forcing the Union's General Grant to end the slaughter," by ending the battle and conceding defeat.[8] The bodies, white and black, were sent to Washington, and many were buried at the national cemetery at Arlington.

The first Civil War burials at Arlington were in the eastern part of Section 27, mostly re-interments from other Washington cemeteries. In July 1864, the western portion of Section 27 became a burial ground for United States Colored Troops.[9] The opening of the western part of Section 27 coincided with USCT participation in one of the bloodiest battles of the war. As the number of African American war dead increased and bodies were sent to Arlington for burial, the lower cemetery was becoming more distinctly divided by race. As the "lower" cemetery was filling with the rising number of black civilians being buried in the area, the section was also becoming separated from that portion of the "upper" cemetery closer to the main house.

As the war progressed and casualties mounted, more and more black soldiers were sent to Arlington for burial. The "upper cemetery" was being recognized as the official cemetery, and the "lower cemetery" was being referred to as the "Contraband Cemetery." As more men from the United States Colored Troops arrived for burial, along with bodies of former enslaved from Washington, Alexandria, and points beyond, the area known today as Section 27 quickly became identified as the "black cemetery," separated by a thick wooded area from the larger, more prestigious national "white cemetery."

In June 1864, General Grant focused his attention on taking Petersburg and destroying the critical railroad junction key to Lee's supply lines. The

Battle of the Crater, on July 30, 1864, was the scene of "the loudest explosion of the war ... opening one of the most spectacular battles of the entire conflict."[10] On his second attempt, Grant looked to the 48th Pennsylvania Regiment for something creative. Utilizing the skill and resources of "Pennsylvania coal miners turned soldiers"[11]:

> General Grant, willing to try anything to breach the rebel defenses, approved the plan to dig a tunnel reaching from the advance unit in the Union force to one of the strongest forts in the rebel lines, and to place under it great magazines of gunpowder. By July 23 about 8000 pounds waited in eight huge magazines. The target was a strong six-gun fort only 150 yards away. Directly behind it, about 400 yards, was Cemetery Hill, another fortified position, whose capture would surely open wide the gate to Richmond.[12]

As planned, the miners dug the underground tunnel under the Confederate fort. But the execution of the attack was poorly planned and mistake on mistake compounded the endeavor. After an initial delay (the fuses leading to the gunpowder fizzled out and had to be relit), the tremendous explosion finally occurred, surprising the Confederate soldiers in the fort. Four tons of powder erupted, tearing a hole that was 150 feet long, 25 feet wide, and 25 feet deep in the Confederate lines.[13]

> The explosion launched earth, debris, men, and matériel hundreds of feet in the air, killing or wounding almost 300 Rebels. Sergeant William H. Thomas of the 5th USCT remembered the explosion as "a never to be forgotten sight of death and devastation."[14]

The night before the explosion, there were disagreements over which of the divisions would lead. "[Union General Ambrose] Burnside sent in three divisions of white troops," some with little time to survey or plan for the attack. Unprepared and inexperienced, "the troops were repulsed, being stopped by the crater."[15] As they attempted to leave the tunnel and climb up on the sides of the crater, the earth gave way all around them, bringing the men back down the crater and creating a bottleneck as troops rushed forward. Having lost the initial element of surprise, as Union soldiers escaped the tunnel, they were quickly mowed down by Confederate soldiers[16]:

> Confederate reinforcements arrived, and a heavy fire began to fall on the Union forces; artillery and musketry decimated their ranks.... [W]hen the other two white divisions were ordered forward, they found their way blocked ... and they, too, merely added to the death and confusion in and around the crater.... When some groups reached the opening they were met with heavy, well-organized fire from artillery and rifles, driving them reeling back into the crater. Within an hour or so, the Confederates had gathered sufficient strength to mount their own offensive, firing directly into the crater, killing and wounding scores of terrified and leaderless men. The crater now had literally become a death trap.[17]

Despite the initial losses, Burnside was determined to take the fort, and he ordered the USCTs under his command to advance.

They made several gallant charges through and around the crater but were driven back, just like the others, by destructive enfilading and crossfire of all enemy weapons from the front and both flanks. Many of them fell back into the crater, where, looking for safety, they met disaster. [According to an eyewitness report], "Some colored men came into the crater and there they found a fate worse than death in the charge. It was believed among the white [soldiers] that the enemy would give no quarter to negroes, or to the whites taken with them so to be shut up with blacks in the crater was equal to a doom of death…. It has been positively asserted that white men bayoneted [their black comrades] in the crater. This was to preserve the whites from Confederate vengeance."[18]

The heavy casualties inflicted upon the USCTs from gunfire was staggering. Colonel George L. Kilmer of the 14th New York reported that "when the colored troops poured into the crater, pandemonium began. Not only were Negroes killed by Confederate troops, but they were slaughtered by men from their own army."[19] Of the 4,500 African Americans who entered the battle, 1,327 were hit, and 436 died. Whites suffered 2,471 casualties, including 227 deaths.[20] Initially the military loss at the Battle of the Crater was blamed on the USCTs, but as more firsthand accounts were documented by officers, it became apparent that the USCT soldiers had demonstrated their persistence and their bravery despite the adversities of the battle.

From the Battle of the Crater to the Battle of New Market Heights on September 29, 1864, the USCT continued to demonstrate their skill and valor; many of their fatalities were sent to Arlington's Section 27. Of the twenty-five African Americans who were awarded the Medal of Honor during the Civil War, fourteen of them were United States Colored Troops who received the medal because of their heroic service during the latter battle.

The Battle of New Market Heights resulted in the largest number of United States Colored Troops to be interred in Arlington's Section 27 from a single unit, the 45th Regiment, USCT. Organized on June 13, 1864, in Philadelphia, Pennsylvania, four companies from the 45th Regiment, USCT, were initially assigned to garrison duty at Arlington Heights as part of the defenses of Washington. On September 20, 1864, the four companies stationed at Arlington Heights joined with the remaining six companies in Philadelphia and moved onto to City Point, Virginia, as part of the Overland Campaign.

On September 29, 1864, "two brigades of General Charles J. Paine's Third Division, Eighteenth Corps, composed of the 4th and 6th USCT and the 5th, 36th and 38th USCT, successfully assailed the Confederate entrenched line of defense at New Market Heights, Virginia, north of the James River."[21] The use of large numbers of African American soldiers was intentional in taking Petersburg and then Richmond. Major General Benjamin Butler, who more than three years earlier on May 24, 1861, had set in motion the migration of tens of thousands of fugitive slaves heading north by labeling them the "contraband" of war, now motivated thousands of United States Colored Troops into the Battle of New Market. Having witnessed the valor of the USCT, after years of hearing how unqualified they were and how they lacked the fortitude to survive and win during the heat of combat while in battle, Butler was determined to show the segregationists and naysayers the value and commitment of the African American soldiers. In his autobiography, Butler exalted the black soldiers:

> This fear was a deep-seated one and spread far and wide, and the negro had had no sufficient opportunity to demonstrate his valor and his staying qualities as a soldier. And the further cry was that the negroes never struck a good blow for their own freedom. Therefore, I determined to put them in a position, to demonstrate the fact of the value of the negro as a soldier, *coûte qui coûte*, and that the experiment should be one of which no man should doubt, if it attained success. Hence the attack by the negro column on New Market Heights. After that in the Army of the James a negro regiment was looked upon as the safest flanking regiment that could be put in line.[22]

As a result of their bravery and heroic deeds, Major General Butler would commission a medal from his own personal funds to honor the brave efforts of African American soldiers in the Battle of Chaffin's Farm and New Market Heights, where fourteen of the USCT were awarded the Medal of Honor (including Sergeant James Harris who is buried in Section 27). Nearly 200 USCT were awarded the so-called Butler Medal, which the general prided himself on awarding "by hand."

Butler was proud of the heroic deeds of his black troops and wanted his medal to acknowledge this bravery. He inscribed the medal with the motto "Freedom Will be Theirs by the Sword," and on the obverse with "Distinguished by Courage." In his autobiography, Butler described his motivation:

> I had the fullest reports made to me of the acts of individual bravery of colored men on that occasion, and I had done for the negro soldiers, by my own order, what the government has never done for its white soldiers—I had a medal struck of like size, weight, quality, fabrication and intrinsic value with those which Queen Victoria gave with her own hand to her distinguished private soldiers of the Crimea.[23]

Several weeks after the men received their medals, General Butler was relieved of his command and the black soldiers were forbidden to wear the medal.[24] The government refused to honor the medal as "official." In 2001 Representative Steny Hoyer (D–Maryland) was petitioned by William Aleshire—a Bowie, Maryland, councilmember—to help in achieving official recognition of the Butler Medal. This attempt and others have yet to succeed.[25] As the war neared its conclusion, the ability and courage of African Americans to make a difference in the outcome of the war was undeniable.

General Benjamin Butler was tagged by the rebels as the "Butcher of New Orleans," for his role in the capture of the city on the Mississippi in 1862 and his disruption of the social order of the slave society. While leading the forces in the Department of the Gulf, Butler spent significant time addressing the safety of African Americans and the need to employ them to assist in Union defenses, although he resisted General Phelps' request to arm them.[26] Butler was dismissed from his command in 1865 after failures at Fort Fisher, North Carolina. He would be elected to the House of Representatives from Massachusetts in time to lead the impeachment trial of President Andrew Johnson, to be a lead author of civil rights legislation in the Grant administration, and to oppose the Ku Klux Klan from his position as chair of the Committee on Reconstruction.

The Confederate Northern Army of Virginia, under Robert E. Lee, was the last major obstacle before the war could come to an end. Union General William T. Sherman successfully took control of the larger rebel cities of Atlanta, Charleston, and Savannah, and now the Confederate capital of Richmond was all that remained before the pitched battles would come to an end. Throughout winter, both sides anticipated each other's tactics. General Lee positioned his men to protect and strengthen the defenses of Richmond in anticipation of the Union attack. With Richmond's fortifications still secure, he fortified his army in Petersburg, 25 miles to the south, where his men were still dug-in.

On Sunday, April 2, 1865, Mary Custis Lee and President of the Confederacy Jefferson Davis found out in the most unusual way that General Grant's Union Army had finally broken through the Richmond defenses:

> Mrs. Lee and her daughters attended communion service at St. Paul's Church, where they saw the sexton walk down the aisle and respectfully bend over to whisper to President [Jefferson] Davis. Davis rose from his pew, followed one after the other by "other important military and government figures." Lee's lines at Petersburg had been broken, and Richmond was lost. By the time Mrs. Lee left church after the service, wagons were already lining up to remove the archives and what remained of the Confederate government's gold bullion. By early afternoon … panic spread through the city. The members of the Confederate government were now fugitives, wanted men, in flight to nowhere. "All of Richmond, rich and poor, highbrow and lowly, seem to be scrambling to leave the city. Wagons and carriages piled high with furniture and barrels jostled the endless stream of heavily laden pedestrians, all intent on getting away, somewhere, anywhere, to escape…."[27]

As the Union Army approached Richmond, Davis and his cabinet fled. They set fire to the entire city, hoping to delay the Union army and destroy any provisions and documents of value that the Union could use to wage war in the future. Once the Union army reached the city from the south and the city leaders surrendered, the Union army put out the massive fire. However, much of the business district and a third of the remaining city was already destroyed.

The Union occupation and subsequent protection of the Confederate capital city were overseen by Generals Edward Ord and Godfrey Weitzel, who commanded the XXV, an entire corps made up of USCTs. On April 2, 1865, as General Weitzel's troops approached Richmond, Confederate forces were retreating. As the USCTs had been one of the first regiments to enter Richmond, the Massachusetts 5th Colored Cavalry, the sister unit to the Massachusetts 54th that had suffered 272 casualties while attempting to overtake the strategic Fort Wagner on July 18, 1863, was honored by being one of the first cavalries to enter the city, to cheers of the African American residents of Richmond.

After the burning of Richmond, the Confederate Army of Northern Virginia under the command of General Robert E. Lee fled and was pursued by the Union army under the command of Union General-in-Chief Ulysses S. Grant. According to Robert E. Lee biographer Douglas Southall Freeman:

> When he evacuated Petersburg on the night of April 2, 1865, Lee had with him probably not more than 12,500 infantry—fewer men than in any of the five Federal corps on the south side of the James [River]—and on the whole of the front he had only from 28,000 to 30,000 infantry moving or preparing to move. After the heavy losses on ... April 1, and the casualties sustained in the Federal assault of April 2, he could not have mustered even that number had not the local defense troops and many of the detailed men and convalescents quit Richmond and joined in the retreat.... Nor, for that matter, could all the units of the veteran army itself be accounted fit.[28]

After Richmond, Union troops were sent to block Lee's escape route to North Carolina. As part of this historic moment, troops deployed to block Lee's escape included United States Colored Troops, many who were former enslaved men from Virginia. "Two divisions of the XXIV Corps under the command of Major General John Gibbon, and troops under the Army of the James commander Major General Edward Ord, including the 8th in Colonel Ulysses Doubleday's 2nd Brigade with the 41st, 45th and 127th USCTs, and the 3rd Brigade, under Colonel William W. Woodward, included the 29th and 31st USCTs." A part of the deployment, "the 1st Brigade's 7th, 109th and 116th USCTs took orders from Colonel James Shaw Jr., entered Petersburg at 6 a.m. on April 3. As General Ulysses S. Grant's troops headed after the [Confederate] Army of Northern Virginia, the Army of the James, including the USCTs, marched to the south of Lee's army.[29]

Grant had successfully weakened the heart of Lee's Army by cutting off desperately needed supply lines and severely reducing his troop strength. Lee ordered his scattered troops to rendezvous at the court house in Amelia County, where he hoped to feed his men and use the "Richmond and Danville Railroad" to transfer his army and join Confederate forces in North Carolina.[30]

Lee's men were fatigued and near starvation, but Lee believed that much needed rations had been stored for his men at the Amelia Courthouse. When he arrived, though, General Lee was deeply disappointed, forcing him to draft an open letter to the citizens of Amelia County where on April 4, 1865, he wrote:

> To the Citizens of Amelia County, Va. The Army of Northern Virginia arrived here today, expecting to find plenty of provisions, which had been ordered to be placed here by the railroad several days since, but to my surprise and regret I find not a pound of subsistence for man or horse. I must therefore appeal to your generosity and charity to supply as far as each one is able the wants of the brave soldiers who have battled for your liberty for four years.[31]

The condition in which General Lee and his men found themselves was deteriorating rapidly, and as "proud as Lee must have been of the spirit his men displayed, he knew that it could not be long sustained in the face of continued hunger and attack."[32] As the Union army was closing in on Lee, he needed to quickly get his men and equipment to the courthouse. However, the weather was not cooperating.

With the Union army in pursuit, Lee needed to get his men to Amelia County as quickly as possible. Rather than have his men, wagons and heavy military equipment travel single file over the same rain-soaked roads, he split them in two parallel columns, under the leadership of two Confederate commanders, General Richard S. Ewell and Major General John B. Gordon. The generals had to cross two small bridges across two branches of Sayler's Creek, tributaries of the Appomattox River.

After a heavy rainstorm, the muddy roads and fields created a bottleneck and slowed the Confederate push forward. The two bridges were weak and narrow, and they eventually gave way under the heavy weight of wagons and military equipment, further delaying the men's arrival. As troops advanced through the bottleneck towards the Amelia County Courthouse, they had to leave the remainder of their supplies behind, causing a breach in the command.

On April 6, 1865, unknown to General Lee, the much larger Union army, including USCT, was closing in from multiple directions and taking steps to block the escape route for the Confederate army stuck at the bottleneck at Sayler's Creek. With Lee's men trapped, aggressive fighting broke out; for the Confederates, it was a humiliating defeat. Many Confederate men were either killed or captured.

However, "Lee did not know the worst of it. Most of Ewell's corps was surrounded and would surrender, and Ewell himself would be captured by the end of the day, as was Lee's oldest son," Major General George Washington Custis Lee, heir to Arlington Plantation, who was "commanding one of the divisions" captured under Ewell.[33]

The losses for General Lee at Sayler's Creek were staggering. According to Civil War historian Andrew A. Humphreys, then a major general in the Union army, Confederate "General Ewell had about 3,600 men…. General Anderson about 6,300, making a total force of about 10,000." At the end of the various battles at the Sayler's Creek, Lee lost anywhere from a quarter to a third of his remaining army: "General Ewell lost about 3,400, General

Anderson about 2,600, making the total loss of both commands about 6,000 in killed, wounded, and prisoners."[34]

General Ulysses S. Grant, realizing that he now surrounded the remainder of the Confederate Army of Northern Virginia and that the end of the war was near, in an attempt to avoid any further loss of life, reached out to General Lee in an attempt to get him to surrender.

Figure 9: Grant Letter of Suggestion to General Lee of Surrender[35]

Headquarters, Armies of the United States
April 7, 1865—5 p.m.
General R. E. Lee
Commanding C. S. Army

General: The results of the last week must convince you of the hopelessness of further resistance on the part of the Army of Northern Virginia in this struggle. I feel that is so, and regard it as my duty to shift from myself the responsibility for any further effusion of blood, by asking of you to surrender that portion of the C. S. Army known as the Army of Northern Virginia.

                Very respectfully,
                Your obedient servant,
                U. S. Grant
                Lieutenant-General
                Commanding Armies of the United States

From a bridge on a bluff high above Sayler's Creek, General Lee witnessed the challenges his men faced and their subsequent capture by the Union troops. As their commanding officer, many thoughts must have gone through Lee's mind, and the thought of surrendering his army must have been difficult. But Lee had to carefully think of the most appropriate response to General Grant, under the circumstances and provided the following:

Figure 10: General Lee's Letter Response Relative to Terms of Surrender[36]

7th Apl' 65
Genl

I have read your note of this date. Though not entertaining the opinion you express of the hopelessness of further resistance on the part of the Army of N. Va.—I reciprocate your desire to avoid useless effusion of blood, & therefore before considering your proposition, ask the terms you will offer on condition of its surrender

                Very respy your obt. Servt
                R .E. Lee
                Genl
                Lt. Genl. U. Grant
                Command Armies of the U. States

On April 8 both men pondered their next steps. They both sent carefully written correspondence back and forth, sensitive to the situation at hand. That evening General Lee received a response and a conciliatory offer in which Grant stated that "peace was his great desire, and that he had only one condition: namely, that the men and officers surrendered shall be disqualified for taking up arms against the Government of the United States, until properly exchanged."[37]

After further deliberation between the two opposing generals, on the morning of April 9, 1865, near the town of Appomattox Court House, Virginia, according to biographer Michael Korda, General Robert E. Lee realized his dire position:

> At first light [General] Lee arose from a brief nap ... wearing his best uniform, a silk sash around his waist, his best sword with a gilded lion's head on its pommel and an ivory grip hanging from a gold-embroidered sword belt.... His knee-high cavalry boots were gleaming, he wore gold spurs with rowels, and he carried a new pair of pale gray gauntlets. "If I am to be General Grant's prisoner today I intend to make my best appearance," he said to Pendleton [an aide], perhaps in jest. Out of an army that was reduced to about 28,000 men, "the mere skeleton, the ghost of the Army of Northern Virginia," Lee now had fewer than 8,000 exhausted, emaciated infantrymen armed and fit for battle and perhaps 2,100 cavalrymen, with which to confront 80,000 Federal troops....[38]

Grant then penned a letter to Lee that essentially brought an end to the war.

Figure 11: General Grant's Terms of Surrender[39]

Appomattox C. H., Va.
Apr 9th, 1865
Gen R. E. Lee,
Comd'g C. S. A
Gen.

In accordance with the substance of my letter to you of the 8th inst., I propose to receive the surrender of the Army of N. Va. on the following terms, to wit: Rolls of all the officers and men to be made in duplicate. One copy to be given to an officer designated by me, the other to be retained by such officer or officers as you may designate. The officers to give their individual paroles not to take up arms against the Government of the United States until properly exchanged, and each company or regimental commander sign a like parole for the men of their commands.

The arms, artillery and public property to be parked and stacked, and turned over to the officer appointed by me to receive them.

This will not embrace the side-arms of the officers, nor their private horses or baggage. This done, each officer and man will be allowed to return to their homes, not to be disturbed by United States authority so long as they observe their paroles and the laws in force where they may reside

Very respectfully,

U. S. GRANT, Lt. Gl

In the late morning of April 9, 1865, the six USCT regiments, consisting of 4,000 to 5,000 men,[40] witnessed one of the most important days in African American history and certainly in their lives as African American men: the surrender of Confederate General Robert E. Lee and his army to Union General Ulysses S. Grant in the parlor of Wilmer McLean's house in Appomattox Court House, Virginia. With the surrender of Lee's army, the two men essentially brought to an end four long and bitter years of fighting between the North and the South, and for the men of the USCTs and all African Americans, the end of slavery as they knew it.

After the terms of the surrender was agreed upon, the two generals each selected three officers to oversee the surrender and parole of Lee's Confederate army. As prescribed by the terms, later that day Lee and six of his staff signed a document granting their parole.

General Grant tried unsuccessfully to capture the Confederate capital for most of 1864, grinding down on supplies and resources of the people and

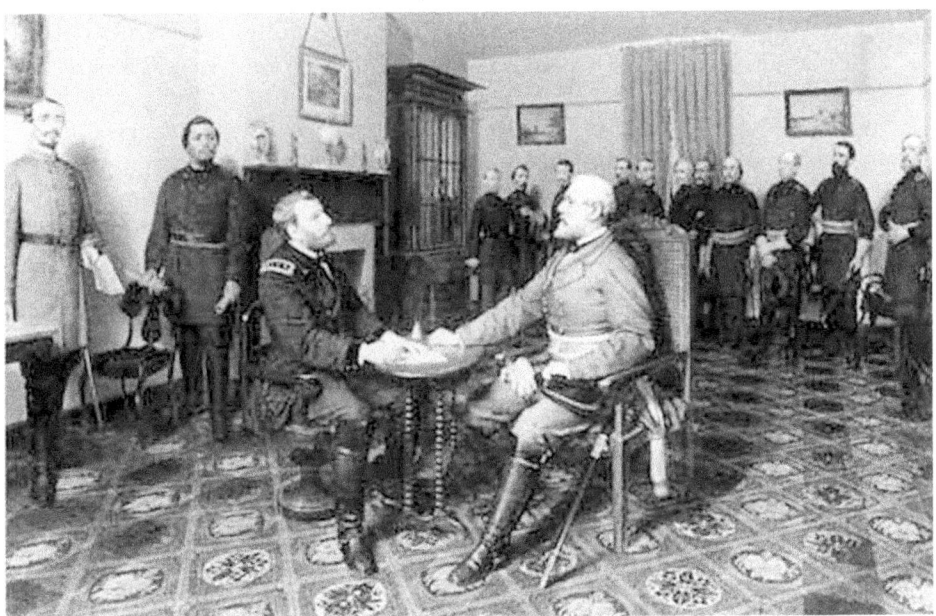

General Lee meets General Grant at Appomattox (courtesy National Park Service).

their army. In the spirit of reconciliation, at Appomattox, Grant would issue "beef, salt, hardtack, coffee and sugar" from the Union commissary to share with the 25,000 hungry Confederates who had subsisted "for days on parched corn." This was, for many of the Confederates, the first real sustenance they had received in a while, and the friendly gesture was well noted by the surrendering troops.[41]

After Robert E. Lee surrendered to Ulysses S. Grant at Appomattox Court House on April 9, 1865, within six short days, President Abraham Lincoln was killed by an assassin's bullet, at which time his Vice President, Andrew Johnson, became president. By May 9 all the Confederate troops throughout the South had surrendered, at which time President Johnson declared that the war had come to an end.

The Civil War was over. This war was the costliest in terms of both American wealth and American lives. The nation's new citizens now had to forge peace with their former enslavers, as well as northern reformers skeptical of their abilities, without the guiding hand of the Great Emancipator. The killing grounds (Antietam, Gettysburg, Vicksburg, Shiloh) and the cemeteries and monuments would be critical in forging the new narratives of justice, freedom, and reconciliation, as well as in developing new social systems, which still included segregation. Arlington would become the greatest of those cemeteries, but not all deaths mattered as much as others.

With the war at an end, William Syphax, son of Maria (Carter Custis) and Charles Syphax, wrote to President Johnson regarding his parent's claim to the seventeen acres given to his mother by George Washington Parke Custis in 1826. His parents lived on their parcel with the real possibility that they may be evicted as Arlington National Cemetery expanded to accommodate the bodies of fallen Civil War soldiers. The Syphax property had also been confiscated by the Federal government when it took the property owned by Maria's half-sister, Mary Custis Lee, after Robert E. Lee left the Union army and joined the Confederacy.

In a firsthand account written May 11, 1865, William Syphax stated that "Mr. G.W.P. Custis manumitted my Mother and her children, and … at the time … gave to her, for the use of herself and heirs, a small parcel of land … on the outer boundary of the Arlington track." Syphax's letter explained the disposition of his parents' property, the circumstances in which they acquired it and the manner in which it was taken from them. Syphax further stated that "My parents have no written evidence of this gift of land made to them by Mr. Custis, but can establish [it], by parol evidence, the facts herein alleged."[42] On behalf of his parents, Syphax set out succinctly what his parents wanted and how they hoped to achieve it:

> What they now desire is that in view of all the facts, they may be permitted to purchase from the Government the small parcel of ground on which they live, and to which they

claim to be equally entitled, at the rate at which the United States purchased the Arlington Estate, and to receive a legal title for the home, so that for free remaining days of their earthly existence, and their children after them, they may enjoy the security and benefits which Mr. Custis benevolently signed they should [share][43]

After the many years of newspaper articles about G.W.P. Custis and his extended and immediate interracial family members, including his daughter Maria Syphax, it took little time and discussion for the United States Congress, on June 12, 1866, to approve an Act for the Relief of Maria Syphax, which supplied "…seventeen acres and fifty-three one-hundredths of an acre of land, be the same more or less … unto the said Maria Syphax, her heirs and assigns," essentially substantiating the family's claim to the land and their lineage.[44]

CHAPTER 11

The Contraband Cemetery

ARLINGTON THE CEMETERY WAS ESTABLISHED as a "purely practical measure" to accommodate the deceased from the District of Columbia who had filled the graveyards of the Soldiers' Home Cemetery, Union Cemetery and the free black Columbia Harmony Cemetery.[1] As the city's population surged with soldiers and support personnel for the war, along with increasing numbers of fleeing slaves, so too did the population of the cemeteries as war dead and sick slaves arrived. The city's cemeteries were now at full capacity.

While war families came to claim their dead, there was no relief for contraband families to claim their loved ones. As the Arlington Estate of the Custis-Lee family had been seen as a respite for the challenges of the healthy contraband, the property was now looked upon as a solution for those dearly departed. As it was originally known, the Contraband Cemetery at Arlington Heights became the final resting place for those who were promised emancipation, even if it had been short lived.

The interchangeable use of the words Contraband and Freedman in some records has muddied some descriptions of who is buried in that portion of the original cemetery known today as Section 27. Despite the presumption, none of the residents from the Freedman's Village, located on the northwest side of the estate, are buried in Section 27, as the village had its own burial plot while it was occupied. Any evidence of those graves or other buildings is entirely vanished from Arlington today, another piece of African American history that has been obscured from contemporary eyes.[2]

The lower cemetery had gone through several name changes, reflecting the nomenclature used for the Americans of African descent buried in the cemetery at the time. First known as a pauper's cemetery, when "the remains of many white soldiers were removed" to the upper cemetery behind the mansion and the lower cemetery "from that time, and continuing after the war, [was for] the burial of black soldiers and civilians," it became known as the Contraband Cemetery.[3] When the military first buried the poor and sick in Washington—military and civilian—they were given simple wooden headboards as grave markers. For the city's black residents, the word "Contraband" rather than their name was originally inscribed on their gravestone.

Customary of the time period, the burial grounds for slaves, freed and free persons of color were always patches of land of little to no value. The Contraband Cemetery at Arlington Heights was no exception; located in the most northeast corner of the plantation, it was also the furthest point from the Custis-Lee mansion. The thin strip of land was divided by a narrow gravel road named after Major Generals Edward Ord and Godfrey Weitzel. The contraband burials are primarily found on the north side of Ord and Weitzel Drive, while on the south side are the original white poor servicemen burials and the subsequent burials of the United States Colored Troops. With the realignment of Ord and Weitzel Drive or the building of the red sandstone north wall, bodies were reinterred to backfill any of the empty grave sites in the section.

Most burials in the lower cemetery occurred between 1863 and 1867; this cemetery became the last resting place of 3,800 African Americans who had made it to the freedom of Washington. According to historian and Arlington National Cemetery archaeologist Timothy Dennee, it is estimated that 58 percent of the civilians buried there are men. Dennee speculates that the majority were adult males because enslaved men would come North first, then bring their families. As many as eight percent of the citizens buried in Section 27 were employees of the quartermaster's office.[4]

As the enslaved continued to migrate to Washington, the number of deaths continued to rise. For many of the contraband, the desire to breathe the fresh air of freedom did not equate to breathing healthy air. Unfortunately, many would become sick from the very freedom they so desired.[5] The grave diggers—men like James Parks, a former slave of the Custis-Lee plantation, along with neighbors Benjamin Green, Thomas Owens and John Wells—were responsible for the digging the graves in the upper and lower cemeteries. They were kept busy burying the contraband, as well as the rising numbers of Union troops. By the middle of 1867 the African Americans in the lower cemetery "were reported to number 3,540. Later, the total was put at 3,639. More than 1,000 were laid to rest in 1864 alone, with 1,391 civilian freedpeople buried from August 1864 through June 1865."[6]

In walking through Section 27, one cannot help but reflect on the challenges of the time period for the enslaved, as reflected by the present day inscriptions on their gravestones which read either "citizen" or "civilian." As in life on the plantation or as part of the African diaspora, enslaved families were permanently separated. Each grave represents a single burial with no apparent surrounding family member or a cluster of names indicating the burial plot being part of a larger family grouping. It is unknown whether James Parks and the other African American grave diggers did so intentionally, but most of the buried are in an east-west pattern, with the stones facing east and presumably the head of the deceased facing west as to observe the falling sunset.

Section 27 provides a deep historical connection between the plights of the fugitives escaping enslavement and the horrific challenges that many faced during the war once they reached the city of Washington. The simplicity of the headstones reflects a time of constant burials void of any dates of burial, as if to indicate the haste of each burial.

By November 1867 "burials of [black] civilians" ceased, "but the reinterment of black troops continued into 1868."[7] Each of the graves was provided with a painted white wooden headboard, two feet in height. The name of the deceased was in black letters and, if known, the date of death. If the deceased was a soldier his military rank, company and regiment were added. If the name of the military deceased was not known, the work "Unknown" was also painted on the headboard, as it was for the contraband.

As fugitive enslaved found their way to the capital city, their families had no funds for proper burials. These were the impoverished forgotten souls sent to the paupers' graves at Arlington. As the expanded Union cavalry needed more space for more horses, some of the contraband indigents buried behind the barns at Giesboro Cemetery in Washington were reinterred at Arlington. In death, as in life, these African Americans' stories were obscured, their conditions harsh, and any record of their lives limited. The lack of proper documentation was due to errors and omissions compounded over the years by changes in record-keeping practices, departmental responsibility, and accountability, all of which has caused many stones to be marked as the burial spot of an "Unknown" person.

For example, at grave number 27:1438, the marker only reads "Unknown"; according to her burial card, she was known as just "Aunty" and was buried on October 26, 1864. She may have cared for many of her slaveholder's children and grandchildren, but here she rests with the marker of "Unknown," her true identity and the reasons she was called "Aunty" now lost to history.[8] In grave number 27:1924, an unknown man was buried on September 9, 1864. There is no record of his hard work or contributions, or even the value he brought to his slaveholder's estate. All that is known is that his last known address was at Mr. Coombs Grindel's house, near the shanties in the rear of K Street SE, between New Jersey Avenue and First Street.[9]

We know from a burial card that on June 5, 1865, Emma's grandson was buried in grave number 27:3336. His grandmother was likely impoverished and unable to bury him properly. She knew her grandchild's name, and probably suffered a broken heart upon his death, but now the child is buried with the caption of "Unknown."[10] Like so many others during this period of hunger, disease and misfortune, a "Newborn" child is buried in grave number 27:2531;

the newer stone designates the child "Citizen," demonstrating how the language of Section 27 continues to evolve. In grave number 27:3252 is the body of an unknown woman who suffered alone in Freedman's Hospital and died on November 12, 1865, of typhoid fever. Because of her health conditions she was probably isolated from her family and buried two days later on November 14, 1865.[11]

In grave number 27:3822, on October 1, 1866, five men were buried together. Perhaps they were all injured at the same time while at work. Perhaps their lives had so little meaning that they were place on the back of a cart akin to sacks of grain and sent over to be buried in a single unmarked grave. The men were originally buried near Union Mills, Virginia. They were exhumed on August 29, 1866, and removed for burial in Arlington.[12] All of these burials are joined by more than 400 other unknown individuals.

On the other side of Arlington National Cemetery, men are entombed in mass graves of solidarity with other unknown soldiers of the Civil War, along with the Tomb of the Unknown Soldier that sits atop one of the rolling hills at Arlington overlooking the city of Washington. The white marble tomb symbolizes the six major campaigns of World War I and honors the dead from the war that was supposed to end all wars. In close proximity, to the west, are memorials to the unknown soldiers who died in World War II and the Korean and Vietnam Wars. But in Section 27, there stands no such memorial to the unknown souls whose imprisonment built a great nation, or whose collective bonds and hours of unpaid slave labor grew the United States economy.

However, not all enslaved were remembered only as "Unknown"; many of them, after reaching Union territory and achieving "freedom," rejected the names given to them by former slaveholders and instead chose their own names, indicating their newly freed status.

By today's standards, it may seem unusual to rename oneself after an important historical figure such as an American president. However, this was

The Unknowns (private collection of Ric Murphy).

The enslaved shed their slave names and took names of important people (private collection of Ric Murphy).

a period in American history when thousands of enslaved men, women and children were asked for the very first time, "What is your last name?" For many, to be able to shed their "slave name" and be able to name themselves after whomever they believed to be important figures in their freedom was indeed an honor. The "enslaved name" of the man interred in grave number 27:3493 has been lost to history. However, this man boldly changed his name to Abraham Lincoln in honor of the 16th President of the United States.

For others, they were so happy to be far from the oppression of their plantation and slaveholder that simply not being identified with their enslaver's surname was a privilege. This explains, in part, why many descendants from these former enslaved have the surname "Freeman."

Another name familiar to families of African American descent is the surname Washington. Arlington National Cemetery's Section 27 is the final resting place for many former enslaved with this last name, including a George and a Martha Washington. Unlike their namesakes, the contributions of these two honorable former enslaved have been lost to history. Of these two, Martha Ann Washington was buried on June 17, 1867, and while the cause of her death is unknown, she died at the house of John Washington on 2nd Street in Washington, D.C.[13] We don't know if any of these Washingtons were descendants of the original enslaved from President George Washington's Mount Vernon plantation, who through the generations of the Washington-Custis family were transferred as chattel property. Perhaps they have no relationship with one another aside from taking the names of the first president and the first lady of the United States.

There are also two John Adams buried in Section 27; one was a white

11. The Contraband Cemetery

Formerly enslaved men that were named after presidents.

Union soldier from New York. The other John Adams had probably been a fugitive slave from one of the Virginia or Maryland plantations. Perhaps each man was named after the second President of the United States, John Adams of Massachusetts.

Arlington National Cemetery is the most sacred of national cemeteries in the nation. The nation takes pride in and from the sacrifices made by our military heroes who are buried in this hallowed ground. Yet so little is known of the sacrifices of thousands of the formerly enslaved also buried under the same hallowed grounds. Two more formerly enslaved men share the names of two well-known American presidents: Thomas Jefferson, the third president of the United States, and James Monroe, the fifth president of the United States, both Virginia-born slave owners. While we know so much about the lives of these two iconic American presidents, we know so little of these two American enslaved men who carry their names. For example, all that is known about the enslaved Thomas Jefferson is that he was buried on November 20, 1865, and that his last known address was across the river at 5th Street NW near Freedman's Hospital.[14]

Chapter 12

The Forgotten Union Blue

The narrow gravel road named after Major Generals Edward Ord and Godfrey Weitzel divides that portion of Section 27 to the north with the contraband dead and to the south with black soldiers that served in the United States Colored Troops. Both generals played significant roles in commanding African American Union soldiers and in bringing the war to its close in Richmond with large numbers of USCT. Earlier Weitzel had been skeptical when given command by Benjamin Butler of black troops in the Department of the Gulf, but he was soon persuaded of their courage.

General Weitzel, like thousands of others, changed his mind in regard to the colored troops. "If he was not convinced by General Butler's reasoning ... he must have been convinced by what he saw of the conduct of those very colored regiments at Port Hudson, where he himself gave such a glorious example of prudence and gallantry."[1]

The USCT would subsequently take charge of policing Richmond in the aftermath of the rebel retreat from their putative capital.

As President Lincoln had allowed African American men to enlist in the United States Colored troops, so they became part of the military dead arriving at the national cemetery in Arlington. The custom of segregation of the races in life and in death meant their burials were separate from the white military dead. Once Meigs' orders were fully enacted and graves dug behind the house, no more white soldiers were buried along with William Christman in the lower cemetery after July 1864.

Section 27 contains the graves of nearly 1,000 USCT soldiers. In addition, the section contains the remains of numerous African American servicemen reinterred or moved into gaps among the civilian graves. Walter P. McClerkin of New York, a private in the 152 Depot Brigade who died on February 8, 1936, is in 27:4748A, near William Harris, an air corps private from the District of Columbia buried at Arlington on December 17, 1936, in 27:4762AA. Neither the USCT nor the other veterans and their stories have been fully or adequately documented as other African Americans, in contrast to those honored at the Philadelphia National Cemetery on April 21, 2018.[2] In the Philadelphia National Cemetery there is now a storyboard, and the military records of each one of the USCT have been researched, documented and archived.

In both the upper and lower cemetery, the wooden headboards quickly deteriorated and needed constant replacement. The two cemeteries were separated by several hills and dense woodlands. The segregated cemeteries received accordingly disparate treatment and maintenance. Special efforts by African Americans were required to ensure the Contraband Cemetery was decorated with flags during the May commemorations.

On May 30, 1868, the Grand Army of the Republic (GAR) organized the first Decoration Day, proclaiming a day of remembrance for those who died in the Civil War "in defense of their country during the late rebellion" and decorating their graves. (The day of remembrance eventually became known as Memorial Day in 1967.) The tolls on the Long Bridge were waived for the day and the Georgetown Corporation reduced its tariffs on the street cars.[3] The fraternal organization developed a reputation for defending the rights for Union soldiers, naval men, and the rights of African Americans. The potential for reopening the wounds of the war and for political strife were apparent:

> Saturday was observed with impressive ceremonies in a great many different parts of the country as a day for the decoration of the graves for the gallant fellows who died for the country.... It is to be hoped that this occasion may grow to be numbered with the national *fasti*, and may not be turned aside from its sacred and peculiar character by the inevitable politician who has already thrust himself into the affairs of the Gettysburg and Antietam cemeteries.[4]

In 1870 the *New Era*, edited by Frederick Douglass, reported:

> Nowhere were the ceremonies fitted the occasion more inspiring probably than at Arlington, where fifteen thousand of the heroic dead lie buried in sight of the capital.[5]

The paper also noted the presence of Hiram Revels, the first African American U.S. Senator (Mississippi, 1870-71), but "regretted and condemned" that the separated lower "colored section" was not a part of the formal ceremony.

The deteriorated condition of the lower cemetery was such that the Grand Army of the Republic and local African American veterans intervened and demanded respect be shown to the United States Colored Troop war dead in the same manner as the upper cemetery. In 1871, they:

> ... petitioned the War Department to relocate hundreds of U.S. Colored Troops to the high ground around Lee's mansion—up from the Lower Cemetery, where black soldiers had been buried unceremoniously among poor white warriors and former slaves. General Meigs, who still kept a firm grip on developments at the national cemetery, fielded the request and advised against the transfer.[6]

Meigs, earlier in the war, went to great lengths to contaminate the grounds and drinking water of the Arlington Plantation with the bodies of war dead, ensuring the Lee family would never return to Arlington. Now, however, he opposed the re-interment of war dead. He professed he regretted moving a single body once interred in the National Cemetery, believing that the dead, once decently buried, should have their final rest. Meigs went further and advocated a full segregation:

> If the colored people generally prefer to have their comrades, who fought for them, taken up again and scattered among the whites, it can be done.... I believe that hereafter it will be more grateful to their descendants to be able to visit and point to the collected graves of these persons, than to find them scattered through a large cemetery and intermingled with another race. The records show that there are in Arlington Cemetery 3,757 contrabands or refugees and 343 colored soldiers.[7]

As the deterioration of the upper and lower cemeteries became more controversial, the Grand Army of the Republic continued to pressure Congress for resolution regarding the lack of maintenance of the lower cemetery, including the replacement of the wooden headboards. The importance of Section 27 to the African American veterans and their memory included work towards the establishment of a monument, as reported 40 years later in 1912, during the height of the creation of the "Cult of the Lost Cause."[8]

> There has long been an agitation among the colored posts of the Grand Army of the Republic for the erection of a monument to the negro dead in this part of the great burial ground, but the shaft has not been reared.[9]

The memorial has still not been raised, yet Arlington was "adorned" by a "warped political movement" with a Confederate monument in 1913.[10] In 1992, in Section 27, the Committee to Memorialize African Americans in the Civil War did finally install a memorial plaque (smaller than many of the gravestones). This African American Civil War Memorial is located at the intersection of Vermont Avenue and 10th Street NW in the District of Columbia.

In 1872, a plan was put in place to ensure that headstones were uniform in appearance and placement. The stones were to be placed in a manner to look like soldiers standing in their ranks at attention. This was the first universal design for stones to be erected in national cemeteries: a permanent slab design of marble or durable stone four inches thick and 10 inches wide, with 12 inches extending above the ground. After the gravestone specifications were agreed upon in 1873 and provided with a $1 million appropriation, each soldier was required to be given an individual gravestone.

> The legislation called for "durable stone of such design and weight as shall keep them in place when set." ... The new tombstones would be fashion from granite or white marble, cut four inches thick, ten inches wide, and a yard long; markers in northern latitudes were made taller by six inches to withstand frost; each tombstone, slightly rounded on top, displayed in an incised shield with the grave number, the name of the deceased, his rank, and his home state.[11]

The replacement of the wooden headboards with permanent gravestones did not begin until 1876 for several administrative reasons, including the investigation of contracts. The USCT in the lower cemetery took the lowest priority with the placement of permanent headstones, though the headstones were specified as being for the military dead. As for the freed enslaved buried in the lower cemetery, even as marble slabs began arriving, the superintendent proposed to the quartermaster general simply to remove the civilians' headboards entirely.[12] In the meantime, the boards rotted out and more of the history was forgotten.

As required, burial reports to the quartermaster were filed for Section 27 and turned in on forms printed with the heading "Contraband Cemetery, Arlington, Va.," instead of the "Arlington National Cemetery" used for the military burials up the hill. The Freedman's Bureau "attempted to provide some additional dignity by referring to it as the "Freedman's Cemetery."[13]

The permanent headstone was referred to as the "Civil War" type, and was furnished for members of the Union army only. The portion of the stone above ground was polished and the top slightly curved. When the military finally replaced the wooden grave markers in Section 27, to ensure uniformity between the grave markers of the military and civilian dead, all the new stone grave markers were of the Civil War type. For the civilian headstones, the usage of the word "contraband" on the marker was revisited.

Initially the inscription may have been acceptable; and though there was some honor in dying freed rather than a slave, after the war the term was derogatory. For unknown buried persons, the practice was reversed and the inscription "citizen" on some and "civilian" on others were replaced on their newer stones. Numerous stones remain inscribed "Unknown" throughout Section 27.

When the marble stones were introduced, any known names of the deceased were carefully placed on each headstone. In walking through Section 27, one realizes what President Abraham Lincoln's time in office came to epitomize for tens of thousands of African American men, women and children: the dream of freedom was possible. On May 24, 1861, Major General Benjamin Butler learned that three slaves belonging to the commander of the local Confederate troops had crossed the battle lines for refuge at his camp; he thereby considered them contraband of war. This classification marked a new beginning for tens of thousands of slaves across the Confederate states. The protection provided by Butler and his regiments at Fort Monroe (recast by the enslaved as "Fort Freedom") was a powerful message to other African Americans: the time to escape was upon them.

Civilians are buried right alongside Union heroes in Section 27. The causes of their deaths were frequently the same infections; more soldiers died from sickness than on the battlefield. Each of the troops now has the permanent Union polished stone engraved with the number of the grave, rank, and the name of the soldier along with the insignia "USCT" for United States Colored Troops cut on the front face of the stone.

At the close of the Civil War, nearly 16,000 of the dead were buried on the property once known as Arlington House, 4,000 of which were unknown soldiers. The hallowed grounds of Arlington's Section 27 have become the final resting place for a number of historic men whose contributions to history have long been forgotten. Some fifty years after the war, the lower cemetery had both been forgotten and embedded with an aura of permanence due to the old trees and worn headstones. Harry Shannon, a writer for the *Washington Evening Star*, on August 17, 1912, described Section 27 as: "An old section of Arlington national cemetery, dedicated to the burial of colored soldiers of the Union before the opening of the new addition to Arlington, is seldom entered by tourists. Though it is a place of great beauty and reverent quiet, it lies off the main track of travel."

He also found it to have a somber immovability:

> A watchman's cottage surrounded by shrubbery and flowers is on the left. The road passes around a brilliant flower circle gorgeously illuminated this season with geraniums, verbenas, roses and petunias. To the westward stretch the ranks of marble headstones, some dark-stained by rains and frosts and some gloomy under a coat of moss. Over all spread somber spruce and sad pine trees. About twenty-five hundred graves are here....
>
> The field of graves lies between the Seneca sandstone north wall and a little stream on the south that trickles down through the impressive woods—woodland yet untouched by the grave digger's spade, and which covers the rough terrain north of the mansion. The timber there is white oak, and the trees, though tall, are not old. Their age is probably forty or fifty years, but the depth of the humous or forest mold would indicate that this is very old, if not primeval, woodland. This woodland is a dreamy place. The sun does not shine there in summer and the snow sifts softly down in winter.
>
> The hard rolled gravel road that runs through these acres of graves and the nearby woods show few wheel tracks, and days and days pass without anybody moving there, except a watchman going his lonely round.[14]

The section retains many of these qualities today, having the most heterogeneous of grave markings, even as the rest of the cemetery has expanded to connect it back into the whole.

Section 27 includes four Medal of Honor recipients, three of whom are African American. Established by the Navy, the Medal of Honor is the nation's highest and most prestigious personal military decoration awarded to U.S. military service members who distinguished themselves by acts of valor. The Medal of Honor was awarded to twenty-five African American men for their valor during the Civil War.[15]

The first Medal of Honor recipient to be buried in Section 27 was a white soldier, Private James Richmond of the 8th Ohio Infantry, U.S. Army. Private Richmond, buried on June 3, 1864, was honored for his bravery during the Battle of Gettysburg when he courageously risked his life by capturing the Confederate flag.

The first African American and second overall Medal of Honor recipient to be buried in Section 27 was Sergeant Thomas Shaw, of the 9th U.S. Cavalry, U.S. Army, on June 23, 1895. Shaw received the Medal of Honor for his heroism on August 12, 1881, as part of the Indian Campaigns, at Carrizo Canyon, New Mexico. Shaw "forced the enemy back after stubbornly holding his ground in an extremely exposed position and prevented the enemy's superior numbers from surrounding his command."[16]

Landsman William H. Brown, of Baltimore, Maryland, served aboard the USS *Brooklyn*, U.S. Navy. He was the second African American Medal of Honor recipient to be buried at Arlington, on November 5, 1896. Brown was honored for his service during successful attacks against Confederate gunboats at Fort Morgan, and the ram *Tennessee* in Mobile Bay on August 5, 1864. "Stationed in the immediate vicinity of the shell whips which were twice cleared of men by bursting shells," according to his commendation, "Brown remained steadfast at his post and performed his duties in the powder division throughout the furious action which resulted in the surrender of the prize rebel ram *Tennessee* and in the damaging and destruction of batteries at Fort Morgan."[17]

The last African American in Section 27 honored with the Medal of Honor was Sergeant James H. Harris (27:985H), of the 38th U.S. Colored Troops, U.S. Army, buried on January 28, 1898. Sergeant Harris, from Saint Mary's County, Maryland, was awarded the Medal of Honor for his valor at the assault on Chaffin's Farm, on September 29, 1864. Sergeant Harris was part of the "two brigades of General J. Paine's Third Division, Eighteenth Corps during the

Section 27 Medal of Honor recipients (private collection of Ric Murphy).

assault on Chaffin's Farm, the Confederate entrenched line of defense at New Market Heights, Virginia, north of the James River."[18] Harris was part of the USCT that were under attack for over 30 minutes. The men charged the Confederate defenses and after an hour of intense combat, most black troops were wounded, captured, or killed.

Of the twenty-five African American men to receive the Medal of Honor for their valor during the Civil War, Milton Holland is the only one to be buried in Section 23. First Sergeant Holland of Austin, Texas (Section 23: 21713), received a Medal of Honor for his valor at Chaffin's Farm, as did James Harris (Section 27: 985H). Holland was "a servant to Colonel Nelson H. Van Vorhes, an officer in the 3rd, 18th and 92nd Ohio Infantry. Once blacks were officially able to be recruited into the Union Army, Holland enlisted in the 127th Ohio Infantry (Colored) in August 1863. The regiment was redesignated as the 5th United States Colored Troops in January 1864."[19]

Milton Holland was recognized for his bravery and leadership when he "took command of Company C, after all the [white] officers had been killed or wounded, and gallantly led it." The Confederate position was captured. Holland's regiment, the 5th USCT, bore the brunt of the New Market Heights attack, suffering the highest casualties of any black regiment that day, 213 killed and wounded, along with 23 missing. Holland's commanding general officer, Major General Benjamin F. Butler, said of Holland: "Had it been within my power I would have conferred upon him in view of it, a brigadier generalship for gallantry in the field."[20]

The skill, tenacity and leadership abilities of Sergeant James Harris and Holland were renowned. Harris and three other black sergeants rose from the ranks and took command of their companies when the white commissioned officers were killed. As the sergeants led their fellow comrades upon the parapet of the southern earthworks, a Confederate officer, attempting to rally his men, waved his sword and shouted, "Hurrah my brave men." Private James Gardiner of the 6th USCT shot the officer and "then ran the bayonet through his body to the muzzle."[21]

Members of the United States Colored Troops were not limited to the burials in Section 27 or 23. There were four iconic men buried in what is now known as Section 1 of the cemetery, representing the pinnacle of African American achievement during the period. They are William H. Hunter, a black minister; Orandatus Simon Bolivar Wall, a black lawyer; Dr. Alexander Augusta, a black doctor; and a professional soldier, Frank Welch.

William H. Hunter was born a slave on June 21, 1831. He was commissioned as Regimental Chaplain of the 4th USCT on October 4, 1863. While stationed with his regiment at the Battle of Petersburg, he witnessed the heroic action and successes of former enslaved, freed, and free African American troops on the battlefield. In his account he said:

The 15th of June, 1864, is the day long to be remembered by the entire colored race on this continent. It is the day when prejudice died in the entire Army of U.S. of America. It is the day when it was admitted that colored men were equal to the severest ordeal. It is the day in which we secured to us the rights of equality in the Army and service of the Government of United States.[22]

Chaplin Hunter was known for his eloquent and inspirational speeches during the war to both the USCTs and civilians alike. While in Wilmington, North Carolina, he "preached to a throng of sixteen hundred people at the Front Street Methodist Church" where he said: "One week ago you were all slaves; now you are free. (Uproarious screamings.) Thank God the armies of the Lord and of Gideon has triumphed like the chaff before the wind. (Amen! Hallelujah!)."[23] Chaplin Hunter died on October 16, 1908, and is buried in Section 1: 123.[24]

The military man who became a lawyer, Orandatus Simon Bolivar Wall, was born a slave on August 12, 1825, in Rockingham, North Carolina, to an enslaved mother and her white slaveholder. Like so many who wanted to volunteer their service to the Union army and serve the needs of other African American men in combat service, Wall wrote letters to Washington volunteering for the United States Colored Troops. In March 1865, O.S.B Wall sent a letter to Union Colonel C.W. Foster of Bureau of Colored Troops volunteering his services:

Figure 12: Requesting to Serve His Country in the United States Colored Troops[25]

Washington D.C. Mar 3rd 1865

Dear Sir I desire to enter the recruiting service. I reside in Ohio. have lived in Ohio since 1846. previous to which time I lived in North Carolina. I am now 39 years old. I took charge of the Col^d recruiting service in Ohio in the spring of 1863. for the State of Massachusetts. I served in the capacity of state Ag^t to organize the colored settlements for the purpose of facilitating colored enlistments. during the time the state of Massachusetts through its agency was allowed to take recruits from the state of Ohio, or about three months. I was then appointed by Gov. Tod to superintend the (Col^d) Recruiting service in the same capacity. in which I had been serving. for the state of Massachusetts I was employed by Gov. Tod about Four months during which time I recruited about 300. of the 5 Regiment USC.T. in the spring of 1864 I was appointed by Gov Brough to assist in raising the 27th Reg. U.S.C.T I was in his service three months during a part of the time. while I was recruiting in Ohio I had the controle of the transportation and subsistence. all of which I did to the entire satisfaction of the gentlemen in authority. if not inconsistent with your orders I wish an appointment to Recruit in some part of the South with a Commission to rank as Captain

Very Respectfully your obedient serv[an]t
O.S.B. Wall

Colonel Foster, upon receiving Wall's request and determining that "he was well qualified to serve as a recruiting officer for black troops," sent orders to the "Commander of the Department of the South and to the War Department's Commissary of Musters ordering Wall's muster as a captain and his assignment to South Carolina for recruiting duty."[26] Wall enrolled into Company K of the 104th USCT and was commissioned as a captain. He served with the Freemen's Bureau until his discharge at Charleston, South Carolina, on February 5, 1866, and was one of twelve known black recruiters of black soldiers.[27] After his discharge, he served as a lawyer in Washington, D.C.

Another officer to be buried in the segregated section of black commissioned officers was Dr. Alexander Augusta, the highest-ranking African American soldier during the Civil War. Dr. Augusta was born a "free man" in Norfolk, Virginia, on March 8, 1825. He moved to Baltimore, Maryland, where he studied elementary medicine. After being "denied admittance to the University of Pennsylvania, Augusta studied privately with faculty members before matriculating at Trinity Medical College of the University of Toronto in Canada, where he graduated in 1856."[28] Augusta then practiced at Toronto City Hospital and became its chief.[29]

On January 7, 1863, Alexander Augusta wrote to President Abraham Lincoln requesting "appointment as surgeon to some of the colored regiments," adding that he had "been in practice for about six years."

Figure 13: A Letter Requesting Appointment as Surgeon to Some of the Colored Regiments[30]

Toronto Canada West Jan 7th 1863

Sir, Having seen that it is intended to garrison the U.S. forts &c with colored troops, I beg to apply to you for an appointment as surgeon to some of the coloured regiments, or as physician to some of the depots of "freedmen." I was compelled to leave my native country, and come to this on account of prejudice against colour, for the purpose of obtaining a knowledge of my profession; and having accomplished that object, at one of the principle educational institutions of this Province, I am now prepared to practice it, and would like to be in a position where I can be of use to my race.

If you will take the matter into favorable consideration, I can give satisfactory reference as to character and qualification from some of the most distinguished members of the profession in this city where I have been in practice for about six years. I Remain Sir Yours

Very Respectfully
A. T. Augusta

Augusta received his commission with the rank of major as a surgeon of the 7th USCT on April 4, 1863.[31] His medical commission made him the first of eight black physicians to obtain a commission during the Civil War. Major

Augusta's initial assignment placed him in charge of the Freedman Hospital in Washington, D.C. (also known as Camp Barker), making him the first black doctor to be in charge of a hospital in the United States.[32] Upon his commission, Major Augusta immediately began to complain of the unequal pay between white and black military doctors.[33] Dr. Augusta's advocacy for equality continued on February 1, 1864, when he again protested inequality when he was removed from a streetcar in Washington, D.C., refusing to sit in the section for African Americans.[34] Later that month, while Augusta was stationed at Camp Stanton in Maryland, several white surgeons of the lower rank of captain complained, in writing, to President Abraham Lincoln. Although they professed the desire for "the elevation and improvement of the colored race, in this country," they would not serve as "subordinates to a colored officer."[35]

Though Major Augusta was able to meet President Lincoln at the White House to discuss race relations in general and address the complaints from his subordinates, the white medical officers with whom Augusta came in contact with pressured commanders, forcing Augusta's transfer to Baltimore, Maryland, and later to South Carolina.[36] However, that spring of 1864, Major Augusta succeeded in obtaining the same pay as that of white officers of equal rank in federal service.[37]

Figure 14: White Medical Officers Complain About Black Doctor[38]

February 1864
Camp Stanton near Bryantown, MD

Sir, We the undersigned, Medical Officers in the Regiments of Colored Troops, under the command of Brig. Gen. Wm Birney at this camp, have the honor most respectfully to ask your attention to the following Statement.

When we made applications for positions in the Colored Services, the understanding was universal that *all* Commissioned Officers were to be white men. Judge of our Surprise and disappointment, when upon joining our respective regiments we found that the *Senior Surgeon* of the command was a Negro.

We claim to be behind no one, in a desire for the elevation and improvement of the Colored race, in this country, and we are willing to sacrifice much, in so grand a cause, as our present positions, may testify. But we cannot in *any* case, willingly compromise what we consider a proper self respect. Nor do we deem that the interests of either country or of the Colored race, can demand this of us. Such degradation, we believe to be involved, in our voluntarily continuing in the Service, as Subordinates to a colored officer. We therefore most respectfully, yet earnestly, request, that this *unexpected, unusual*, and most unpleasant relationship in which we have been placed, may in some way be terminated. Most Respectfully Your Obt. Servants,

J. B. McPherson	E.M. Pease
Chas C. Topliff	Joel Morse
M. O. Carter	Henry Grange

Augusta overcame more racial barriers when, on March 13, 1865, he was promoted to brevet lieutenant colonel, making him the highest ranking black officer in the Civil War era.[39] In October 1866, Augusta was mustered out of the military, whereupon he returned to Washington, D.C., and started a private practice.[40]

In 1868, Dr. Augusta was elected to the faculty of the medical department of Howard University, making him the first black faculty member of an American medical school.[41] An honorary medical degree was conferred upon Professor Augusta by the university in 1869.[42] For the next eight years, he served as a professor and was on the Freedman's Hospital staff. However, he was refused admission to the Medical Society of the District of Columbia, which was supposed to be open to all races[43] After the war, Freedman's Hospital "became the teaching hospital for Howard University Medical School, [and] Dr. Augusta was offered a place on the faculty—the first black to hold such a position at any medical school in the U.S."[44]

The fourth commissioned officer to be buried in the segregated section of Arlington National Cemetery's Section 1 Civil War Officers was Frank Welch, who was part of the Fort Wagner advance. Sergeant Welch (Section 1: 123-A), was born in Philadelphia, Pennsylvania. Before the war, he worked as a barber in West Meridian, Connecticut. On May 12, 1863, he enlisted into Company A of the 54th Massachusetts infantry, where on the next day he became a sergeant.[45]

On July 18, 1863, under the leadership of Massachusetts native Colonel Robert G. Shaw, Welch advanced with 624 members of his regiment along the beach at Morris Island, South Carolina, in an assault of Fort Wagner. The fort was impregnable, and during this assault the Massachusetts 54th saw the war's first heavy casualties. Casualties in the 54th Massachusetts Regiment were 45 percent and included Frank Welch, who was wounded in the neck and taken to a hospital in Beaufort, South Carolina.[46] Welch was granted a commission as second lieutenant and later appointed first lieutenant on July 22, 1865.[47] After the Civil War, Welch stayed in the military where he served briefly as a lieutenant in the 14th U.S. Colored Heavy Artillery. He was appointed captain of the Welch Guard in Bridgeport, Connecticut, and served as a major in the Connecticut National Guard.[48]

Chapter 13

Eviction

AFTER THE CIVIL WAR, following the death of her husband General Robert E. Lee in 1870, Mary Custis Lee had likely realized that with her advancing years and infirmities, she would be unable to restore Arlington House to the grandeur she remembered. The deterioration of the house after being used as billet for Union officers and the thousands of graves around it made the property uninhabitable.[1]

Perhaps after seeing how her African-American nephew William Syphax successfully negotiated the inherited ownership of her half-sister's land at Arlington Plantation, Mary Custis Lee decided to also petition the United States Congress. Mrs. Lee made the decision to contest the loss of the title to the family's property and offered to sell it back to the federal government so that her son would be able to inherit the value of the property. Based on her father's will, upon Mary's death, the property was to revert to her son, George Washington Park Lee. With the assistance of family, friends and acquaintances, she took steps to be compensated for her family's property.

Mrs. Lee agreed with the federal government that the constitution allowed for the forfeiture of property in the case of treason. However, she asserted that *if* treason was committed, it was committed by her late husband, and since Robert E. Lee never owned title to the Arlington House, her property was illegally taken.

In an attempt to move the stalemate over the property and the question of its title ownership, on behalf of Mrs. Lee and her family, "on January 22, 1872, Senator John W. Johnston of Virginia presented the United States Senate with a petition from Mary Custis Lee that offered to acknowledge the validity of the government's legal title to Arlington, if in return the government provided reasonable compensation for the property."[2] According to another entry in the *Congressional Record* regarding Mary Custis Lee's petition:

> But assuming the most favorable view for the United States possible under the circumstances, it cannot be doubted but that a serious cloud rests upon the title. To remove

this cloud and quiet the title to the property would appear to be the evident interest of the Government of United States.

Your petitioner, and her son, G. W. Custis Lee (the owner of the reversion,) are willing to avoid, however, all litigation on the subject, and to have an amicable settlement of this matter. With this in view, they now offer to the Government of the United States, through your honorable bodies, that upon the receipt of three hundred thousand dollars they will execute and deliver such necessary releases and conveyances as may be adjudged sufficient to sanction and quiet any claim which the Government may now have, by making a legal and valid title to the property.

Your petitioner therefore prays your honorable bodies for the passage of the above offer.

                Respectfully submitted.
                Mary A. R. Lee.[3]

Mary died on November 5, 1873, without the Committee on the Judiciary ever taking any action on her request. Upon his mother's death, G.W.C. Lee was assigned. He, in turn, on April 6, 1874, petitioned the Committee on the Judiciary. Lee presented the facts and "gave his reasons for believing the sale void, and that the property belonged, in law and equity, to himself." He wrote:

The Government by its agents is in procession of the "Arlington–home estate" claiming title under the tax-sale certificate. It has been devoted, as your petitioner is informed, to the purpose, in part at least, of a national cemetery for soldiers who died during the civil war. Your petitioner's remedy through the courts of the country is, as he is advised, clear and compete. But while the associations of his early life would make the recovery of the estate peculiarly agreeable to him, he is frank to say that as Congress has devoted it to the purpose of a national cemetery, and naturally desires to preserve in their graves under the guard of the Federal authority, the remains of those who lost their lives in the service of the country, your petitioner is willing to avoid litigation, by the release of his title to the estate, upon the payment of a joint compensation. Such a purpose was expressed by Mrs. A. R. Lee, the life tenant, and your petitioner renews the proposal to release and convey to the United States, by valid deed, his fee-simple title of the estate, upon the payment to him of its fair and just value. Your petitioner has thus candidly presented his views of his claim, and respectfully asks for the passage of a law making the necessary appropriation for the purchase of said estate by Congress, upon the execution of a legal deed conveying a complete and valid title to the same to the United States.

                All of which is respectfully submitted.
                G. W. C. Lee.[4]

After Lee failed upon his request with Congress, he then took his grievance directly to the courts, arguing:

The Constitution allowed for the forfeiture of property in the case of treason, but since the United States never actually tried generally for treason, it was found that they had no right to retain the property in the manner which it had. The suit was heard in United States District Court in Alexandria, which found in favor of the federal government, Lee appealed, in 1882, and the case was then heard by the United States Supreme Court.

The court ruled on December 5, 1882, [sic—ruling was Dec. 4] that the property had been unfairly taken and returned title of the Alexandria stayed to the Lee family.[5]

Upon the decision of the Supreme Court, Congress appropriated funds to purchase title to the property. After receiving $125,000 (nearly $3M in today's currency), George Washington Custis Lee transferred a clear title to the federal government in May 1883, ending a 20-year debate over a clouded title and 105 years of Custis-Lee family ownership.

By 1883, the Freedman's Bureau had been long ago disbanded by Congress. Formalized on March 3, 1865, as the Bureau of Refugees, Freedmen and Abandoned Lands within the War Department, the bureau carried on the activities that had been improvised in the field under General Butler and others to bring African American civilians into the war effort. General Oliver Otis Howard was appointed by President Johnson to lead the bureau in May 1865. General Howard would remain in charge until the bureau's charter was revoked in 1872.[6]

The development of African American self-sufficiency has peculiar resonance in the history of Arlington. The records of the bureau provide us extensive insight into the official actions of the administrators and some insight into the lives of the formerly enslaved. The bureau, modeled after the army's "experience in the occupied South," was a critical agency in helping the newly freed enslaved navigate challenges they faced as new citizens in an overtly hostile region that had only months ago treated them as chattel property.[7] "The Republicans from the North reasoned that since they had taken the lead in seeing the successful conclusion of the war, they should take the lead in shaping the peace."[8]

The Freedman's Bureau was set up to ensure that the rights of the newly freed men were protected. Northern Republicans believed that the objectives of the Freedman's Bureau aligned with the major outcome of the Civil War. "The war had not only preserved the Union—it had also created a nation," where all People of Color were free, and in which black suffrage had to be ensured.[9] The bureau recorded their marriages from the time of enslavement, documented pay claims and rents paid for the lots secured at Arlington, Barry Farm in the District and Camp Distribution (the successor name to Camp Misery/Convalescent) outside of Alexandria.

The members of the Freedman's Bureau knew that once African Americans were given the right to vote, they would favorably remember the bureau and vote Republican for generations to come. Southern state legislatures and former Confederates were well aware of the political advantages this bureau could gain, and because of this, the Freedman's Bureau was subject to resistance by whites in the South, who demanded it be disbanded.[10]

The Freedman's Village at Arlington would be a major symbol of liberation and a model for lives transformed by the end of enslavement. Close to the seat of American power, senators, executive branch officials, and the prominent stalwarts of the abolitionist and relief organizations would tour the village and give laudatory speeches at numerous celebrations and anniversary events. Their speeches would be peppered with allusions to the dramatic transformation of Arlington, from plantation to a healthy location for a freedman's home and place of livelihood. Representative Samuel Moulton of Illinois would wrap himself in Lincoln's memory and expressed his honor in addressing an assembly on New Year's Day, 1867: "My Fellow-Countrymen.... I esteem it a privilege and pleasure to speak to you a few earnest words of congratulations and encouragement on this to you deeply interesting and happy occasion. This is the anniversary of your emancipation. It is your jubilee."[11]

While the Representative R.W. Clarke of Ohio warned at the same event of the fragile nature of freedom and their occupancy:

> The colored race in our country had suffered long and patiently.... The battle has been fought, well fought, and victory has declared for the right. You are sharers with the white men and all races of men in common humanity.... And the boon of freedom once bestowed, is not easily taken away. No force will dare wrench it from you. Take care that, by your own improvidence, you do not give it back to your masters, who, while there is the faintest hope of recovering their lost estate, will not cease to watch with eager eyes, and seize upon the earliest occasion that may promise them success.[12]

General C.H. Howard, an assistant commissioner of the bureau, would share that he was ready to help any of the citizens who wanted to move North, where "some of your number have found good homes."[13] Howard ordered that food distribution was to end in the fall of 1866, except in the bureau's hospitals and orphanages. The federal government did provide a basic protection under the law that had not existed, but it did not fundamentally change economic circumstances, labor rights or land ownership. Historian Eric Foner declared:

> Throughout its existence the Bureau regarded poor relief as a temptation to idleness. Blacks, declared Virginia Bureau head Orlando Brown, must "feel the spur of necessity, if it be needed to make them self-reliant, industrious and provident." Clearly, this position reflected not only attitudes toward black, but also a more general Northern belief in the dangers of encouraging dependency among the lower classes.[14]

When the right to the title to Arlington National Cemetery was resolved with the Custis family, the superintendent of the national cemetery determined it was time to remove the former enslaved people residing at Freedman's Village. The major additional usage claim to the original Custis acreage was Freedman's Village, but it now was inside a military reservation and subject to federal property regulation.

The National Cemetery System, originally enacted in July 1862, would be reauthorized by the Radical Congress; $750,000 was appropriated for fencing, headstones, and the purchase lands. In 1872, the reauthorization stipulated that there would be a place for everyone honorably discharged who "[died] in a destitute state."[15] After the Civil War, General Meigs continued as the quartermaster of the United States Army. His span of responsibility grew after the war, as did his resentment towards the South. Although Meigs and his comrades endeavored to ensure that Arlington would become a permanent shrine to the war dead, "there was no suggestion that John Meigs would be buried at Arlington; that was a place for poor unfortunates far from home and loved ones."[16]

The Union Army had denuded the property of most of the trees on the southern and western sides out of necessity. After the war, caretaker James Parks led the work to replant the ornamental and specimen trees, including elm, beech, chestnut and oak trees,[17] as found before the Union Army occupied the Heights. The very trees that Marquis de Lafayette had so admired would be used as a device to force the eviction of the villagers.

On November 12, 1887, J.A. Commerford, the superintendent of the National Cemetery, wrote to the Army's Deputy Quartermaster, Lieutenant Colonel George B. Dandy, that:

> ... some of the colored people who live on the reservation have been in the habit of entering the cemetery during the late hours of the night for the purpose of getting wood for fuel.... I was informed that several hundred young forest trees, from 2 to 6 inches in diameter were cut down and carried away. The remains of these trees can yet be seen.... It is said, that very few of these squatters buy any fuel, and depend mostly on what they can pick up within the enclosure. It would be necessary for a man to remain on watch all night, to arrest the guilty parties. It has been suggested, that the most effective way of preventing such thefts, is to cause the removal of these people from the reservation.[18]

By 1888, this once temporary, model village was now a vibrant community. According to the Arlington County, Virginia, Department of Community Planning, Housing and Development, Freedman's Village was well established, subject to the norms of many southern communities:

> In 1888, the village consisted of 124 dwellings, 3 shops, 2 churches, 1 school, and 170 families totaling a population of 763. There were two justices of the peace, one constable, and two special policemen. Most of the adult males voted and paid taxes (personal property, poll, school, and road taxes). Over 50 percent of the families who lived at the village had resided on the property for at least 15 years.[19]

The pressure to hold onto their community was mounting, and the residents turned to help from neighbors who could speak on their behalf with the various government agents and tier departments. They chose an able and qualified man as their representative, John B. Syphax, the son of Maria Syphax and the grandson of G.W.P. Custis. John Syphax had served on the Arlington Board of Supervisors (1872), as a clerk of the court (1872), and was the county treasurer from 1875 to 1879. Having also served as a Republican member of the House of Delegates from 1873–5,[20] John Syphax was well known in black and white communities throughout Virginia and within the offices of the federal government agencies.

On January 18, 1888, Syphax wrote to the Secretary of War William C. Endicott on behalf of the residents, offering facts about the property and its present condition:

> As the army advanced, during the war, several thousand colored people, men, women, and children, of all ages, and every condition, were quartered on this place by the agents of the government. Many of this number were employed by the United States, a portion of their pay being withheld for the support of the aged and infirm. When buildings were erected, Gen. O. O. Howard entered into contract with each tenant, demanding payment in money for rent of land. After the abolition of the Freedman's Bureau, they were required to work out rent at Fort Myer which they have continued to do until the present time. Agents representing the government fully impressed upon the people the idea that in some way they would come to possess a valid claim to a part of Arlington.[21]

Syphax sought to establish a clear understanding with the secretary of war about how the residents came upon the military reservation and their current living conditions. It was essential to convey that the residents were a hardworking, industrious people that wanted to improve their condition in life; their living at the village allowed them to do that. Most of the fugitive enslaved came to Washington on their own volition, having escaped from the plantations in Virginia and Maryland. Others had been brought to Freedman's Village by the federal government after a botched attempt to resettle the island nation of Haiti.

The reference by J.A. Commerford, the superintendent of the national cemetery, in his November 12, 1887, letter, that the men and women who resided at Freedman's Village were "squatters," could not go unanswered. In his letter to the secretary of war, Syphax continued by writing:

> When many of them were taken with a colony to Hayti [sic], and returned after the scenario was exposed, and their sufferings made known, they were told, perhaps as an apology, that they would remain here. Many began to plant trees, and make such other improvements as their scanty means would permit. They paid in ready money for their houses, churches, and other buildings, which were all sold to them by the government through its agent.[22]

Since his family owned the land adjacent to Freemen's Village, Syphax knew many of its residents from his earliest of memories. He was well aware of the construction of many of the buildings on the property and the adversities that residents had faced while creating a viable community that they believed belonged to them. According to Syphax:

> About nine years ago, Lieut. R.P. Strong, then commanding at Fort Myer, gave permission to erect a brick church on the reservation, costing nearly two thousand dollars,

and here again, they were made to believe that their stay would be indefinitely prolonged, therefore, several houses were built, and the spirit of improvement again revived.[23]

Syphax was all too familiar with the rumors and exaggerations made by white neighbors and outside agitators at the expense of the residents of the village. These detractors contributed to the belief that residents were taking advantage of the government and were a drain on the resources of the community. Syphax knew firsthand that despite the condition of their birth and the challenges they faced as black men and women:

> Many of these people [the residents of the village] have been soldiers, teamsters, workers on fortifications and sufferers by the freedman's bank swindle. Although no taxes have been paid on the Arlington land, yet the colored people have been fully taxed upon their general property, and have been no unjust burden upon the community, because the small amount paid for labor enabled others to help in the work of education and care of the helpless. Coming from the shades of the past, these people have proven, in their new condition of self-reliance, more thrifty, and less vicious than could be reasonably anticipated; and they have failed, after the teachings, and traditions of their fathers, to implore Almighty God for help and protection.[24]

The residents of Freedman's Village were unfamiliar with the complexities of home and land ownership. They did not have role models or extended family members whose wisdom they could seek counsel from. They soon came to learn the nuances of owning land separate from owning buildings, in particular that the ownership of the physical building did not constitute ownership of the land. The military and the federal government were not going to give the residents of Freedman's Village title to the land under their homes, even if they had resided in them for over twenty years.

Because these residents had been chattel property only a few years earlier, and because they were still being victimized by government bureaucracy despite being free American citizens, Syphax knew he must be both respectful of the families he represented and assertive in the face of the government. In his letter to Endicott, Syphax set to inform the secretary of war the condition of the buildings for which residents continued to make payments to the federal government:

> There are about one hundred families here, who own their dwellings. Nearly all of these houses are so constructed, and in such condition of decay, as to be useless to take down and move away; besides, contemplated improvements such as the Memorial Bridge, Mount Vernon Avenue, the Aqueduct and the Potomac flats, have made the price of the land, in this vicinity, beyond the reach of the poor. I know not what may be the purpose of the government, or the pleasure of the Honorable Secretary in the premises, but if it be to take this property wholly for National use, I most respectfully ask that an appropriation be recommended of not less than three hundred and fifty dollars a-piece for each owner of a house, but to be apportioned according to merit, and the various conditions and circumstances by the "Board of Protection," consisting of five of their number which they have chosen to look after their local interests.[25]

Syphax concluded his letter to the secretary by stating that after "twenty-four years residence at Arlington, with all the elements involved in this case inspire the hope that full and simple justice will be done even to the weakest members of this great Republic."[26] As hard as they tried to defend their homes and their right to live there, the residents had no longer any legal recourse to stay in their properties. How the government treated Custis Lee in his recent Supreme Court victory "had not been lost on John Syphax or his constituents. If they could not prevent the evictions at Arlington, at least they might expect compensation for their property."[27] Two days before Christmas, the War Department took steps to survey, record physical improvements, and assess the value of each property. Upon completion, General Holabird authorized:

> ... the purchase of land held by "unauthorized citizens or others as squatters or for residence, under the color of any permission or otherwise." Then he ordered that the freedmen's occupation of the village be "made to cease and desist."
>
> The first wave of black residents pulled up stakes in the spring of 1888—most of them with trifling payments for their Arlington property. Lucy Harris received $35 for her house; Martha Smith, a former Custis slave, got $40.34 for hers, along with $3 for the trees and vines she had planted. Her neighbor James Parks, who occupied half of the duplex built in the first days of Freedman's Village, received $13.20 for his home, while his brothers Lawrence and William were paid $63.09 and $78.09, respectively. The unfortunate William Winston, lot 83, got nothing at all. Members of the Mt. Olive Baptist Church were paid $1,040 for their brick building, which provided seed money for the replacement they would soon raise down the road in Alexandria.[28]

The federal government compensated the residents $10,936, for the buildings and property, based on an outdated 1868 appraised value, and an additional "$75,000 to reimburse residents and their heirs for the contraband taxes they had been required to pay during and after the war."[29]

After 30 years, an active and vibrant community was cleared from Arlington. There is very little in Arlington National Cemetery to show for the historic lives of the black men, women and children who once lived in Freedman's Village. The only current remembrance of the fugitive enslaved who lived and worked at the Arlington Plantation are the 3,800 marble headstones in Section 27. The state of Virginia has erected a small marker in a neighborhood park across the street from the cemetery.[30]

After the village was emptied in 1900, it was re-graded and used for military burials in what are now Sections 3, 4, 8, and 18. Today's section of Grant Drive, Clayton Drive, and Jessup Drive are in the same location as the main road of Freedman's Village and are the only indication of the village's earlier presence, inside Arlington National Cemetery.

CHAPTER 14

Reconstruction, Reconciliation and Retribution

ON OCTOBER 2, 1865, former Confederate General Robert E. Lee was inaugurated as president of Washington College in Lexington, Virginia. That same day he signed his Amnesty Oath, complying with the provisions of President Andrew Johnson's Proclamation of Amnesty and Pardons. Lee was never pardoned in his lifetime. According to the National Archives:

> More than a hundred years later, in 1970, an archivist at the National Archives discovered Lee's Amnesty Oath among State Department records.... Apparently Secretary of State William H. Seward had given Lee's application to a friend as a souvenir, and the State Department had pigeonholed the oath.
> In 1975, Lee's full rights of citizenship were posthumously restored by a joint congressional resolution effective June 13, 1865.
> At the August 5, 1975, signing ceremony, President Gerald R. Ford acknowledged the discovery of Lee's Oath of Allegiance in the National Archives and remarked: "General Lee's character has been an example to succeeding generations, making the restoration of his citizenship an event in which every American can take pride."[1]

Lee never returned to Arlington, yet the property he never owned would become a memorial to him. To contemporaries like Meigs at the end of the war this would seem incredible. How did the traitor get this place of honor, but not Meigs, Lincoln or the USCT who had fought to end the slave economy and extend civil rights to all Americans?

From the beginning of the National Cemetery, Confederate dead would be interred in Arlington, challenging the very concept of the nation while their generals were still marshalling them to secede and divide the Union. "L. Reinhart, Rebel, N.C." was recorded dead on May 17, 1864, in the official Arlington Memorial history and follows William Christman (Section 27, Grave 19) in burial at Arlington, though Reinhart of the North Carolina 23rd is no longer in the database of the dead buried at Arlington.[2] Reinhart might have been part of the storied sacrifice of 50 percent of the regiment at Chancellorsville, their engagement at Gettysburg, and died as a result of injuries at Spotsylvania Court House, where it is reported by the regimental history "the men refused to go forward 'til General Lee, then in the field, went to the rear."[3] Reinhart is not discoverable in the regimental rolls.

The regimental histories, published in 1901 in the middle of the production of the documents of the Lost Cause, would be full of the creation myths of the time: pliant negroes, pillaging Union forces, gallant southern men all staying true to the cause. These narratives would dominate the post-war generations, and obscure the other narratives of Section 27.

The former enslaved were now honored at Section 27 with the inscription "Citizen" to acknowledge their American citizenship pursuant to the 14th Amendment to the United States Constitution. Considered part of the Reconstruction Amendments, the 14th Amendment addressed the citizenship rights of the former enslaved and provided equal protection of the nation's laws to them. The 14th Amendment reads:

> All persons born or naturalized in the United States and subject to the jurisdiction thereof, are citizens of the United States and of the State wherein they reside. No State shall make or enforce any law which shall abridge the privileges or immunities of citizens of the United States; nor shall any State deprive any person of life, liberty, or property, without due process of law; nor deny to any person within its jurisdiction the equal protection of the laws.[4]

Even in the fog of war, integration of burials at Arlington, by regiment, gender and race was controversial, and so it would remain.[5] The process of national reconstruction, the subsequent era of reconciliation that was led by prominent veterans, and the retribution on the black community disguised as legislation and social concern would go on until well after the last veteran died. Many commentators on American history and society say it has never stopped, simply taken other forms. The public health emergency had a long tail; the violence of war, the post-traumatic stress, the stoked feelings of partisan polarization, and the need for remembrance and justification would take many more turns up until the present day.[6] Monuments would become memorials, bodies would be moved, and heroes documented, traitors denounced and Lost Causes born.

Just as the rhetoric of the observers of the wars in the contemporary newspapers drove suspicion and division, so would battle lines be drawn for the post-conflict spoils.[7] In 1866 Congress would enact a Reconstruction of the nation and attempt to impeach President Johnson for lacking resolve in implementing their intent. Ten years later all the states had been accepted back into the Union having passed the required 14th and 15th Amendments, yet an economic depression and unwavering resistance throughout the south to civil rights would lead to massive widespread violence. Rutherford Hayes became president but was shorn of powers to support civil rights, and southern control over Congress would return.

By 1900 African Americans would be thoroughly disenfranchised and have no representation in the Congress. "Separate but equal" would become the rule in the South, and African Americans were increasingly sidelined. By 1901, George White, a black congressman, had introduced an anti-lynching bill, pointing out America's hypocrisy in fighting for citizens' freedom in the Philippines and Cuba but not providing that same freedom to citizens at home. Congressman White was gerrymandered out of office and would be the last African American in Congress for 28 years. In the congressional debate in February 1900, he asked:

> Should not a nation be just to all her citizens, protect them alike in all their rights, on every foot of her soil!—in a word, show herself capable of governing all within her domain before she undertakes to exercise sovereign authority over those of a foreign land?—with foreign notions and habits not at all in harmony with our American system of government? Or, to be more explicit, should not charity first begin at home?[8]

White delivered his final speech in the House of Representatives on January 29, 1901:

> This, Mr. Chairman, is perhaps the negroes' temporary farewell to the American Congress; but let me say, Phoenix-like he will rise up some day and come again. These parting words are in behalf of an outraged, heart-broken, bruised and bleeding, but God-fearing people, faithful, industrious, loyal people—rising people, full of potential force.[9]

These rights were stripped in an organized, concerted and deliberate effort, centered on a belief in white supremacy. The state of Virginia was represented by John Warwick Daniel in the Senate for 24 years beginning in 1887. In his long address at the 1892 Convention of the United Confederate Veterans, he insisted "there was no treason in being a Confederate," claiming slavery had been helpful for black Americans:

> It had a peculiar institution, slavery. I will not discuss it further than to say, that whatever else the war did, it vindicated the beneficence of the institution to the subject race. Our own race found the black man a wanderer in the wilderness and gave him a home; it found him naked and clothed him; it found him a savage, a cannibal, and a heathen and it made him a Christian; it found him muttering a gibberish and gave him a language; it found him empty-minded and it filled him with instruction. When he ceased to be a slave, so had he been elevated from his barbarous state that he was declared fit to assume the great prerogatives and responsibilities of an American citizen. What prouder monument could there be to the civilization and humanizing genius of a people?
>
> ... The Confederate principles were three-fold: first, local self-government represented by the sovereignty of the State; second, race purity represented by the sovereignty of the race; third, the union of States represented by a confederated, union and constitution.[10]

In 1876, Virginia's white representatives amended the Constitution to require a poll tax of African Americans; this was repealed by a multi-ethnic majority of Readjusters in 1882, but in 1884 the Democrats, back in control of the legislature, passed an act giving Democratic party workers control over the polls. In 1902, the final steps at a Constitutional Convention, where Senator Daniel was a leader, were taken to wrest democratic control from the people, as reported in the *Lexington Gazette*:

> In the language of the Supreme Court of Mississippi they swept the field of expedients. They have adopted a plan of suffrage which will accomplish the paramount object for which the Convention was called, a plan which will effectually eliminate illiterate negro suffrage, and at the same time preserve the rights of the white man....[11]

The number of black voters would be reduced by 90 percent by the constitutional change, while white voters would be reduced by 50 percent between 1900 and 1902 as the poor were disenfranchised.[12]

Tempestuous political changes would be reflected at Arlington through the lens of traditions that grew in the latter part of the nineteenth century, including the development of a new monument in Section 16, the so-called Confederate section. Robert E. Lee wanted no monuments, believing they would not advance post-war harmony. He wrote in response to a proposal to erect a monument made by General (CSA) Rosser:

> As regards the erection of such a monument as is contemplated; my conviction is, that however grateful it would be to the feelings of the South, the attempt in the present condition of the Country, would have the effect of retarding, instead of accelerating its accomplishment; & of continuing, if not adding to, the difficulties under which the Southern people labour.[13]

As Lee did not want monuments celebrating an otherwise gruesome and tragic war, instead hoping the aftermath would lead to peace, so had President Lincoln spent much of his presidency attempting reconciliation. In his thoughtful, deliberative process, Lincoln was still planning to end the war by reimbursing the enslavers for their losses. In his February 1865 inaugural address, Lincoln offered a conciliatory tone, and an open hand to the secessionists. He reminded those in the audience that there was a fundamental justification for such a costly war, and that was to preserve the Union and liberate the enslaved. Promising his audience that he would be short, President Lincoln stated the common fear of war that gripped the nation:

> On the occasion corresponding to this four years ago all thoughts were anxiously directed to an impending civil war. All dreaded it—all sought to avert it. While the inaugural address was being delivered from this place, devoted altogether to saving the Union without war, insurgent agents were in the city seeking to destroy it without war—seeking to dissolve the Union, and divide effects, by negotiation. Both parties deprecated war, but one of them would make war rather than let the nation survive, and the other would accept war rather than let it perish. And the war came.

> One-eighth of the whole population were colored slaves, not distributed generally over the Union, but localized in the southern part of it. These slaves constituted a peculiar and powerful interest. All knew that this interest was, somehow, the cause of the war. To strengthen, perpetuate, and extend this interest was the object for which the insurgents would rend the Union even by war; while the Government claimed no right to do more than to restrict the territorial enlargement of it. Neither party expected for the war the magnitude or the duration which it has already attained. Neither anticipated that the cause of the conflict might cease with or even before the conflict itself should cease. Each looked for an easier triumph and a result less fundamental and astounding. Both read the same Bible and pray to the same God, and each invokes His aid against the other. It may seem strange that any men should dare to ask a just God's assistance in wringing their bread from the sweat of other men's faces, but let us judge not, that we be not judged.[14]

Lincoln concluded that the nation must focus on reconciliation without regard for side taken in the war, but only with the "offense" of slavery removed forever from the sight of the "providence of God." Then, and only then:

> Fondly do we hope, fervently do we pray, that this mighty scourge of war may speedily pass away. Yet, if God wills that it continue until all the wealth piled by the bondsman's two hundred and fifty years of unrequited toil shall be sunk, and until every drop of blood drawn with the lash shall be paid by another drawn with the sword, as was said three thousand years ago, so still it must be said "the judgments of the Lord are true and righteous altogether."
>
> With malice toward none, with charity for all, with firmness in the right as God gives us to see the right, let us strive on to finish the work we are in, to bind up the nation's wounds, to care for him who shall have borne the battle and for his widow and his orphan, to do all which may achieve and cherish a just and lasting peace among ourselves and with all nations.[15]

Lincoln would live to see the surrender of Lee at Appomattox and walk among the USCT in Richmond, but he would not be given opportunity to define further peace. In a little more than a month, President Lincoln would be struck by an assassin's bullet. The president had many enemies and detractors. Enslavement was at its apex at the beginning of the Civil War, a war that wiped out the commercial value in excess of $2.4 billion to the slavers of their human chattel. Lincoln's focus on ending the war reflected a lack of planning for the post-war economic replacement system.

On April 15, 1865, a day after the president's death, Vice President Andrew Johnson became the seventeenth president of the United States. Dubbed by many as the "accidental President," Andrew Johnson "began his fortunes as a tailor in Tennessee and had great affection for struggling white men who were trying to succeed. In contrast, he did not trust wealthy white southerners or African Americans."[16] His political philosophy reflected his poor upbringing and his deep-seated belief that the southern aristocracy had dragged the South into war; he, like Lincoln, rejected the slave economy in favor of free labor and the "self-made man."

The Constitution's Thirteenth Amendment was ratified on December 6, 1865, and the institution of slavery was abolished in the United States. New President Johnson was immediately confronted with the awesome burden of reuniting an extremely polarized country and had little time to consider the long-term impact of his decisions. For any president, reconstruction would have been difficult, but for Johnson the challenge was even greater. Johnson knew that Lincoln wanted to take all measures necessary to restore order nationally and to restore full citizenship to the residents of the secessionist states as soon as possible, "so that peace, order, and freedom might be established."[17]

On May 29, 1865, as a continuation of Lincoln's policies towards national reconciliation, President Andrew Johnson issued his own form of amnesty, declaring that any former Confederate who hadn't taken advantage of the previous amnesty offered by President Lincoln in 1863 could now declare their allegiance and take an oath to defend the Constitution of the United States.[18] The Johnson Amnesty Proclamation was intended to be a direct blow to the hated planter aristocracy and anyone of importance in the antebellum South, whom he personally blamed for the war; his proclamation would force each person to seek a special pardon directly from the president.[19]

On June 13, 1865, former Confederate General Robert E. Lee sent Ulysses S. Grant his application for amnesty; Grant forwarded it on to President Johnson for approval. In his application request, Lee wrote:

> Being excluded from the provisions of amnesty & pardon contained in the proclamation of the 29th Ulto; I hereby apply for the benefits, & full restoration of all rights & privileges extended to those included in its terms. I graduated at the Mil. Academy at West Point in June 1829. Resigned from the U.S. Army April '61. Was a General in the Confederate Army, & included in the surrender of the Army of N. Va. 9 April '65.[20]

To support Lincoln's policies towards national reconciliation, Senator Trumbull, a moderate from Illinois, supported a bill to extend the life of the Freedman's Bureau for the simple reason that it was "not intended to be a permanent institution." The senator believed that no state law or custom should deprive any citizen of these "fundamental rights belonging to every man as a free man."[21] The bill and a Civil Rights Bill were sent to Andrew Johnson, who vetoed them both. Congress overrode the vetoes, increased their Radical numbers in the 1866 congressional election (run on an anti–Johnson platform), and passed the 14th Amendment (guaranteeing due process and establishing citizenship for blacks and women).[22] African Americans standing for election in 1866 were threatened and assassinated by the Ku Klux Klan and other terrorists; Arkansas Congressman James Hinds was murdered, as were three South Carolina state legislators; while General Rousseau, a Johnson ally and commander in Louisiana, is reported to have been pleased that the "ascendance of the negro in this state is approaching its end."[23]

Robert E. Lee's Amnesty Oath (courtesy of the National Archives, Records of the Department of State, G 94).

When Johnson fired Secretary of War Stanton in February 1868, the House Republicans unanimously voted to impeach the president. Benjamin Butler would be the lead prosecutor in the Senate but would not secure impeachment. Andrew Johnson on acquittal displayed a "brazen show of presidential indifference"[24] to the expanding violence directed at blacks in the South, failing to use his authority to oppose the Ku Klux Klan. The radical opposition was diluted by the acquittal, but Grant would bring numerous examples to Johnson's attention during the last nine months of Johnson's presidency. Subsequently, Grant would be president and oversaw the southern states re-entering the Union, upon developing state constitutions in compliance with the 13th, 14th and 15th amendments. The 14th Amendment passed in July 1868 guaranteed equal process and bestowed citizenship on black men, women and children born in the United States. A month later the radical leader in the House, Thaddeus Stevens, passed away and was buried in an integrated cemetery in Pennsylvania "…to illustrate in my death the principles which I advocated through a long life. Equality of Man before his Creator."[25]

Congress further required the senior military official, General Grant, to approve all orders to subordinates, taking the authority away from the Commander-in-Chief Johnson. Grant was being widely discussed as a candidate for the upcoming election, and he became the Republican nomination for President on a "Let Us Have Peace" platform. President Grant, in league with Butler in the Congress, would wage a successful battle against the Klan. At the end of his term, Reconstruction collapsed and "...left southern blacks for eighty years at the mercy of Jim Crow, segregation, lynchings, poll taxes, literacy tests and other tactics."[26]

Violence against blacks seeking to participate in the political process was prevalent. The same issue of the paper that reported John Meigs' death casually reports "another Democratic Murder": "That notorious and bloodthirsty Democratic organization known as the Ku Klux Klan, have just committed another cruel murder. The victim was loyal man of course. These infamous wretches murder no others. He is ex–Senator Stephens of North Carolina."[27]

Arlington, however, was becoming a site of reconciliation even as white terrorism was making demands for a return to supremacy. In 1874 Meigs would build the amphitheater for the Grand Army of the Republic ceremonies, inscribed with the national heroes of the war, to the annoyance of Mildred Lee, daughter of Robert E. and Mary Lee Custis: "In place of the jasmine arbour was a hideous pavilion with the names of Lincoln, Grant, Sherman, Sheridan, etc.... Everything was gone."[28]

"Everything" was defined by Mildred as the pre-war plantation and the slave economy. Meigs was able to accomplish another objective—removing war dead from the battlefields within thirty-five miles around the capital city. According to the National Park Service:

> ... the work of recovering the remains of the dead from battlefields and interring them at the newly formed national cemeteries continued several years after the Civil War fighting ended. By the time they were recovered, many of the individuals found could not be identified, but nonetheless, efforts were made to give every soldier a proper burial ... to ensure that there may not be a single body of a deceased soldier that does not receive the grateful care and protection of the government for which he sacrificed his life.... The scattered bones and disorganized remains of 2,111 unknown Civil War soldiers [were] found on the battlefields of Bull Run and Manassas.[29]

At the order of General Meigs, the remains found were placed in a single vault built at the southern end of Mrs. Lee's flower garden. The remains of Federal soldiers, and though never intended, the remains of Confederate soldiers as well, were entombed in what became known as the Tomb of the Civil War Unknowns, as designed by Meigs (Section 26).

Still grieving over the death of his son and his anger over the actions of the Confederacy, Meigs did not allow memorial flowers to be placed at Con-

Civil War Unknowns Memorial (private collection of Ric Murphy).

federate graves at Arlington National Cemetery on Decoration Day. Meigs' action at Arlington and the actions of others across national cemeteries in the North only served to further anger and alienate the families of the Confederate war dead. For a period, "families of Confederate soldiers were not always allowed to decorate the graves of their soldiers and, at times, were not allowed to enter the cemetery."[30] Even as criticism mounted, in "1873, Secretary of War William Belknap had turned the cemetery over to the GAR on Decoration Day. Because the event honored the soldiers who fell in defense of the Union, the decoration of Confederate graves was restricted by an order on May 24, 1873."[31]

As the tenth anniversary of the end of the Civil War approached, white attitudes and anger began to soften, and a nation began to heal and reconcile. Historian William A. Blair in reflecting upon the mood of the day captured the sentiment of a northern correspondent who wrote about Arlington Cemetery and how it still evolved raw emotions of the war and of its dead:

> The place is sad beyond description. The graves create a somber mood that promotes refection ... it is quite impossible not to image that a spirit of true revengefulness had much to do with the selection of this place for the holy purpose to which it is put. He was a blind man who chose this spot for the last resting-place of our soldiers, thinking that retaliation upon the Lees would always be an object to be desired, and he was bar-

ren of honor to cause the revered dead to play so ignoble a part in the scheme of procuring pain for a foe.[32]

The following year, in 1877, President Rutherford B. Hayes opened the gates of Arlington Cemetery on Decoration Day to all who wished to honor their dead, Union or Confederate.

After the Civil War, the Republican Party, at its political height, was a party of the North, along with a small coalition of Freedmen and sympathizers in the South. Hayes, a former Union general, won the presidency in a contested Electoral College dispute. The outcome of the election was determined by a compromise in which Hayes agreed to withdraw Federal troops from southern states, put there to enforce the 14th and 15th Amendments, if he got the necessary Democratic votes to win the Electoral College.[33] The year 1877 was marked by violence and would be one of the most "tumultuous in American history": a "white woman was jailed for two years" for marrying a black man, "industrialism would dominate national discourse, while the rights of African Americans would be largely forgotten."[34] The era of Reconstruction had come to an end; northern politicians no longer used their energy to assert equal rights and instead focused on the shared narratives of sacrifice on the battlefield. Meigs continued to have "singular authority over the direction and design of the national cemetery," from "graves and racial segregation to roadway names": "Meigs devoted much of the 1870s and 1880s to making Arlington patriotism's high church and most sacred terrain."[35]

The old Confederate headstones bearing the offensive inscription, "Rebel," were replaced with stones similar to those of Federal soldiers.[36] Necessarily for a Union cemetery with a few scattered Confederates, there was no monument to Confederate soldiers until the early twentieth century, after Meigs had passed away.

In 1884, the city of New Orleans erected a monument—arms crossed, looking north at his "adversaries"—to Lee. This monument, as well as a White League obelisk and monument to PGT Beauregard and Jefferson Davis, would be removed in 2017.[37] In 1890, the city of Richmond installed a statue to Robert E. Lee, 16 inches taller than George Washington's in front of the Virginia state capital,[38] before an enormous crowd (estimates range from 25,000 to more than 100,000). The Richmond event required a coordinated effort by the "Boarding House Committee" to find accommodation for people coming to Richmond.[39] For the first Decoration Day at Arlington the crowd estimate was 25,000, a third of the population of the capital. The reported crowd in Richmond was larger than the population of the city's 1890 census, and the city's now historic Monument Avenue would become the established name of the street in 1906.[40]

Reaction to the statue and the events was immediate and hostile from congressmen: "the rebellion was a conspiracy organized in the interest of human slavery," and "let me say that the broad sky over our country is broad enough only for one flag, and that the stars and stripes, and when a man waves any other his is in his hearty as much a traitor as he was thirty years ago," and "in view of the things that transpired within the past few days I believe that the only regret our adversaries feel is that they failed to succeed." The outrage was compounded by a statue of George Washington having been draped in a Confederate flag.[41] Prior to the unveiling, the Richmond press was full of stories connecting the Lee statue to the one of Washington, continuing to emphasize the historical connection even as Lee had served in the rebellion.[42]

The apologists for secession were well served by newspapers highlighting a claim that the source of the money was fitting with their virtue:

> The Lee Statue, paid for with money raised principally through the efforts of the ladies of Virginia, was, with their assistance, removed from the depot in Richmond on last Wednesday, to the granite monument which it is intended to surmount. An occasion more interesting is not recorded in the annals of Virginia than this evidence of devotion of the noble women of Virginia for the hero of "the lost cause," and it is safe to say that the memory of the gallant men who followed him and principles for which they fought, will not suffer as long as it is in the keeping of such women. Children taught by such women can never cease to revere the memory of the patriots, who fell in the defence [sic] of the rights of the South.[43]

The role and importance of women in contrast to men was a thread through the war. Women had been essential to the creation and regulation of the care system. The hospital organization and techniques of Florence Nightingale were studied, such as descriptions of hospital layout and ventilation, as well as handwashing practices. Nightingale's *Notes on Nursing* was published in 1860 and paved the way for Victorian women to work and overcome social strictures. Nightingale's example is cited by Civil War nurses as a common reference, including Louisa May Alcott in *Hospital Sketches*.[44] Clara Barton was one who "shrank from service" because of the stigma attached to women in military camps. Attitudes and social restrictions changed, and women were encouraged to serve, inspired to an extent by Alcott's account, an inspiration to American nurses and the medical profession.[45]

Women would also take an increasing role in the fight to define the peace through monuments and have their sacrifices recognized. In 1899, hearings on the role of women in the military were held, leading to the establishment in 1901 of the Army Nurse Corps. The Spanish American War would see women nurses taught in Washington at the Freedman's Hospital serve alongside black regiments. For many, their service was predicated on the notion that African Americans had a peculiar racial immunity to yellow fever.[46] When no nurses who had died in the Spanish American War were interred at Arlington, they began the advocacy for a monument to complement the "distinguished right of burial with the army and navy in beautiful Arlington."[47]

Civil War historian William A. Blair describes how the Spanish American War was central to the "origins of the Confederate section in Arlington" driven by President McKinley's "desire for three things: reconciliation of the sectional heart, consolidation of southern support for overseas expansion, and reclamation of his reputation in racial affairs."[48] The United Daughters of the Confederacy were instrumental in the development, design and fundraising for the Confederate monument. During the war, Rutherford Hayes was McKinley's regimental commanding officer in the Ohio 23rd Infantry; and after the war, Hayes served as a political mentor to McKinley. Ohio gained influence nationally in political circles, particularly at the presidential level, producing Hayes in 1876, followed by James A. Garfield in 1880, and then William McKinley in 1896.[49]

During the four-month Spanish American War, military men from the North and the South came together to serve under commanding officers who once served in either the Union or Confederate armies. Antietam and especially Gettysburg were annually becoming great gathering places for veterans, though significantly these were both battles in which there were few if any African American regiments engaged.

After the Civil War, the United States became more involved in international trade and the diplomatic issues of its neighbors. Cuba was a Spanish colony; once the most powerful colonial power, Spain now possessed only the Philippine islands, Guam, Puerto Rico, and Cuba. As the Cuban island revolted against Spain, many Americans were sympathetic to the Cuban people.[50] President William McKinley ordered the USS *Maine* to rescue the United States citizens on the island, bring them home and protect American interests on the island. On February 15, 1898, the USS *Maine,* while docked in Cuba's Havana Harbor, was destroyed in an explosion that killed more than 260 Americans, mostly men of African descent.[51] The national newspapers were filled with the slogan, "Remember the Maine," a rallying cry for vengeance and war. The American response was quick and resolute. On April 22, 1898, the U.S. Navy blockaded Santiago Harbor and declared war on Spain two days later.[52] As with the Revolutionary and Civil Wars, recognition, honor, and leadership were some of the prime reasons African Americans wanted to serve in the U.S. military.[53] In support of their black brethren, large numbers of African-American men enlisted for military service, dedicated patriots ready to serve and fight for their country.

The United States Congress activated ten regiments of all black troops: the 6th, 7th, 8th, 9th, 10th, 3rd Alabama, 3rd North Carolina, 23rd, 24th, and 25th. Only the 9th, 10th, 24th, and 25th Regiments saw actual combat in this short-lived war. Two men of the 10th Cavalry, Dennis Bell and George H.

Wanton, Medal of Honor recipients for heroism, volunteered to go ashore, four months after the USS *Maine* explosion, to provide critical reconnaissance on the enemy. Upon landing on the Cuban island, despite coming under heavy fire, the two men were able to provide critical information that enabled the rescue of wounded compatriots.

The Spanish American War was short, and after four months ended in August, with the signing of the Treaty of Paris on December 10, 1898. At Arlington National Cemetery, in Section 24, is the USS *Maine* Memorial, where twenty-two African American sailors are interred with 163 sailors who were killed during the bombing of the *Maine*.

Despite its brevity, the actual war was costly for Spain, ending its entire overseas empire including its prized islands of Cuba and Puerto Rico in the Atlantic, and the Philippines and Guam in the Pacific. After the war, the United States established itself as a world naval power.[54]

Before the Treaty of Paris could be signed, President McKinley toured the nation to garner support. As he toured the South, he heard about and saw firsthand the deplorable condition of the Confederate cemeteries. On December 14, 1898, McKinley delivered his address to the Atlanta Peach Jubilee from the hall of the Georgia state legislature:

> The president opened by declaring that the war had proven that sectional ties no longer existed. The nation stood as one. He was also pleased to attend a celebration that marked the signing of the treaty with Spain (even if the agreement still required ratifying). He then led into the section of the speech that received so much acclaim throughout the former Confederate states. "Every soldier's grave made during our unfortunate civil war is a tribute to American valor," said the president. He acknowledged that when those graves were dug, wide differences existed between the sections. But he added that "the time has now come in the evolution of sentiment and feeling under the providence of God, when in the spirit of fraternity we should share with you in the care of the graves of the Confederate soldiers."[55]

Many in the audience and beyond were pleased with McKinley's pronouncement. According to art historians Cynthia Mills and Pamela Simpson:

> ... [McKinley's] words were salve for the wounded egos of white southerners, who had witnessed the Federal government's development of national cemeteries for Union casualties over the decades and heard former Confederates berated as "traitors" and "rebels." McKinley's comments also were timely, given the "romance of reunion" currently taking place between the North and South. Northerners and southerners had defeated a common enemy during the Spanish-American War, and in the 1890s white men from both regions were reveling in ... "the cult of Anglo-Saxonism." These shared experiences contributed to a new respect among northerners for Confederate veterans, an important step in reunification as well as vindication for southern men.[56]

Dr. Samuel Lewis of Washington, D.C., "seized upon the president's words and in June 5, 1899, asked that the remains of the southern soldiers at

Arlington be gathered in a section and marked appropriately."[57] Lewis, who was a surgeon during the war for the Confederate States Army, took a special interest in Confederate graves, particularly on the battlefields of northern Virginia and around Washington. There were ready ears for Lewis' proposal to re-segregate Arlington, as the spurious science of eugenics was being widely propagated by medical professionals from all parts of the nation. The seminal Eugenics Records Office funded by the Carnegie Institute would soon be opened in Cold Harbor Spring, New York.[58]

Separate but equal would become enshrined in law, and Arlington would be an arbiter of that triumph:

> As the adornment of the Confederate Section was underway, Arlington received the last USS Maine remains and the ship's mast for a memorial. The simultaneous repatriation of bodies from overseas suggested a similar sort of homecoming for the former rebels, making manifest in the land popular assertions that shared white valor and racially exclusive nationalism were the central legacies of the Civil War.[59]

Fear of the African American body and its supposed unique immunities and characteristics was commonly discussed:

> Another case of death from the bite of a "blue gummed" negro is reported. Ever since negroes were first brought to this country instances of such cases have been narrated and believed. Indeed the belief was so prevalent throughout all the South during the time of slavery, that few white men ever thought of striking a negro on the mouth, and in every instance in which those suffered who failed to observe this rule, it was found that the negro whose teeth cause the abrasion had blue gums. Some consider this another evidence of the physiological fact that the color of the skin is not the only difference between the white and the black race.[60]

The fears provided Lewis and others the narrative to achieve their supremacist goals. Lewis was bothered that the bodies were scattered across Arlington Cemetery, "intermingled with federal soldiers—white and black—and their graves undistinguished by any mark or characteristic from those of [quartermaster] employees, citizen refugees or negro contrabands." In 1899, the group discovered another 128 bodies buried in the cemetery of the Soldiers' Home before it had reached capacity and Arlington had become a soldiers' cemetery.[61]

Health leaders would be at the forefront of implementing segregation policies. The Virginia assembly would pass SB219 "The Racial Integrity Act," in 1924, and the State Health Department and Registrar of Vital Statistics were willing implementers of a core provision that ensured that all children with "a single drop" of African American blood would be removed from "white schools."[62] The same year, Congress passed the National Origins Law, immigration restrictions that barred Southern and Eastern Europeans on racial hygiene grounds, for being "dysgenic."[63] The same Congress initiated a joint resolution for the "restoration of the Lee Mansion."

In a relatively short time, the Confederate section became a reality. According the National Park Service, in June 1900:

> ... a section of the cemetery was authorized by Congress to be used for the burial of confederate dead. During the next year and a half, soldiers who had been buried in national cemeteries in Alexandria and the Soldiers' Home in Washington, D.C. were moved to the Confederate section of Arlington National Cemetery. In total, 482 persons are buried in the section, 46 officers, 351 enlisted men, 58 wives, 15 Southern civilians, and 12 unknowns.[64]

Unlike the remainder of the cemetery, where the Union dead were buried in straight rows, the reinterred Confederate dead were buried in a "concentric circle of graves" with new headstones. The grave markers were designed to also differ from the remainder of the cemetery, with pointed tops that were meant to be easily distinguishable from the rounded tops of Union soldiers' headstones.

As soldiers' interments took place, disputes within the different groups representing Confederate war dead were resolved, funds were raised and architect Moses J. Ezekiel, a former Confederate soldier and internationally recognized artist, was commissioned to construct the monument.

> Ezekiel was born in Virginia ... and attended Virginia Military Institute (VMI) as its first Jewish cadet at the outbreak of the Civil War. Ezekiel fought at the Battle of New Market in 1864 and in the trenches outside Richmond near the war's close. After he finished his education at VMI ... he moved to Berlin in 1868 to study at the Royal Academy of Art. Ezekiel moved to Rome after winning the Michel-Beer Prix de Rome from the Academy in 1874.[65]

By contrast, the remains of black Union heroes interred were largely unnoticed. Captain Edwin Belcher was born in South Carolina, but he was sent north to attend white schools in Philadelphia. His interment at Arlington is reported only in the African American press in November 1900: "The remains of Captain Edwin Belcher who served as captain of a company of Pennsylvania volunteers during the Civil War were removed from Augusta, Ga. And buried Friday November 2nd at Arlington Cemetery without ceremony."[66]

Captain Belcher "passed" as white throughout the war, was injured at Chancellorsville, fought in Georgia, and was employed in the Freedman's Bureau until his race was uncovered in 1867, at which point he chose to embrace his blackness and appeal to Benjamin Butler for employment. His appearance on both sides of the race line illustrates how powerfully skin color defines a life. Currently the Arlington "Find a Grave" index has no record of Captain Belcher, further staining the treatment of this soldier.[67]

Upon accepting his commission, Ezekiel advised the United Daughters of the Confederacy (UDC) that he would make a "heroic bronze statue" and that he would construct it in Rome; they would have to trust his judgment for its design, for he would not accept any input or suggestions.[68]

According to art historians Cynthia Mills and Pamela H. Simpson, the construction of a Confederate monument at Arlington National Cemetery had a special and profound meaning to the UDC. Its purpose and meaning were greater "than sectional peace for white southerners. For them, it also was about Confederate vindication. Vindication, after all, was the clearest path southerners could see to reconciliation and a truly united country."

> Ever since the United Daughters of the Confederacy formed in 1894, the organization's underlying goal had been to vindicate the actions of its members' parents and grandparents, often referred to as the "generation of the sixties." Confederate monuments served as one means of attaining this goal, and it is no coincidence that the Daughters placed them in the most publicly visible locations—on the grounds surrounding state capitols and county courthouses. By erecting images of their heroes on a political landscape, the Daughters insisted that the ideals of the Old South must be present in the creation of the New.[69]

On June 4, 1914, the statue was revealed, on a day to coincide with the 106th anniversary of the birth of the president of the Confederacy, Jefferson Davis. By all accounts, those in attendance were pleased with the majestic figure. According to the National Park Service, the Confederate Memorial:

> Stands 32 feet tall and is dominated by a larger-than-life statue of a woman representing the South. Crowned with olive leaves, her left hand extends a laurel wreath southward in acknowledgement of the sacrifice of those who died in the war ... at the front of the monument, the panoplied figure of Minerva, goddess of war and wisdom, tries to hold up the figure of a fallen woman (the South) who is resting on her shield, the Constitution.[70]

Directly below the statue are a number of life-size reliefs, each with their own symbolic meaning to the South and her former days of glory. Below the statue on a cylindrical mount are a series of 32 eight-foot figures representing the various races and classes of people of the South. The profound meaning of some of the relief figures and the original intent of the monument are best described by Hilary A. Herbert, chairman of the executive committee of the United Daughters of the Confederacy (UDC) Arlington Confederate Monument Association (ACMA)[71]:

> ... there is another story told here, illustrating the kindly relations that existed all over the South between the master and the slave—a story that can not be too often repeated to generations in which "Uncle Tom's Cabin" survives and is still manufacturing false ideas as to the South and slavery.... The astonishing fidelity of the slaves everywhere during the war to the wives and children of those who were absent in the army was convincing proof of the kindly relations between master and slave in the old South. One leading purpose of the UDC is to correct history. Ezekiel is here writing it for them, in characters that will tell their story to generation after generation.[72]

Confederate Memorial (private collection of Ric Murphy).

As chairmen of the executive committee of the ACMA, Herbert could provide insight into race relations prior to and during the war, and the continuum of desire to segregate the races fifty years after the war's end. In his record of Confederate monuments at Arlington, he explains that the young black man in uniform is not a Confederate soldier, but "a faithful negro-body-servant following his young master" in his new Confederate uniform.[73]

Herbert further explains that next to the black servant man, stands "an officer, kissing his child in the arms of an old negro 'mammy.' Another child holds on to the skirts of 'mammy' and is crying, perhaps without knowing why." For Herbert, and many of the period, there was "no allegory in all this, no wings of angels, no imaginary beings are anywhere in all the monument, excepting only the classic and familiar Minerva and the Furies, the monument is a faithful picture of real things—things that actually happened."[74]

In capturing what was believed to be the face of the South prior to the war, Herbert describes the remaining reliefs under the statue as:

> There is also the clergyman in his robes, his hand resting tenderly on the shoulder of his weeping wife, who holds her school-boy son's right hand in her own, as he goes off from his books and his home to the war. The boy's gun is on his shoulder, while his father's hand rests with a blessing on his head. This typifies the deep religious feeling that pervaded the Confederate armies, the soldiers, who knelt in prayer and rose, musket in hand, to go forward into line of battle. A strong oak tree overshadows with its branches at the same time the two groups, the preacher and his wife taking leave of their schoolboy son, and the blacksmith bidding good-bye to his forge and his loved ones.
>
> Another group is the young bride of war times, her bridal gown hooped and flounced as in those days, binding his sword and sash around her lover's waist, as he tenderly bends his head towards her.[75]

Confederate monument relief panel: "Mammy" (private collection of Ric Murphy).

At the base of the monument are the head stones of four notable Confederates, each buried at the compass points. One such burial is that of Moses Ezekiel, the monument's architect, who was flown from Italy to be buried on the east side of the monument at Arlington National Cemetery.

Directly across from Jackson Circle and across from McPherson Drive is Section 23, where one finds the headstones of soldiers who fought for the Union, and whose service did not automatically grant them the full rights as citizens. Section 23 also contains the remains of United States Colored Troops, where men like Thomas Francis (23-14869), Benjamin Hines (23-14868), Robert Coats, Samuel Kendall, Randall Skinner (23-14866), James Allen, and Edward Hoar provide a watchful guard against this intrusion in the national cemetery, a testimony to enslavement's legacy in the United States.

The Confederate Monument to the rebels is offset by these stalwart servants in a segregated army. Their headstones line the road in Section 23 that separates the monument from the rest of Arlington National Cemetery. While the monument continues the Lost Cause's trope of looking south, the headstones of Section 23 show their backs to the circle of CSA soldiers that fought against the United States.

In addition to the "guard" provided by the USCT, juxtaposed to the north of the Confederate Monument is the headstone of Lt. Colonel James Longstreet, Jr., and Major Robert Lee Longstreet, sons of the Confederate's deputy field commander. General James Longstreet was a "reconstructed rebel," who endorsed General Grant in the 1868 election, joined the Republican party, and was appointed by President Grant as the superintendent of customs in New Orleans. In that role he led state militia to defend the election of the Republican Governor Kellogg of Louisiana in the face of White League violence and lynchings in 1874. By 1875, Longstreet had to leave New Orleans fearing for his security.[76] Longstreet's memoirs criticized Robert E. Lee for tactical errors at Gettysburg, so Longstreet had long been assaulted by those seeking to burnish the image of the Lost Cause's main hero.

Confederate monument relief panel: "Faithful Servant Following Young Master" (private collection of Ric Murphy).

Section 23 to the east and Section 17 to the south are full of graves of African American sons who fought for the liberty of the United States in Havana, Manila, France and the other international engagements after the Civil War. Their burial and service was segregated. Not until 1948, after President Truman issued order 4444 integrating the army, would the nation honor its heroes side-by-side, without regard to race. The proximity of the segregated sections to the monument to the Lost Cause is ironic and significant.

Epilogue

The estate that surrounds Arlington House, today known as Arlington National Cemetery, is now home to the remains of military men of the American Revolutionary War and the War of 1812, having been reinterred on the site, giving grace and dignity to American service in every war fought. Each Memorial Day, American flags are individually placed at each marble headstone in honor of the service of those buried in the nation's most important military cemetery.

Each year, over four million visitors honor those heroes and heroines who have fallen during service to our nation, including those original men who served during the Civil War. The bodies of the dead from the Union army, the United States Colored Troops, and the Confederate army grace the tree-lined rolling hills, reflecting upon a period when differences were more important than the sacrifices their families would ultimately endure.

On many days, the silence is broken by the distinct sound of the hoofs of the horse-drawn carriages carrying the remains of another to their final place of rest, as the family follows the slow procession to the designated gravesite. Then, in tribute to the fallen, a lone bugler pays homage by playing the "Taps" at the end of the funeral.

Today, Arlington National Cemetery consists of over 624 acres and includes over 400,000 people buried, including over 3,000 former enslaved citizens buried in the cemetery's Section 27; and it represents every American conflict, including reburials of those from the Revolutionary War.[1] The cemetery has also become the final resting place for many iconic figures, including two presidents. William Howard Taft, the 27th president of the United States, was the first president to be buried at Arlington National Cemetery on March 8, 1930, to be followed by John F. Kennedy, the 35th president of the United States, on November 22, 1963.

The former Custis-Lee mansion (known since 1972 by congressional mandate as Arlington House, the Robert E. Lee Memorial) sits perched above the Potomac River, upon a 200-foot hill overlooking the massive Washington,

D.C., metropolitan area. The surrounding cemetery honors those brave men and women who gave their lives as the ultimate sacrifice serving our nation honorably.

At Arlington, the mansion has been restored as a congressionally mandated Confederate memorial. While some of the enslaved quarters are described, what has been lost in the current configuration are the Freedman's Village, the explication of Section 27, a full enumeration of the USCT, and the larger consequences of having our most hallowed ground be segregated for more years than it has been integrated.

Section 27 contains the remains of almost 3,800 formerly enslaved men, women and children who escaped from plantations in Virginia and Maryland, alongside hundreds of U.S. Colored Troops. Their story will always continue to inform how Americans find and hold their freedom. The current National Cemetery also contains the remains of many other great Americans who have continued to defend and extend freedom. These heroes are buried all across Arlington, in segregated sections until 1948, and from then until now interspersed with their fallen comrades without regard to race or color.

Men who served in our nation's Armed Forces, but will be forever known for their historic accomplishments outside of the military, are buried at Arlington National Cemetery. They include such men as former Army Sergeant Joseph Louis Barrow, who is best known as Joe Louis (Section 7A-Grave 177) the legendary world heavyweight boxing champion of the world. Another is former World War II Army Sergeant Medgar Evers, who was engaged in the European theater where he was part of the largest amphibious invasion in world history and fought on the beaches of France in June 1944, in the Battle of Normandy.[2] After the war, Evers returned home and became a civil rights activist, advocating for voter rights, integrated schools and equal access to public facilities. Having outlived over 113,000 German Axis and over 120,000 Allied casualties while serving for his country at the Battle of Normandy, at the age of 37 in 1963, Evers was shot in the back in his driveway by a convicted member of the White Citizen's Council, or the Ku Klux Klan, while getting out of his vehicle.[3]

The cemetery is also the final resting place for civilians and historic figures who changed societal norms for the better, such as the civil rights pioneer and first African American Justice of the Supreme Court of the United States, Justice Thurgood Marshall (Section 5: 40–3), who was appointed to the Supreme Court in 1967. Justice Marshall was the National Association for the Advancement of Colored People lead attorney and blazed a trail for civil rights litigation across the country. In 1940, he won the first of his 32 cases before the Supreme Court. In 1954, he was the lead attorney in *Brown vs Board of Education Topeka 347 U.S. 483*, the key case that established that separate but equal was not equal.[4]

Tomb of General Montgomery C. Meigs (private collection of Ric Murphy).

Americans of African descent who paved the way for so many to follow in their footsteps are also honored at Arlington National Cemetery. They include Benjamin O. Davis, Sr., who was the first African American to attain the rank of general in the United States armed forces (Section 2: E478B). Born in 1877 in Washington, D.C., General Davis served in the United States Army with the segregated black units "until his elevation to brigadier general by President Roosevelt in 1940." During World War II, Davis "coordinated the war effort recruitment of black soldiers into the U.S. Army—increasing the ranks from 3,640 in 1939 to almost 100,000 two years later. In 1942 Davis joined General Dwight Eisenhower, serving as liaison between black soldiers and the British citizenry."[5]

Over 400,000 men and women who wore the uniform are honored for their service and buried at Arlington National Cemetery. However, only one man can be said to embody the historic purpose of the cemetery. He did not set policy like Meigs, did not own any piece of it like G.W.P. Custis, nor did Congress intervene to name the property after him to burnish the myth of the Lost Cause like General Robert E. Lee. But James Parks has left us a profound legacy as the digger of graves, planter of trees and the single strongest link between the Antebellum South, Civil War, Reconstruction, Eviction and Jim Crow. He ranks among the highest of those who shaped Arlington.

Parks is perhaps one of the last individuals who knew how profoundly Arlington House changed during its transition from a plantation to a military camp, to a Freedman's Village, to a contraband cemetery and finally to a national cemetery. He was born a slave of the Custis-Lee family, lived his entire life on the former Arlington House Plantation, and lived through the war years at Freedman's Village.

On Sunday, November 4, 1928, James Parks, born a slave of the Custis-Lee family, provided the local newspaper an interview about his time as an enslaved man on the Custis-Lee Arlington House Plantation and provided a firsthand account of his interaction with George Washington Parke Custis and his daughter Mary Custis Lee, as well as information about his own parents and grandfather.

Honored citizen James Parks grave site (**private collection of Ric Murphy**).

In Enoch Aquila Chase's *Washington Star* newspaper article, Mr. Parks confirmed that he was in fact born at Arlington Plantation and that all his ancestors are buried in the slave cemetery, down in the grove of trees near the river shore, including his "father and mother, his grandfathers and grandmothers, including the renowned George Clark, who cooked for Mr. Custis at the mansion house the greater portion of his life." According to Chase, Mr. Parks' grandfather George Clark was "a gift from [President] George Washington to Major Custis, and was the family cook before the big house on the hill was built, when Mr. Custis first lived in the little house not far from the spring" during construction of the plantation.[6]

Having seen the plantation's transformation to a military cemetery, James Parks was able to provide interesting tidbits, informing Chase that the red stones used for the wall around the oldest part of the cemetery "came from the Seneca quarry in Maryland and had been transported over the Chesapeake and Ohio canal right into the Arlington reservation in the days when a branch of that important artery of commerce crossed the Potomac at Georgetown over the Aqueduct Bridge."[7]

Parks was a leader among the gravediggers that included Thornton Gray (Selena's husband), Wesley Norris (G.W.P. Custis' valet), and Shorter Syphax (descendant of G.W.P. Custis and Maria Syphax).[8] Parks would dig many of the graves in Section 27 and throughout the main portion of the cemetery; he also dug the holes for many of today's majestic trees that provide shade and protection to thousands of gravesites. One gravesite that was dug by James Parks "with his own hands" was the grave of Quartermaster General Montgomery C. Meigs, "the man who probably did more than anyone else to convert a large part of the plantation into a national cemetery, where sleep a legion of America's heroic dead."[9]

On August 21, 1929, James Parks died.[10] The secretary of war had granted special dispensation to bury Mr. Parks at Arlington "out of recognition of his service to the Government." He is buried in the otherwise all-white Section 15, near the Selfridge Gate.[11] The newspaper notice of his funeral describes how this former "Custis slave, 'Uncle Jim' had played as boy on Arlington's 'hallowed ground.'" The chaplain of Fort Myer presided at the funeral, and Fort Myer provided a firing squad and a bugler. The American Legion would erect a headstone. The final line of the notice tells that five of Parks' sons served in the World War.[12]

Mr. Parks, born enslaved, saw Arlington House as a plantation, then as a military camp, a home for freed people, and then as a national cemetery. He is the only person known to have been born, lived and worked, and buried at Arlington National Cemetery.

On behalf of Mr. Parks, we pay homage to all of the enslaved people born and buried at Arlington National Cemetery.

Appendix I

Chronology

1754

November 27—Birth of John Parke Custis, son of John Custis and Martha Dandridge Custis, New Kent County, Virginia, British North America.

1759

January 6—Martha Dandridge Custis marries George Washington.

1778

July 1—John Parke Custis, son of Martha Custis Washington, purchases 1,000 acres of tract of land to be known as Arlington.

1781

November 5—John Parke Custis dies after the Battle of Yorktown.

1802

Date Unknown—George Washington Parke Custis, son of John Parke Custis, begins construction of Arlington House.

1824

October 15—The Marquis de Lafayette, while on tour of the United States, visits Arlington Plantation.

1826

Date Unknown—Maria Syphax, daughter of G.W.P. Custis and born enslaved, granted 17 acres of Arlington Plantation and freed.

1831

June 30—Mary Custis, daughter of G.W.P. Custis, marries Robert E. Lee at Arlington House.

1843

Date Unknown—James Parks born enslaved at Arlington.

1846

September 7—Alexandria and Arlington vote for retrocession from the District of Columbia.

1850

September 20—District of Columbia outlaws slave trading, Alexandria trade flourishes.

1857

March 6—Supreme Court issues Dred Scott Decision declaring Missouri Compromise of 1820 unconstitutional.

October 10—George Washington Parke Custis dies, daughter Mary Custis Lee inherits Arlington.

1858

January 2—Custis enslaved people were inventoried at the Arlington Plantation by executor Robert E. Lee.

1861

March 4—President Lincoln inaugurated.

March 11—Constitution of the Confederate States of America was signed in its capital city of Montgomery, Alabama.

April 12—Confederate forces fire on Fort Sumter precipitating the Civil War.

April 12—Virginia officially secedes from the Union.

April 17—Virginia convention votes to succeed from the Union.

April 18—Robert E. Lee is offered command of Union forces in the field by Francis P. Blair.

April 20—Colonel Robert E. Lee resigns his commission in the U.S. Army.

April 22—Robert E. Lee leaves Arlington for Richmond and takes command of the armed forces of the Commonwealth of Virginia.

May 3—Brigadier General Irvin McDowell ordered to clear Arlington and the city of Alexandria, Virginia, of troops not loyal to the Union.

May 4—General Benjamin Butler treats enslaved men as "contraband" of war.

May 7—Virginia militia occupied Arlington and Arlington House.

May 12—Virginia House of Burgesses votes to secede from the Union.

May 14—Mary Custis Lee leaves Arlington Planation for Fairfax, Virginia.

May 24—Some 14,000 federal troops cross the Potomac River to Virginia, taking control of Alexandria and bridge crossings. General Irvin McDowell takes control of Arlington Plantation.

May 24—General Benjamin Butler allows three enslaved safe passage behind his lines at Fort Monroe, deeming them "contraband of war."

July 21—First Battle at Bull Run/Manassas where Federals suffer 2,700 casualties in a disappointing loss.

August 6—Confiscation Act signed by President Lincoln allowing for the confiscation of any property being used to support the independence of the Confederate states, including confiscating and freeing slaves.

1862

April 14—President Lincoln signs bill emancipating the enslaved people in the District of Columbia.

June 7—U.S. Congress passed "An Act for the Collection of Taxes in the Insurrectionary Districts."

Date Unknown—A tax is levied against the Arlington property, Mary Custis is unable to pay in person and the property is auctioned off by the U.S. government.

July 16—Congress authorizes federal government to purchase land for national cemeteries.

July 17—New cemeteries created in Alexandria, Virgina, and the District of Columbia to accommodate rising number of fallen soldiers.

September 17—Lincoln announces Emancipation Proclamation freeing slaves in Confederate states if they don't return to Union by January 1, 1863.

1863

January 1—Emancipation for all enslaved in Confederate states, contraband flows north in to District of Columbia.

May 5—Colonel Elias M. Greene proposes Freedman's Village at Arlington.

July 2—Battle of Gettysburg.

July 4—First United States Colored Troops recruited, trained and deployed.

July 18—Colonel Shaw leads African American 54th Massachusetts in assault on Fort Wagner.

September 22—President Lincoln announced that if the secessionist states did not rejoin the Union, he would free all of the enslaved people on January 1, 1863.

October 17—President Lincoln delivers the Gettysburg Address.

December 4—Freedman's Village at Arlington dedicated, population reaches 1,500.

1864

January 11—Arlington Plantation was sold off at auction to pay the tax of $92.07 enacted by the Act for the Collection of Taxes in the Insurrectionary Districts (12 Stat. at L. 422); federal government was the only bidder, purchased the property for $26,800.

May 4—General Ulysses S. Grant crosses Rapidan River of Virginia to confront Robert E. Lee in forty days of continuous combat, with more than 80,000 casualties. Cemeteries in Washington run out of space and Brigadier General Montgomery C. Meigs unofficially begins to bury war dead at Arlington House.

May 13—Arlington becomes a national cemetery.

May 13—Private William Henry Christman first military burial at Arlington National Cemetery at Northeast Gate Section 27.

June 15—Meigs recommends that 200 acres of the Arlington property be used as a national cemetery.

November 8—President Lincoln re-elected.

1865

March 3—Congress sets up Bureau of Refugees, Freedmen and Abandoned Lands.

March 4—Second Inauguration of President Lincoln.

April 9—Confederate General Robert E. Lee surrenders to General Ulysses S. Grant at Appomattox Court House.

April 14—Assassination of President Lincoln.

May 11—William Syphax writes letter to President Andrew Johnson regarding his family's claim to the 17 acres given by George Washington Parke Custis.

October 2—Robert E. Lee was sworn in as the president of Washington College in Lexington, Virginia. The same day, he signed his Amnesty Oath complying with President Johnson's Proclamation of Amnesty and Pardons.

December 18—Thirteenth Amendment goes into effect.

1866

April—2,111 unknown soldiers from the Battle at Bull Run and other nearby battles are buried in a crypt in Mrs. Lee's Arlington House Rose Garden.

June 11—U.S. Congress approved the Act for Relief of Maria Syphax, ensuring her family's claim to the land presented to them by George Washington Parke Custis.

1868

May 30—The first Decoration Day observed at Arlington by Grand Army of the Republic.

December 25—President Andrew Johnson announces amnesty for all former Confederates, except the very wealthy 2,000 citizens who he blamed for the war.

1870

October 12—General Robert E. Lee (CSA) dies in Lynchburg, Virginia.

(*specific date unknown*) Mary Custis Lee petitions U. S. Senate to disinter thousands of those buried and return to the land to her possession.

1872

Date Unknown—Uniform headstones begin to be used to mark graves at Arlington.

1873

Date Unknown—Congress approves white marble marker for each service member buried at Arlington.

June—Mary Custis Lee visits Arlington one last time.

November 5—Mary Custis Lee dies in Richmond, Virginia.

1878

April—After Congress turned the family down, George Washington Custis petitions U.S. Supreme Court to return Arlington to the Lee family.

1882

December 4—U.S. Supreme Court ruled that Arlington was seized illegally, and rules in favor of Custis family.

1883

March 3—U.S. Congress enacted legislation to fund the purchase of Arlington.

March 31—George Washington Custis Lee sells Arlington to the federal government for $150,000.

1887

December 7—Residents of Freedman's Village are ordered to leave.

1892

January 2—Brigadier General Montgomery C. Meigs dies and is buried at Arlington Cemetery near Custis-Lee mansion.

1898

February 16—USS *Maine* explodes and sinks in Havana Harbor, Cuba, killing 260 sailors, catalyst for Spanish American War.

1900

Date Unknown—Last of former freedmen leave Arlington.

1909

April 28—Pierre L'Enfant, the designer of the nation's capital, is buried at Arlington National Cemetery overlooking the city of Washington, D.C.

1912

November 12—Cornerstone laid for Confederate Memorial.

1929

August 21—James Parks dies in Arlington, buried in Section 15.

Appendix II

Inventory of Slaves at Arlington Plantation Belonging to G.W.P. Custis, January 1, 1858[1]

1. Austin Bingham
2. Louisa Bingham
3. Harrison Bingham
4. Reuben Bingham
5. Parke Bingham
6. Edward Bingham
7. Henry Bingham
8. Austin Bingham
9. Leanthe Bingham
10. Lucius Bingham
11. Caroline Bingham
12. Jim her child
13. Louisa her child
14. Baby her child
15. Lon Norris
16. Sally Norris His wife
17. Wesley Norris
18. Mary Norris
19. Sally Norris child
20. Thornton Grey
21. Selina Grey His wife
22. Emma Grey
23. Sarah Grey
24. Harry Grey
25. Annie Grey
26. Ada Grey
27. Selina Grey child
28. Julia Ann Cheek
29. Catherine Cheek
30. Louis Cheek
31. Henry Cheek
32. Catherine Burke
33. Fanny Burke
34. Mary Ann Burke
35. Agnes Burke
36. Obadiah Grey
37. Gideon Lancaster
38. Shack Check
39. Michael Meredith
40. Lawrence Parks
41. Patsy Parks
42. George Parks
43. Amanda Parks
44. Perry Parks
45. Robert Parks
46. Martha Parks
47. Laurence Parks
48. James Parks
49. Magdaiena Parks
50. Louina Parks
51. Matilda Parks
52. William Parks
53. Margaret Taylor
54. Dandridge Richardson
55. John Richardson
56. Billy Taylor
57. Quincy Taylor
58. Austin Grey
59. Austin Branham
60. Charles Sifax
61. George Clark
62. Daniel Dotson
63. Ephraim Derricks

Alexandria County Court September 11th 1858 returned to Court and ordered to be recorded. The foregoing inventories were Teste: B. H. Berry Clerk

Appendix III

Emancipation by R.E. Lee of G.W.P. Custis' Enslaved

(A complete transcription of the original document)

Know all men by these presents, that I, Robert E. Lee, executor of the last will and testament of George W. P. Custis deceased, acting by and under the authority and direction of the provisions of the said will, do hereby manumit, emancipate and forever set free from slavery the following named slaves belonging to the Arlington estate, viz: Eleanor Harris, Ephraim Derricks, George Clarke, Charles Syphax; Selina and Thornton Grey and their six children Emma, Sarah, Harry, Anise, Ada, Thornton; Margaret Taylor and her four children Dandridge, John, Billy, Quincy; Lawrence Parks and his nine children—Perry, George, Amanda, Martha, Lawrence, James, Magdalena, Leno, William; Julia Ann Check and her three children Catharine, Louis, Henry and an infant of the said Catharine; Sally Norris and Len Norris and their three children Mary, Sally, and Wesley; Old Shaack Check; Austin Bingham and Louisa Bingham and their twelve children Harrison, Parks, Reuben, Henry, Edward, Austin, Lucius, Leanthe Austin Bingham and Louisa Bingham, Louisa, Caroline, Jem, and an infant; Obadiah Grey; Austin Banham, Michael Merriday, Catharine Burk and her child; Marianne Burke and Agnes Burke: Also the following slaves belonging to the White House estate, viz: Robert Crider and Desiah his wife, Locky, Zack Young and two other children, Fleming Randolph and child; Maria Meredith and Henry her husband and their three children Nelson, Henry, and Austin; Lorenzo Webb, Old Daniel, Clavert Dandridge, Claiborne Johnson, Mary and John Stewart, Harrison, Jeff, Pat and Gadsby, Dick, Joe, Robert, Anthony, Davy, Bill Crump, Peyton, Dandridge, Old Davy and Eloy his wife, Milly and her two children [,] Leanthe and her five children; Jasper, Elisha and

Rachael his wife, Lavinia and her two children, Major, Phill, Miles, Mike and Scilla his wife and their five children Lavinia, Israel, Isaiah, Loksey [?] and Delphy; Old Fanny and her husband, Patsy, [L]ittle Daniel, and Cloe, James Henry, Milly, Ailsey and her two children, Susan Pollard [,] Armistead and Molly his wife, Airy, Jane Piler [?], Bob, Polly, Betsy and her child, Molly, Charity, John Reuben, George Crump, Minny, Grace, Martha and Matilda: Also the following belonging to the Romancoke estate, viz: Louis, Jem, Edward, Kitty and her children[,] Mary Dandridge and an infant; Nancy; Dolly, Esther, Serica[?], Macon and Louisa his wife, Walker, Peggy, Ebbee, Fanny, Chloe Custis and her child Julia Ann, Elvey Young and her child Charles, Airy Johnson, Anne Johnson, William and Sarah Johnston and their children Ailey, Crump, Molly, and George, James Henry and Anderson Crump, Major Custis and Lucy Custis, Nelson Meredith and Phoebe his wife, and their children Robert, Elisha, Nat, Rose and Sally, Ebbee Macon, Martha Jones & her children Davy & Austin; Patsey Braxton, Susan Smith and Mildred her child, Anne Brown, Jack Johnson, Marwell Bingham and Henry Baker.

And I do hereby release the aforesaid slaves from all and every claim which I may have upon their services as executor aforesaid.

Witness my hand and seal this 29th day of December in the year of our Lord eighteen hundred sixty-two

    [signed] R. E. Lee [seal]
    Ex. of G. W. P. Custis

State of Virginia, County of Spotsylvania to wit:

I, Benj[amin] S. Cason, Justice of the Peace in and for the said County, do hereby certify that Robert E. Lee, executor of the last will and testament of George W. P. Custis, a party to the foregoing deed of manumission, this day appeared before me, and acknowledge the same to be his act and deed.

Given under my hand this 29 day of Dec 1862.

    [signed] Benj[amin] S. Cason J. P.

City of Richmond, to wit:
 In the Office of the Court of Hustings for the said City, the 2d day
  of January 1863
 This deed was presented and with the Certificate annexed, admitted
  to record at twelve o'clock N. Teste

    Ro[bert] Howard, Clerk

SOURCE: Robert Edward Lee Papers, Museum of the Confederacy, Richmond, Virginia.

Appendix IV

Growth of Employment in Washington, D.C., from 1850 to 1870[1]

Census Year	1850	1860	1870	1850–70 increase
Population of Washington, D.C.	51,687	75,080	131,700	255%
Percent Increase per Decade		45%	75%	
Agriculture				
Farmers and Planters	246	246	255	104%
Gardeners, Nurserymen, and Vine Growers	175	266	347	198%
Miscellaneous Titles	14	51	763	5450%
	435	563	1,365	314%
Percent Increase per Decade		29%	142%	
Professional and Personal Services				
Barbers and Hairdressers	93	93	227	244%
Boarding & Lodging House Keepers	96	149	111	116%
Clergymen	94	71	174	185%
Domestic servants	507	3,672	9,107	1796%
Hotel & Restaurant Keepers and Employees	96	67	1,052	1096%
Laborers	2,071	3,426	7,839	379%
Launderers and Laundresses	488	1,287	2,470	506%
Officials and Employees (civil) of Government	451	513	5,824	1291%
Physicians, Surgeons and Nurses	104	276	326	313%

Appendix IV. Growth of Employment in Washington, D.C., 1850–1870

Census Year	1850	1860	1870	1850–70 increase
Soldiers (U.S.A.)			253	
Miscellaneous Titles	1,017	1,892	2,462	242%
	5,017	11,446	29,845	595%
Percent Increase per Decade		128%	161%	
Trade and Transportation				
Traders and Dealers		3	1,973	
Hucksters, Peddlers, & Commercial Travelers	94	178	398	423%
Clerks, Salesmen, and Accountants (in Stores)	887	1,509	1,590	179%
Officials and Employees of Railroad Companies	3	13	110	3667%
Carmen, Draymen, Teamsters, etc.	161	57	762	473%
Sailors, Steam Boatmen, Watermen, etc.	3	12	265	8833%
Miscellaneous Titles	503	910	1,028	204%
	1,651	2,682	6,126	371%
Percent Increase per Decade		62%	128%	
Manufacturing and Mining				
Bakers	123	185	339	276%
Blacksmiths	302	426	518	172%
Bookbinders and Finishers	50	97	180	360%
Boot and Shoemakers (Cordwainers)	359	387	618	172%
Brick and Tile Makers	29	133	289	997%
Butchers	133	224	396	298%
Carpenters and Joiners	847	1,163	1,707	202%
Painters and Varnishers	191	331	562	294%
Plasterers	57	186	334	586%
Plumbers and Gasfitters	2	51	198	9900%
Tailors, Tailoresses, and Seamstresses	512	900	1,018	199%
Miscellaneous Titles	1,501	5,469	5,546	369%
	4,106	9,552	11,705	285%
Percent Increase per Decade		133%	23%	
Total	11,209	24,243	49,041	438%

Appendix V

An African American Walking Tour of Arlington Cemetery

Section   Grave   Honored and Historical Significance

27   —   **Section 27.** Site of the first burials of Arlington National Cemetery. The site contains the remains of over 1,500 United States Colored Troops from the Civil War and contains over 3,800 former enslaved men, women and children who are honored as "citizens" at the site.

27   19   **William H. Christman,** Civil War Army Private, Company G, 67th Pennsylvania Volunteer Infantry (1843–1864). A poor farm boy who enlisted to help the family financially, Private Christman was the first soldier to be buried at Arlington National Cemetery, in Section 27, on May 13, 1864, after succumbing to illness.

27   98   **William McKinney,** Civil War Army Private, Company F, 17th Pennsylvania Volunteer Cavalry. At the age of seventeen, Private McKinney was the first soldier to be interred at Arlington National Cemetery, whose family was present at the burial, establishing a long tradition. Also buried on May 13, 1864, he was the second to be buried at the cemetery.

27   565-A   **William H. Brown,** Civil War Navy Landsman (1836–1896), Baltimore, Maryland. **Service Award(s):** Medal of Honor for his actions aboard the USS *Brooklyn* against Fort Morgan rebel gun boat attacks at the Battle of Mobile Bay.

27   886   **James Richmond,** Civil War, Private Army 8th Ohio Infantry (1843–1864). **Service Award(s):** Medal of Honor, for his actions at the Battle of Gettysburg citation reads: "Capture of Flag."

Appendix V. African American Walking Tour of Arlington Cemetery 189

Section   Grave   Honored and Historical Significance

27   952-B   **Thomas Shaw,** American/Indian War, Sergeant, Company K 9th Cavalry Regiment (1846–1895). **Service Award(s):** Medal of Honor, citation reads: "forcing enemy back after stubbornly holding his ground in an extremely exposed position and prevented the enemy's superior numbers from surrounding his command."

27   985-H   **James H. Harris,** Civil War, Sergeant, 38th United States Colored Troops (1828–1898), Saint Mary's County, Maryland. **Service Award(s):** Medal of Honor, for service in Battle of Chaffin's Farm, citation Reads "Gallantry in the assault."

1   123-D-RH   **William H. Hunter,** Civil War, Regimental Chaplin, 4th USCT (1831–1908). Commissioned as regimental chaplain of the 4th USCT, on October 4, 1863. While stationed with his regiment at the Battle of Petersburg, he witnessed the heroic action and successes of former enslaved, freed, and free African American troops on the battlefield, and rallied their support with his eloquent sermons.

1   124-B   **Orandatus Simon Bolivar Wall,** Civil War, Captain, Company K of the 104th USCT (1825–1891), Rockingham, North Carolina. Born a slave on August 12, 1825, to an enslaved mother and her white slaveholder. Commissioned as a captain of Company K of the 104th, served with the Freemen's Bureau until his discharge, and was one of twelve known black recruiters of black soldiers.

1   124-C   **Dr. Alexander Augusta,** Civil War, Brevet Lieutenant Colonel, 7th USCT (1825–1890), Norfolk, Virginia. Dr. Alexander Augusta was the highest-ranking black officer in the Civil War era. He served as the head of the Freedman's Hospital at Camp Barker, Washington, D.C.

1   123-A   **Frank M. Welch,** Civil War, 1st Lieutenant, 54th Massachusetts Colored Infantry (1841–1907), Philadelphia, Pennsylvania. Served under the leadership of Massachusetts native, Colonel Robert G. Shaw, Welch advanced with 624 members of his regiment along the beach at Morris Island, South Carolina, in an assault of Fort Wagner.

1   630-B   **Isaiah Mays,** Corporal, 24th Infantry, Buffalo Soldier, U.S. Army (1858–1925), Carters Bridge, Virginia. Battles/Wars: American Indian Wars, Wham Paymaster Robbery. **Service Award(s):** Medal of Honor, citation reads: "Gallantry in the fight between Paymaster Wham's escort and robbers. Mays walked and crawled 2 miles to a ranch for help."

2   4968-B-LH   **Daniel "Chappie" James, Jr.,** Four Star General, USAF (1920–1978), Pensacola, Florida. Having served in World War II, the Korean War and the Vietnam War, James became the first African American Four Star General in the United States Air Force. General James' distinguished career included the Defense Disfigured Service Medal, two Air Force Distinguished Service Medals, two Legion of Merits, three Distinguished Flying Crosses, Meritorious Service medals, along with other commendations and Air Medals.

Section   Grave   Honored and Historical Significance

    2   E-311-RH   **Benjamin O. Davis, Jr.**, Four Star General, U.S. Army; U.S. Air Force (1912–2002), Washington, D.C. First African American general in the United States Air Force. General and Commander of the Tuskegee Airmen in World War II. Battles/Wars: World War II, Korean War, Vietnam War. **Service Award(s):** Air Force Distinguished Service Medal, Army Distinguished Service Medal Silver Star, Legion of Merit, Distinguished Flying Cross, Air Medal, Army Commendation Medal, Langley Fold Medal.

    2   E-478-B   **Benjamin O. Davis, Sr.**, U.S. Brigadier General, 9th Cavalry (1877–1970), Washington, D.C. First African American to reach the rank of general in the U.S. Armed Forces. Battles/Wars: Spanish-American War, Philippine-American War, World War I, World War II. **Service Award(s):** Distinguished Service Medal, the Bronze Star, French Croix de Guerre, Africa Star.

    3   1730-B   **Charles Young**, Colonel U.S. Army 9th Cavalry Regiment (1864–1922), Mays Lick, Kentucky. Born as an enslaved person, he became the third graduate of the U.S. Military Academy at West Point. He became the first colonel in the U.S. Army where he served in the American Indian Wars, Spanish-American War, Philippine-American War, Pancho Villa Expedition, and World War I. After his military retirement, he served as the first African American U.S. National Park Superintendent.

    4   2749   **George H Wanton**, Spanish-American War, Master Sergeant, 10th Cavalry Regiment, U.S. Army (1868–1940), Patterson, New Jersey. Sergeant Wanton served in the Spanish-American War, and for his service at the Battle of Tayacoba he was awarded the Medal of Honor. His citation reads: "Voluntarily went ashore in the face of the enemy and aided in the rescue of his wounded comrades; this after several previous attempts at rescue had been frustrated."

    5   40-3   **Thurgood Marshall** (1908–1993), Baltimore, Maryland. Appointed as Associate Justice of the Supreme Court of the United States in 1967. Denied entry to Maryland's School of Law he attended Howard University and used his education to sue his birth state of Maryland for denying his educational rights. Served as the National Association for the Advancement of Colored People lead attorney, blazed a trail of civil rights litigation across the country. In 1940, he argued (and won) the first of his 32 cases before the Supreme Court. In 1954 he was the lead attorney in *Brown vs Board of Education, Topeka 347 U.S. 483*, the key case that established separate was not equal. In his 1987 address on the bicentennial of the Constitution he declared the document was "defective from the start," and that the "living document" required a "civil war and major social transformations to attain the system of constitutional government."

    7A   177   **Joe Louis Barrow**, Private, Technical Sergeant, U.S. Army (1914–1981), Lafayette, Alabama. He was the legendary world heavyweight boxing champion of the world. Born Joseph Louis Barrow, "the Champ" and his family lived in Lafayette, Alabama. After the family had a confrontation with the local

Appendix V. African American Walking Tour of Arlington Cemetery

Section   Grave   Honored and Historical Significance

Ku Klux Klan, they moved to Detroit, Michigan. He served as a sergeant in the United States Army during World War II. Prior to enlisting "he donated the purses from two fights—nearly $100,000—to the army and navy relief societies in 1942. When he joined the Army later that year, he would embark upon a schedule of staging 96 boxing exhibitions during nearly four years of service at installations all over the world including Fort Lee on September 15, 1943.

7A   18   **Roscoe Robinson, Jr.,** Four Star General, U.S. Army, (1928–1993), St. Louis, Missouri. A West Point graduate, Robinson became the first African American to achieve the rank of four-star general in the United State Army. General Robinson served in the Korean War and Vietnam Wars. General Robinson's distinguished career included the Distinguished Service Medal, two Silver Star medals, three Legion of Merit medals, the Bronze Star, the Distinguished Flying Cross and the Combat Infantry Badge Second Award.

8   —   **Freedman's Village** (1863–1901). Located on the once abandoned plantation of Robert E. Lee's wife, Mary Custis Lee. The village served as home to a 1,000 former enslaved people who were refugees of the Civil War. The village became a permanent settlement with a hospital, churches and schools. The only physical reminder of this home to many is a marker on the outer parameters of the property located outside of Section 8 of the Arlington National Cemetery.

8   S-15-1   **Matthew Henson** (1866–1955), Nanjemoy, Maryland. African-American explorer who co-discoverer the North Pole in 1909. Henson was born in Nanjemoy, Maryland in 1866. Both of his parents died when he was a child, and he was shuttled around with different relatives at a young age. Henson reached the North Pole in 1909, nine years after Freedman's Village officially closed. Henson died in 1955, in New York. Ironically, Henson, who became the first African American to reach the top of the world, is buried at the top of a hill in Section 8, the very land that once was home to over a thousand fugitive slaves at Freedman's Village.

13   6513   **George Washington Parke Custis,** civilian (1781–1857), Mount Airy, Maryland. The grandson of First Lady Martha Washington and the adopted son of President George Washington, he inherited 1,100 acres from his father that became known as Arlington Plantation. Upon his death he left the property to his daughter Mary Custis Lee, the wife of Confederate States of America General Robert E. Lee. After the Lee family abandoned the property, the Union army confiscated it and transformed it into a military camp, Freedman's Village, a pauper cemetery than a national cemetery to bury the war dead from the Civil War.

15   2   **James Parks,** an honored citizen and civilian (1843–1929), Arlington, Virginia. Born enslaved on the Arlington Plantation, as the property of George Washington Parke Custis. Lived most of his life on the property and saw the transformation of the land use from a plantation, to a military camp, to a freedman's village, to a pauper's cemetery, to the hallowed grounds of Arlington

Section   Grave   Honored and Historical Significance

National Cemetery. Recognized as the man who buried many of the original grave sites, and as the only man to bury and be buried on the site.

23   21712   **Milton Holland,** Civil War, Sergeant Major, 5th USCT (1844–1910), Carthage, Texas. **Service Award(s):** Medal of Honor, citation Reads: "Took command of Company C, after all the officers had been killed or wounded, and gallantly led it."

25   64   **Henry Johnson,** Sergeant, 9th Cavalry Regiment, U.S. Army (1897–1929), Winston-Salem, North Carolina. Battles/Wars: World War I, Champagne-Marne, Meuse-Argonne. **Service Award(s):** Recipient of the Medal of Honor, Purple Heart, Croix de guerre (with bronze palm and bronze star).

31   349   **Dennis Bell,** Private, 10th Cavalry Regiment (1866–1953), Washington, D.C. Battles/Wars: Spanish-American War, Battle of Tayacoba, Cuba. **Service Award(s):** Medal of Honor, citation reads: "Voluntary went ashore in the face of the enemy and aided in the rescue of his wounded comrades; this after several previous attempts at rescue had been frustrated."

36   1431   **Medgar Evers,** World War II, U.S. Army Sergeant (1925–1963), Decatur, Mississippi. He served in the United States Army during World War II, and was engaged in the European theater where he was part of the largest amphibious invasion in world history and fought on the beaches of France in June 1944, in the Battle of Normandy. After the war, Evers returned home and became a civil rights activist, advocating for voter rights, integrated schools and equal access to public facilities. Having survived over 113,000 German Axis casualties and over 120,000 Allied casualties while serving for his country at the Battle of Normandy, at the age of 37 in 1963, Evers was murdered by a shot in his back by a convicted member of the White Citizen's Council (KKK) in his driveway while getting out of is vehicle.

60   9836   **Hazel Johnson-Brown,** Brigadier General, U.S. Army (1927–2011), West Chester, Pennsylvania. General Brown's distinguished career included the Distinguished Service Medal, the Legion of Merit medal, the Meritorious Medal and the Army Commendation Medal.

Sources: Henry Louis Gates, Jr., and Evelyn Brooks Higginbotham (editors), *African American National Biography*, Oxford University Press, New York, NY, 2008. *See Also* Medal of Honor recipients, United States Army Center of Military History, available at: https://www.army.mil/medalofhonor/recipients.html; and Gale Group (Creator), *Who's Who Among African Americans*, Gale Group, Farmington Hills, MI.

Chapter Notes

Introduction

1. "The Greatest Memorial Service is at Arlington Cemetery," *The Sunday Star* (Washington, D.C., May 26, 1912), 3.

2. Dave Philips, "Arlington Cemetery, Nearly Full, May Become More Exclusive," *New York Times* (May 28, 2018). Accessed at nytimes.com, May 28, 2018.

3. Colonel Elias Greene describes the "salutary effects of good, pure country air" to Major General S.P. Heintzelman in his letter of May 5, 1863. National Archives, RG 92: Records of the Office of the Quartermaster General, Records Relating to Functions: Cemeterial, 1829–1929. General Correspondence and Reports Relating to National and Post Cemeteries ("Cemetery File"), 1865–c.1914. Arlington, VA. Box 7, NM-81, Entry 576.

4. *Rand McNally & Co.'s Pictorial Guide to Washington* (Rand McNally: Chicago, Illinois and New York, 1904), 5.

5. Jonathan Horn, *The Man Who Would Not Be Washington: Robert E. Lee's Civil War and His Decision That Changed American History* (Scribner: New York, 2015), 75.

6. Blassingame, John W. (ed.): *Slave Testimony: Two Centuries of Letters, Speeches, and Interviews, and Autobiographies*, ed. John W. Blassingame (Louisiana State University Press: Baton Rouge, LA, 1977), 467–468. ISBN 0-8071-0273-3.

7. Robert M. Poole, *On Hallowed Ground* (Bloomsbury: New York, 2009), 20.

8. Horn, *The Man Who Would Not Be Washington*, 104–109.

9. New Year's Festival to the Freedmen on Arlington Heights and Statistics and Statements of the Educational Condition of the Colored People in the Southern States and Other Facts (McGill and Witherow: Washington, D.C., 1867).

10. C.B. Rose, Jr., "The Map of Arlington in 1878—Places and People," *Arlington Historical Magazine* (Arlington, VA, Vol. 2, October 1962), 32–33.

11. Frederick Douglass, *The Life and Times of Frederick Douglass Written by Himself: His Early Life as a Slave, His Escape from Bondage, and His Complete History to the Present Time* (DeWolfe, Fiske & Co.: Boston, 1895), 507.

12. "Decoration of Soldiers' Graves," *Alexandria Gazette* (Alexandria, VA, May 27, 1874), 2.

13. Lucinda Prout Janke, *A Guide to Civil War Washington, D.C.* (History Press: Charleston, SC, 2013), 35.

14. *The National Tribune*, Washington, D.C. was published for forty years from 1877 to 1917. The November 30, 1882, No. ("Soldiers to the Front," Page 9) is a particularly strong call to "arms" to the veterans to remain united in the face of the Democrat press.

15. Kathleen, L. Gorman, "Civil War Pensions," *Essential Civil War Curriculum* (Virginia Tech University Press: Blacksburg, 2012), 2.

16. Public Law 84-107: JOINT RESOLUTION: Designating the Lee Mansion in Arlington National Cemetery as a permanent memorial to Robert E. Lee. https://www.gpo.gov/fdsys/pkg/STATUTE-69/pdf/STATUTE-69-Pg190.pdf Accessed May 28, 2018.

Chapter 1

1. John Clagett Proctor, "Master of Arlington House Striking Figure in Virginia History," *The Sunday Star* (Washington, D.C., February 26, 1928), Part 7, 2.
2. *Ibid.*
3. Enoch Aquila Chase, "Ancient Custis Slave Remembers Brilliant Arlington Events," *The Sunday Star* (Washington, D.C., November 4, 1928) Part 7, 5.
4. *Ibid.*
5. *Ibid.*
6. *Ibid.*
7. *Ibid.*
8. *Ibid.*
9. *Ibid.*
10. Joseph P. Reidy, "Coming From the Shadow of the Past: The Transition from Slavery to Freedom at Freedman's Village," *The Virginia Magazine of History and Biography*, Vol. 95, Number 4 (October 1987), 405.
11. Felix James "The Establishment of Freedman's Village in Arlington, Virginia," *Negro History Bulletin* (Washington, D.C., April 1970) Vol. 33 No. 4. 5.
12. Micki McElya, *The Politics of Mourning: Death and Honor at Arlington National Cemetery* (Harvard University Press: Cambridge, MA, 2016), 95–96.

Chapter 2

1. Reidy, Joseph, P., "Coming From the Shadow of the Past: The Transition from Slavery to Freedom at Freedman's Village," *The Virginia Magazine of History and Biography* (Richmond, VA, Vol. 95, Number 4 October 1987, 404.
2. Dennee, "A District of Columbia Freedmen's Cemetery in Virginia? African-American Civilians in Section 27 of Arlington National Cemetery, 1864–1867," (Friends of Freedmen's Cemetery). Accessed April 10, 2017, at http://www.freedmenscemetery.org/resources/documents/arlington-section27.pdf.
3. Janke, *A Guide to Civil War Washington, D.C.: The Capital of the Union*, 93.
4. Dennee, "African American Civilians in Section 27 of Arlington National Cemetery, 1864–1867," 40.
5. Voyages Database. 2017. *Voyages: The Trans-Atlantic Slave Trade Database, Assessing the Slave Trade, Estimates.* http://www.slavevoyages.org/assessment/estimates. Accessed February 24, 2017.
6. *Ibid.*
7. Sven Beckert, *Empire of Cotton: A Global History* (Vintage Books, New York, 2014).
8. *A Century of Population Growth: From the First Census of the United States to the Twelfth* (United States Department of Commerce and Labor, Bureau of the Census, Government Printing Office: Washington, D.C., 1909), 132.
9. Edward E. Baptist, *The Half has Never Been Told: Slavery and the Making America* (Basic Books, New York, 2016), 343. ISBN 978-0-465-04966-0.
10. Michael Korda, *Clouds of Glory; the Life and Legend of Robert E. Lee* (Harper Collins, New York, 2014), 203. ISBN: 978-0-06-2 11629-1.
11. "Making the Case for Racial Reparations: Does America Owe a Debt to the Descendants of Its Slaves?" Ed. Jack Hitt, *Harper's Magazine* (November 2000).
12. Robert Pierce Forbes, *The Missouri Compromise and Its Aftermath: Slavery and the Meaning of America* (University of North Carolina Press: Chapel Hill, NC, 2007), 5.
13. Harold Holzer, *Lincoln And the Power of the Press* (Simon & Schuster, New York, 2014), 151.
14. James Fuller, *The Election of 1860 Reconsidered* (Kent State University Press: Kent, Ohio, 2013).
15. Harold Holzer, *Lincoln President Elect: Abraham Lincoln and the Great Secession Winter of 1860–1861* (Simon & Schuster: New York, 2008), 243–4. ISBN 978-0-7432-8947-4.
16. "Mr. Hunter's Proposition," *Alexandria Gazette* (January 8, 1861), 3.
17. Holzer, *Lincoln and the Power of the Press*.
18. "Jeff. Davis's Northern Conspiracy," *Chicago Daily Tribune* (June 25, 1861), 2.
19. "The 'Protection of Washington'—Gen. Scott Carries Out the Black Republican Policy," *Richmond Enquirer* (Richmond, VA, January 18, 1861), 4.
20. U.S. Census for 1859, 1860 and 1870, www.census.gov.
21. John David Hoptak, *First in Defense of the Union: The Civil War History of the*

First Defenders (AuthorHouse: Bloomington, IN, 2004), 7.
  22. Benjamin Franklin Cooling III, and Walton H. Owen II, *Mr. Lincoln's Forts: A Guide to the Civil War Defenses of Washington* (White Mane Publishing: Shippensburg, PA), 94–99.
  23. Elizabeth Keckley, *Behind the Scenes, or, Thirty Years a Slave, and Four in the White House* (G.W. Carleton: New York, 1868), 139.
  24. Heather Butts, *African American Medicine in Washington, D.C.* (History Press: Charleston, SC, 2014), 17.
  25. "Hydrant Water," *The National Republican* (Washington, D.C., March 31, 1862), 3.
  26. "Senator Wilson's Description of the Jail," *The National Republican* (Washington, D.C., December 7, 1861), 1.
  27. "Arrest of the Mayor of Washington on Charge of Disloyalty," *Evening Star* (Washington, D.C., August 24, 1861), 3.
  28. "Descent Upon a Ranche," *Evening Star* (Washington, D.C., November 4, 1861), 3.
  29. "A Horse Dealer," *Evening Star* (Washington, D.C., November 4, 1861), 3.
  30. "Our Military Budget," *Evening Star* (Washington, D.C., February 26, 1862), 3.
  31. Kate Masur, *An Example for All the Land: Emancipation and the Struggle Over Equality in Washington D.C.* (University of North Carolina, Chapel Hill, NC, 2012).
  32. Dennee, "A District of Columbia Freedmen's Cemetery in Virginia?"

Chapter 3

  1. John Keegan, *The American Civil War* (Alfred A. Knopf, New York, NY, 2009), 334.
  2. Bruce Levine, *Half Slave and Half Free: The Roots of the Civil War* (Hill and Wang: New York, 2005), 37–38.
  3. Dorothy Schneider, and Carl J. Schneider, *First Ladies: A Biographical Dictionary* (Infobase Publishing: New York, 2010), 2. ISBN 1-438-12750-2.
  4. Patricia Brady, *Martha Washington* (Penguin Press: New York, 2005), 39. ISBN 0-670-03430-4.
  5. Helen Bryan, *Martha Washington, First Lady of Liberty* (Wiley 2002), 26–7. ISBN 978-0-471-15892-9.
  6. Henry Wiencek, *An Imperfect God: George Washington, His Slaves, and the Creation of America* (Macmillan Publishers: New York, 2013), 67. ISBN 1-466-8565-9.
  7. *Ibid.*, 49.
  8. Cynthia Parzych, *Arlington National Cemetery: Trace the Path of America's Heritage* (Rowman & Littlefield: Guilford, CT, 2015), 1. ISBN 978-1-4930-1300-5.
  9. Bernice-Marie Yates, *The Perfect Gentleman: The Life and Letters of George Washington Custis Lee* (Xulon Press: Maitland, FL, 2003), 34–39. ISBN 1-5916-0451-6.
  10. Poole, *On Hallowed Ground*, 11.
  11. Henry Lee, *Funeral Oration on the Death of General Washington, Delivered at the Request of the Congress* (Printed for Joseph Nancrede and Manning & Loring: Boston, 1800).
  12. Note: The word slave is not used; in reference to Africans and their increase, "all other Persons" is used.
  13. Parzych, *Arlington National Cemetery*, 3–4.
  14. Poole, *On Hallowed Ground*, 11–12.
  15. C.B. Rose Jr., *Arlington County Virginia: A History* (Arlington Historical Society, Port City Press: Baltimore, 1976), 68. LCCCN 76-5938.
  16. McElya, *The Politics of Mourning*, 15–17.
  17. "Christening," *The Daily Republic* (Washington, D.C., August 6, 1853), 3.
  18. Murray H. Nelligan, *Arlington House: The Story of the Lee Mansion Historical Monument* (Chatelaine Press: Burke, VA, 2005), 143.
  19. *Ibid.*, 109.
  20. Lee Standiford, *Washington Burning: How a Frenchman's Vision for Our Nation's Capital Survived Congress, the Founding Fathers, and the Invading British Army* (Three Rivers Press: New York, 2008), 282.
  21. Nelligan, *Arlington House*, 126.
  22. *Ibid.*, 143.
  23. *Catalogue No. 712: Relics of General Washington and a Variety of Historical Chinaware to Be Sold at 2:30 O'Clock*, at Thos. Birch Son's Book Auction Room, 1100 Chestnut Street, Philadelphia, PA, December 14, 1893.
  24. "Museum of the American Revolution Names Theater in Hopnor of $8 Million Gift from Alan B. and Jill Miller," *Museum of the American Revolution Press Release*, March 15, 2018. https://www.amrevmuseum.

org/press-room/press-releases/museum-american-revolution-names-theater-honor-8-million-gift-alan-b-and. Accessed June 28, 2018.
  25. "Custis, George Washington Parke," *Dictionary of Virginia Biography*, Vol. 3, Sara B. Bearss, Ed. (Library of Virginia: Richmond), 631.
  26. Nelligan, *Arlington House*, 96–97.
  27. Ibid., 129.
  28. "Custis, George Washington Parke," 632.
  29. Nelligan, *Arlington House*, 109.
  30. Korda, 12, and Sean Wilentz, *The Rise of American Democracy* (WW Norton: New York, 2005), 62–65.
  31. Clifford Dowdey, *Lee* (Bonanza Books: New York, 1965), 3. LCCCN 65-20743.
  32. Ibid., 31.
  33. James Edward Peters, *Arlington National Cemetery: Shrine to America's Heroes* (Woodbine, MD, 1986), 10. ISBN 0-9331-149-042.
  34. Enoch Aquila Chase, "Ancient Custis Slave Remembers Brilliant Arlington Events," *The Sunday Star* (Washington, D.C., November 4, 1928), Part 7, 5.
  35. "George Washington Parke Custis Obituary," *Port Tobacco Times* (Port Tobacco, MD, October 12, 1857), 2.
  36. "Georgetown Affairs," *Evening Star* (Washington, D.C., October 12, 1857), 3.
  37. "Death of Mr. Custis," *Weekly National Intelligencer* (Washington, D.C., October 17, 1857), 1.
  38. Chase, "Ancient Custis Slave Remembers Brilliant Arlington Events," 5.
  39. "The Funeral of G.W.P. Custis," *Evening Star* (District of Columbia, October 13, 1857), 3.
  40. "Death of Mr. Custis," *Weekly National Intelligencer* (Washington, D.C., October 17, 1857), 1.
  41. Jennifer Hanna (*Arlington House, The Robert E. Lee Memorial* (Washington D.C., U. S. Department of the Interior, 2001), 62. Accessed January 26, 2017.
  42. Alexandria City Court Record, Will Book 7, George Washington Parke Custis, January 1, 1858.
  43. Alexandria City Court Record, Arlington House Slave Inventory of George Washington Parke Custis, September 11, 1858.
  44. McElya, *The Politics of Mourning*, 30, quoting from Helen Nicolay, *Our Capital on the Potomac* (Century: New York, 1924), 375, ellipsis in the original.
  45. David Glenn Brasher, "The Myth of Robert E. Lee and the Good Slave Master," *Daily Beast* (www.dailybeast.com). Accessed September 23, 2017.
  46. Eric Foner, "The Making and Breaking of the Myth of Robert E. Lee," *New York Times* (www.nytimes.com). Accessed August 28, 2017.
  47. Hartford Fire Insurance Company Policy, Hartford, CT, Robert E. Lee, Arlington House, October 17, 1859.
  48. Ibid.
  49. McElya, *The Politics of Mourning*, 21.

Chapter 4

  1. Ron Chernow, *Grant* (Penguin Press: New York, 2017), 795. ISBN 9781594204876.
  2. Holzer, *Lincoln and the Power of the Press*, 152–153.
  3. "Southern Monitor" *Daily Dispatch* (Richmond, VA, May 28, 1857), 4.
  4. "Lemmon Case the New York Tribune," *Richmond Enquirer* (Richmond, VA, October 9, 1857), 1.
  5. "Speech of A. Lincoln," *The Kansas News* (Emporia, KS, August 8, 1857), 1.
  6. Samuel H. Williamson, and Louis P. Cain, *Measuring Slavery in 2016 Dollars* (University of Chicago-Northwestern University). Accessed May 4, 2017. https://www.measuringworth.com/slavery.php.
  7. Elizabeth Brown Pryor. *Reading the Man: A Portrait of Robert E Lee Through His Private Letters* (Penguin Group: New York 2007), 137–138.
  8. Wiencek, *An Imperfect God*, 73.
  9. Ibid., 77.
  10. Pryor, *Reading the Man*, 137–38.
  11. Arlington House, Robert E. Lee Memorial, National Park Service.
  12. Dorothy S. Provine, *Alexandria County, Virginia, Free Negro Registers, 1791–1861* (Heritage Books: Bowie, MD, 1990), 206. ISBN 1-55613-416-9.
  13. Poole, *On Hallowed Ground*, 86.
  14. Rose, *Arlington County Virginia: A History*, 122.
  15. Insights from descendants, Craig Syphax and Stephen Hammond, November 7, 2017. Arlington, VA.

16. Poole, *On Hallowed Ground*, 11.

17. Ric Murphy, *Freedom Road: An American Family Saga from Jamestown to World War* (AuthorHouse: Bloomington, IN, 2014-Edition 1), 155. ISBN 978-1-4969-2051-5.

18. John Liebertz, *A Guide to the African American Heritage of Arlington County* (Virginia, Department of Community Planning, Housing and Development, 2016), 2.

19. Enoch Aquila Chase, "Ancient Custis Slave Remembers Brilliant Arlington Events," 5.

20. *Ibid.*

21. *Ibid.*

22. *Ibid.*

23. Dowdey, *Lee*, 108.

24. Karl Decker, and Angus McSween, with contributions from Leslie S. Smyth, *Historic Arlington* (Creative Media Partners: Sacramento, CA), 80–81.

25. "Manumission" *Evening Star*, Washington, D.C., December 11, 1857, 1.

26. "The Slaves of Mr. Custis," *New York Times* (December 30, 1857), 8.

27. "The Will of Mr. Custis," *New York Times* (January 8, 1858), 4.

28. Dowdey, *Lee*, 112.

29. *Ibid.*

30. *Ibid.*, 113.

31. Pryor, *Reading the Man*, 123–124.

32. Alexandria County (Virginia) Probate Court, 1858.

33. Alexandria County (Virginia) Probate Court, 1858.

34. As posted on the Commonwealth of Virginia Library website: A chancery cause is a case of equity where "Justice is administered according to fairness as contrasted with the strictly formulated rules of common law." In layman's terms, a chancery case was one that could not be readily decided by existing written laws. A judge, not a jury, determines the outcome of the case. These types of court documents are useful when researching genealogical information and land or estate divisions and may contain correspondence, lists of heirs, or vital statistics, among other items. Cases in chancery often address estate and business disputes, debt, the resolution of land disputes, and divorce. A chancery case began with the bill of complaint, explaining the background of the action, followed by an answer from the parties being sued. Court appointed commissioners decided a fair and equitable settlement of the case based on the evidence presented and reported their findings to the court. The court's decision or final decree was the last step in the proceedings of a chancery case. The earliest Virginia court records are those of the county courts. The end of primogeniture in Virginia in 1786 and the creation of general inheritance laws caused an increase in chancery cases; as a result, additional courts were created in which cases could be heard, including District Courts (1789–1808), Superior Courts of Chancery (1802–1831), Circuit Superior Courts of Law and Chancery (1831–1851), and Circuit Courts (1852–present). See http://www.lva.virginia.gov/chancery/faq.htm. Accessed June 30, 2018.

35. Arlington County (Va.) Chancery Causes, 1753–1911. EXR OF George Washington Parke Custis vs. Mary Ann Randolph Lee ETC., 1859-017. Local Government Records Collection, Arlington County Court Records. The Library of Virginia, Richmond, Virginia.

36. Custis EXR vs. Lee and Others, "Note of Argument for Appellant," [1858], Supreme Court of Appeals of Virginia, copy in Local History/Special Collections, Legal Papers, Kate Waller Barrett Branch Library, Alexandria, VA.

37. Blassingame, *Slave Testimony*, 467–468.

38. *Ibid.*

39. Liebertz, *A Guide to the African American Heritage of Arlington County*, 3.

40. Blassingame, *Slave Testimony*, 467–468.

41. *Ibid.*

42. Douglas Southall Freeman, *R.E. Lee: A Biography*, Vol. 1 (Charles Scribner's Sons: New York, 1935), 390.

43. *Ibid.*, 392.

44. Holzer, *Lincoln and the Power of the Press*, 303.

45. Levine, *Half Slave and Half Free*.

Chapter 5

1. Holzer, *Lincoln and the Power of the Press*, 291.

2. "Howell Cobb on Resistance," *Keowee Courier* (Pickens Court House, SC, December 22, 1860).

3. "The Treachery of the Government," *The National Republican* (Washington, D.C., December 27, 1861), 2.

4. James G. Barber, *Alexandria in the Civil War* (H.E. Howard, Inc.: Lynchburg, VA, 1988), 3. ISBN 0-930919-69-2.

5. "Forward," *Weekly Trinity Journal* (Weaverville, CA, July 30, 1864), 1.

6. Ric Murphy, *Freedom Road: An American Family Saga from Jamestown to World War* (Franklin Pearson Publishing: Alexandria, VA 2019), 177.

7. John G. Nicolay, and John Hay. *Abraham Lincoln: A History*, Vol. 4 (New Century Press: New York, 2009), 160.

8. Joshua Zeitz, *Lincoln's Boys: John Hay, John Nicolay and the War for Lincoln's Image* (Viking Press: New York, 2014), 273.

9. Nicolay and Hay, *Abraham Lincoln: A History*, 416.

10. Poole, *On Hallowed Ground, The Story of Arlington National Cemetery*, 296.

11. *Ibid.*, 11.

12. "Record of Council Minutes November 9, 1863," *Richmond at War: The Minutes of the City Council, 1861–1865*, Ed. Louis H. Manarin (University of North Carolina Press: Chapel Hill, 1966), 391.

13. Rick Atkinson, *Where Valor Rests: Arlington National Cemetery* (National Geographic Society: Washington, D.C., 2007), 22. ISBN 1-4262-0089-7.

14. Liebertz, *A Guide to the African American Heritage of Arlington County*, Virginia, 3.

15. Adjutant General's Office Report: *Mount Vernon Relics*, 41st Congress, 2nd Session, House of Representatives, Report No. 36, Washington, January 29, 1870.

16. McElya, The *Politics of Mourning*, 40.

17. *Ibid.*, 35.

18. Nelligan, *Arlington House*, 399.

19. McElya, *The Politics of Mourning*, 39–40.

20. Atkinson, *Where Valor Rests*, 25.

21. Chase, "Ancient Custis Slave Remembers Brilliant Arlington Events," 5.

22. Cooling, III, and Owen, II, *Mr. Lincoln's Forts*, 94–100.

23. David W. Miller, *Second Only to Grant: Quartermaster General Montgomery C. Meigs* (White Mane Books: Shippensburg, PA, 2000), 95. ISBN 1-57249-212-0.

24. Civil War battles were named differently by the Union and Confederate armies. The Union named battles for natural features such as bodies of water near or at the battle. The Confederates named battles after the closest town or man-made landmark.

25. David W. Miller *Second Only to Grant: Quartermaster General Montgomery C. Meigs* (White Mane Books: Shippensburg, PA, 2000), 258. ISBN 1-57249-212-0.

26. Parzych, *Arlington National Cemetery*, 21–22.

Chapter 6

1. *Abraham Lincoln's Great Speeches* (Dover Thrift Editions: Toronto, Canada, 1991), 50.

2. Holzer, *Lincoln President Elect*.

3. Stanley Harrold, *Lincoln and the Abolitionists*.

4. *Abraham Lincoln's Great Speeches*, 56.

5. Chandra Manning, *What This Cruel War Was Over: Soldiers, Slavery and the Civil War* (Alfred A. Knopf: New York, 2007), 21.

6. John Keegan, *The American Civil War: A Military History* (Alfred A. Knopf: New York, 2009), 333–334.

7. Jaime Amanda Martinez, "Slavery During the Civil War," *Encyclopedia Virginia* (Richmond, VA, 2015).

8. "The Contrabands at Fort Monroe," *Atlantic Monthly* (Vol. 0008, No. 49, November 1861), 627.

9. "Monthly Record of Current Events," *Harpers New Monthly Magazine* (Vol. 0023, No. 134, July 1861), 257.

10. "Where Will the Rebellion Leave Us?" *Atlantic Monthly* (Vol. 08, No. 46, August 1861), 241.

11. James M. McPherson, *For Cause and Comrades: Why Men Fought the Civil War* (Oxford University Press: New York, 1997), 117.

12. Joseph Wheelan, *Libby Prison Breakout: The Daring Escape from the Notorious Civil War Prison* (Public Affairs: New York, 2010), 131.

13. Frederick Douglass, "How to Win the War," *Douglass Monthly* (May 1861). Transcript at http://rbscp.lib.rochester.edu/4373. Accessed June 25, 2017.

14. *Ibid.*

15. United States War Department, *The War of the Rebellion: A Compilation of the*

Official Records of the Union and Confederate Armies; Series 1, Vol. 2, 668. Letter of Major General Benjamin F. Butler to Lieutenant General Scott, June 6, 1861. Accessed at http://ebooks.library.cornell.edu on June 24, 2017.

16. "The Contrabands at Fort Monroe," *Atlantic Monthly* (Vol. 0008, No. 49 November 1861), 628.

17. "Contrabands on a War Footing," *The National Republican* (Washington, D.C., January 1, 1862), 2.

18. "The Blacks at Washington," *Winchester Daily Bulletin* (Winchester, VA, February 7, 1863), 4.

19. Butts, *African American Medicine in Washington, D.C.*, 55–57.

20. "The Contrabands at Fort Monroe," 630.

21. "General News," *Alexandria Gazette* (Alexandria, VA, October 25, 1862), 1.

22. "Contrabands," *Evening Star* (Washington, D.C., February 13, 1862), 3.

23. Joseph P. Reidy, "Coming from the Shadow of the Past: The Transition from Slavery to Freedom at Freedmen's Village," *The Virginia Magazine of History and Biography* (October 1987, Vol. 95, Number 4), 405.

24. Reidy, "Coming from the Shadow of the Past," 407.

25. Jim Downs, *Sick from Freedom: African American Illness and Suffering During the Civil War and Reconstruction* (Oxford University Press: New York, 2012), 6. ISBN 978-0-19-975872-2.

26. "The Blacks at Washington," *Winchester Daily Bulletin* (Winchester, TN, February 7, 1863), 4.

27. Janke, *A Guide to the Civil War Washington, D.C.*, 99.

28. Frederick Douglass, "What Shall be Done with the Slaves If Emancipated" *Douglass Monthly* (Rochester, NY, January 2, 1862).

29. United State War Department, *The War of the Rebellion: A Compilation of the Official Records of the Union and Confederate Armies*, 40–41.

30. "Death of Col. Ellsworth," *The National Republican* (Washington, D.C. May 25, 1861), 2.

31. "President's Persistent Sorrow," *Evening Star* (Washington, D.C., May 27, 1861), 2.

32. "Reception of Col. Ellsworth's Remains at New York," *Evening Star* (Washington, D.C., May 27, 1861), 3.

33. "General News," *Alexandria Gazette* (Alexandria, VA, May 17, 1862), 1.

34. Roberta Schildt, "Freedman's Village: Arlington, Virginia, 1863–1900," (Arlington Historical Society, Vol. 7, Number 4), 11. Accessed January 2017, Arlington's Civil War Memorial Website.

35. "Council Proceedings," *The Evening Star* (Washington, D.C., May 13, 1862), 3.

36. Sandra Fitzpatrick, and Maria Goodwin, *The Guide to Black Washington* (Hippocrene Books: New York, 1990), 148. ISBN: 0-87052-832-7.

37. *Freedom: A Documentary History of Emancipation, Series 1, Vol. II, The Wartime Genesis of Free Labor*, Ed. Ira Berlin et al (Cambridge University Press, New York, 1993), 246–248.

38. Dennee, "African-American Civilians in Section 27 of Arlington National Cemetery, 1864–1867," 2.

39. Schildt, "Freedman's Village: Arlington, Virginia, 1863–1900," 11.

40. Fitzpatrick and Goodwin, *The Guide to Black Washington*, 148.

41. Anthony Waskie, *Philadelphia and the Civil War: Arsenal of the Union* (History Press: Charleston, SC, 2011), 52–62.

42. "Contrabands," *Alexandria Gazette* (Alexandria, VA, December 10, 1863), 1.

43. "The Sufferings of the 'Contrabands,'" *Alexandria Gazette* (Alexandria, VA, November 12, 1863), 3.

44. Schildt, "Freedman's Village: Arlington, Virginia, 1863–1900," 11.

Chapter 7

1. *Freedom: A Documentary History of Emancipation, Series 1, Vol. II, The Wartime Genesis of Free Labor*, 76–77.

2. "How the Proclamation Works in Virginia," *Chicago Tribune* (January 16, 1862), 3.

3. United States Census, Population by Color and Condition, 588. United States Census, 1870, Table I., Population of the United States (By States and Territories) in the Aggregate, and as White, Colored, Free Colored, Slave, Chinese, and Indian at Each Census.

4. Smallpox, a highly infectious disease, passed between humans when the infected had visible rash. The most infectious version,

variola major, had a mortality rate of up to 35 percent, and was responsible for more than 300 million deaths worldwide in the twentieth century alone. The disease circulated for thousands of years, but was finally eliminated with the last case diagnosed in 1977.

5. Stephen Coss, *The Fever of 1721: The Epidemic That Revolutionized Medicine and American Politics* (Simon & Schuster: New York, 2016). ISBN 978 147678308X.

6. "Another Small-Pox Case," *Evening Star* (Washington, D.C., January 21, 1862), Image 3, Column 3.

7. Downs, *Sick from Freedom*, 99.

8. *Ibid.*, 211.

9. *Ibid.*, 107.

10. Kathryn Shively Meier, *Nature's Civil War: Common Soldiers and the Environment in 1862 Virginia* (University of North Carolina Press: Chapel Hill, 2003).

11. Downs, *Sick from Freedom*, 3–4.

12. *Freedom: A Documentary History of Emancipation, Series 1, Vol. II, The Wartime Genesis of Free Labor*, 78.

13. Cooling, III, and Owen, II, *Mr. Lincoln's Forts*, 94–99.

14. Shauna Devine, *Learning from the Wounded: The Civil War and the Rise of American Medical Science* (University of North Carolina Press, Chapel Hill, 2014), 5–8.

15. David Hacker, "A Census-Based Count of the Civil War Dead," *Civil War History* (Vol. 57, Number 4, December 2011, Project MUSE, Baltimore) 307–348.

16. Drew Gilpin Faust, *Death and Dying* (National Park Service, U.S. Department of the Interior) https://www.nps.gov/nr/travel/national_cemeteries/death.html. Accessed September 22, 2017.

17. Stephen B. Oates, *A Woman of Valor: Clara Barton and the Civil War* (The Free Press: New York, 1994), 95. ISBN 0-02-923405-0.

18. Robert E. Denny, *The Civil War Years: A Day-by-Day Chronicle* (Gramercy Books: New York, 1998), 199. ISBN 0-517-18945-3.

19. Pamela D. Toler, *Heroines of Mercy Street: The Real Nurses of the Civil War* (Little, Brown & Co.: New York, 2016), 180. ISBN 978-0-316-39207-5.

20. *Ibid.*

21. Drew Gilpin Faust, *This Republic of Suffering: Death and the American Civil War* (Vintage Books: New York, 2008).

22. John Harley Warner, and Lawrence Rizzolo, "Anatomical Instruction and Training for Professionalism from the 19th to the 21st Centuries," *Clinical Anatomy 19* (2006), 403–414.

23. Devine, *Learning from the Wounded*, 53–57.

24. Michael Sappol, *A Traffic of Dead Bodies: Anatomy and Embodied Social Identity in Nineteenth-Century America* (Princeton University Press: Princeton, NJ, 2004).

25. Stanley B. Burns, "Wound Infection," (Technical Notes to PBS's *Mercy Street*, 2014). http://www.pbs.org/mercy-street/uncover-history/behind-lens/wound-infection/. Accessed June 7, 2017.

26. J.N. Hays, *The Burdens of Disease: Epidemics and Human Response in Western History* (Rutgers University Press: Piscataway, NJ, 2009), 214–42 ISBN 978-0-8135-4613-1.

27. Robert E. Hicks, "'The Popular Dose with Doctors:' Quinine and the American Civil War," *Distillations* (Chemical Heritage Foundation)https://www.chemheritage.org/distillations/magazine/the-popular-dose-with-doctors-quinine-and-the-american-civil-war. Accessed June 17, 2017.

28. Hicks, "The Popular Dose with Doctors."

29. "The Evolution of Penn's Medical School in the Middle and Late Nineteenth Century," *The 1860s: The Civil War*. University of Pennsylvania Medical School Archives. http://www.archives.upenn.edu/histy/features/medschool_evolution/5_1860s.html. Accessed June 17, 2017.

30. Jane E. Schultz, *Women at the Front: Hospital Workers in Civil War America* (University of North Carolina Press: Chapel Hill, 2004), 1, 169–170.

31. Robert G. Slawson, "African American Physicians in the Civil War Era," National Civil War Medicine Museum, http://www.civilwarmed.org/africanamericandrs. Accessed September 21, 2017.

32. Gates and Higginbotham, Vol. 1, 6.

33. "Anderson Ruffin Abbot (1837–1913)" http://www.blackpast.org/aah/abbott-anderson-ruffin-1837-1913. Accessed October 19, 2017.

34. Harry S. Robinson "Anderson Ruffin Abbott, MD, 1837–1913," *Journal of the National Medical Association*, Vol. 72, No. 2 (Silver Spring, MD, 1980), 713.

35. *Ibid.*, 715.
36. Butts, *African American Medicine in Washington D.C.*, 123.
37. *Ibid.*, 53–58.
38. John David Smith, *Black Soldiers in Blue: African American Troops in the Civil War Era* (University of North Carolina Press, Chapel Hill, 2002), xvi–xviii ISBN 0-8078-2741-X.
39. Gretchen Long, *Doctoring Freedom: The Politics of African American Medical Care in Slavery and Emancipation* (University of North Carolina Press, Chapel Hill, 2012), 74. ISBN: 978-1-4696-2833-2.
40. *Ibid.*, 51.
41. Joseph J. Ellis, *His Excellency George Washington* (Alfred A. Knopf: New York, 2004), 87.
42. "The Washington Star Says," *Alexandria Gazette* (Alexandria, VA, May 23, 1863), 2.
43. Schultz, *Women at the Front*, 31.
44. R. Gregory Lande, *Psychological Consequences of the American Civil War* (McFarland: Jefferson, NC, 2016), 10.
45. Michael A. Bellesiles, *1877: America's Year of Living Violently* (The New Press: New York, 2010).

Chapter 8

1. Murphy, *Freedom Road*, 181.
2. Rose, *Arlington County Virginia*, 122.
3. Schildt, *Freedman's Village: Arlington, Virginia, 1863–1900*, 11–14.
4. Rose, *Arlington County Virginia: A History*, 122–124.
5. Reidy, "Coming from the Shadow of the Past," 409.
6. Consolidated Statement of Contraband Tax, Captain C. H. Tompkins, A.Q.M., U.S. Army, from 1st February to 31st Decembers 1863. (CQMGT. MSS. R. G. 92). Courtesy of Arlington Public Library.
7. Graham D. Welch, "Ile À Vache and Colonization: the Tragic End of Lincoln's 'Suicidal Folly,'" *The Gettysburg College Journal of the Civil War Era*, Vol. 4, Article 5 (Gettysburg, PA, April 2014), 45–81.
8. Eric Foner, "Lincoln and Colonization," *Our Lincoln: New Perspectives on Lincoln and His World* (W.W. Norton: New York, 2009), 135–66.ISBN 978-0-393-06756-9.
9. Welch, "Ile À Vache and Colonization," 53.
10. *Ibid.*, 56–63.
11. "Failure of the A Vache Colonization Scheme," *Alexandria Gazette* (Alexandria, VA, March 22, 1864), 1.
12. "The Wartime Genesis of Free Labor," *Freedom: A Documentary History of Emancipation*, 308.
13. Schildt, *Freedman's Village: Arlington, Virginia, 1863–1900*, 14.
14. McElya, *The Politics of Mourning*, 62.
15. McElya, *The Politics of Mourning*, 61.
16. Schildt, *Freedman's Village: Arlington, Virginia, 1863–1900*, 14.
17. *Ibid.*, 11–14.
18. *Ibid.*, 17.
19. Margaret Washington, *Sojourner Truth's America* (University of Illinois Press: Chicago, 2009), 318. ISBN 978-0-252-03419-0.
20. *Ibid.*, 317.
21. Kate Clifford Larson, *Bound for the Promised Land: Harriet Tubman, Portrait of an American Hero* (Random House: New York, 2004), 46. ISBN 0-345-45627-0.
22. Washington, *Sojourner Truth's America*, 318.
23. *Ibid.*, 319.
24. Schildt, *Freedman's Village: Arlington, Virginia, 1863–1900*, 14.
25. Nell Irvin Painter, *Sojourner Truth: A Life, a Symbol* (W.W. Norton: New York, 1996), 215, quoting a letter to Amy Post, October 1, 1865.
26. Eric Foner, *A Short History of Reconstruction* (Harper & Row: New York, 1990), 223. ISBN 0-06-096431-6.
27. "Letter of John C. Underwood," *Alexz* 2.
28. Bren Tarter, "Disenfranchisement," *Encyclopedia Virginia* (Virginia Foundation of the Humanities: Richmond, 19 July 2016). Accessed 31 March 2018.
29. Liebertz, *A Guide to the African American Heritage of Arlington County*, 8.
30. *Ibid.*
31. McElya, *The Politics of Mourning*, 95–96.

Chapter 9

1. From the folder 1 of the Profitt Family Letters, #3408-z, Southern Historical Col-

lection, The Wilson Library, University of North Carolina at Chapel Hill.

2. Douglas E. Campbell, and Thomas B. Sherman, *On the Potomac* (Lulu Publishing Services: Morrisville, NC, 2014), 49.

3. David W. Miller, *Second Only to Grant: Quartermaster General Montgomery C. Meigs* (White Mane Books, Shippensburg, PA, 2000), 101. ISBN 1-57249-212-0.

4. "As Might Have Been Expected," *The Potter Journal* (Coudersport, PA, August 14, 1861), 2.

5. Thomas M. O'Brien, and Oliver Diefendorf, *General Orders of the War Department, Embracing the Years 1861, 1862 & 1863, Adapted Specifically for the Use of the Army and Navy of the United States*, Vol. 1 (Derby & Miller: New York, 1864), 158.

6. Mark E. Neely Jr., *The Civil War and the Limits of Destruction* (Harvard University Press: Cambridge, MA, 2007), 166–167.

7. *Ibid.*, 211–213.

8. "Mortality of Federal Prisoners in Rebel Hospitals," *Soldiers Journal* (Camp Distribution, Virginia, May 13, 1864), 4.

9. "The Effect of the Hatteras Affair on Naval Stores," *Newbern Weekly Progress* (New Bern, NC, September 17, 1861), 4.

10. Hanna, *Arlington House: The Robert E. Lee Memorial*, 84.

11. Civil War Casualties, https://www.civilwar.org/learn/articles/civil-war-casualties. Accessed December 15, 2017.

12. A.L. Long, *Memoirs of Robert E. Lee: His Military and Personal History* (The Blue and Grey Press: Secaucus, NJ, 1983), 40. ISBN 0-89009-694-5.

13. Pryor, *Reading the Man*, 312–313.

14. *National Register of Historic Places Registration Form* (United States Department of the Interior, National Park Service, February 24, 2014), 39.

15. Arlington National Cemetery has developed a numbering system for all graves. William Henry Christman (27:19) is buried in Section 27, Grave 19. A searchable list of graves is located at: http://ancexplorer.army.mil/publicwmv/. This book will use the format Name (Section-Grave) to denote all of the soldiers buried at Arlington National Cemetery.

16. Rick Bodenschatz, "The William Henry Christman Story," http://www.tobyhannatwphistory.org/assets/William Christ-manHistory.pdf. Accessed November 30, 2017.

17. Atkinson, *Where Valor Rests*, 21.

18. Miller, *Second Only to Grant*, 259.

19. Poole, *On Hallowed Ground*, 63.

20. "Gen. Lee's Land," *The Liberator* (Boston, July 15, 1864), 3.

21. Miller, *Second Only to Grant*, 241.

22. Poole, *On Hallowed Ground*, 64–65.

23. "Rebel Soldiers," *Alexandria Gazette* (Alexandria, VA, May 31, 1871), 2.

24. R.D.B., "Letter from Virginia," *New National Era* (Washington, D.C., June 8, 1871), 1.

25. McElya, *The Politics of Mourning*, 128.

Chapter 10

1. Martin Binkin et al, *Blacks and the Military* (Brookings Institute: Washington, D.C., 1982), 14–15. ISBN 0-8157-0974-9.

2. *Ibid.*, 15.

3. "Confederate Memorial," https://www.arlingtoncemetery.mil/Explore/Monuments-and-Memorials/Confederate-Memorial. Accessed March 31, 2018.

4. Murphy, *Freedom Road*, 192.

5. *Ibid.*, 196.

6. William K. Klingaman, *Abraham Lincoln and the Road to Emancipation, 1861–1865* (Viking Penguin Books: New York, 2001), 276. ISBN 0-670-86754-3.

7. *Ibid.*

8. *Ibid.*

9. Dodge, George, W., "The Burial of United States Colored Troops at Arlington National Cemetery," *Arlington Historical Magazine* (October 1997), 46.

10. Hondon B. Hargrove, *Black Union Soldiers in the Civil War* (McFarland: Jefferson, NC), 183. ISBN 0-89950-337-3.

11. Salmon, John S., *The Official Virginia Civil War Battlefield Guide* (Stackpole Books: Mechanicsburg, PA, 2001), 398. ISBN 0-8117-2868-4.

12. Hargrove, *Black Union Soldiers in the Civil War*, 183.

13. Charles H. Wesley, and Patricia W. Romero, *Negro Americans in the Civil War: From Slavery to Citizenship* (Publishers Company, Inc: New York, 1967), 93.

14. John David Smith, *Black Soldiers in Blue: African American Troops in the Civil War Era* (University of North Carolina Press,

Chapel Hill, 2002), 59. ISBN 0-8078-2741-X.

15. George Washington Williams, and John David Smith, *A History of the Negro Troops in the War of the Rebellion, 1861-1865* (Fordham University Press: New York, reprint, 2012), 248.

16. Wesley and Romero, *Negro Americans in the Civil War: From Slavery to Citizenship*, 93.

17. Hargrove, *Black Union Soldiers in the Civil War*, 185.

18. Hargrove, *Black Union Soldiers in the Civil War*, 185.

19. Wesley and Romero, *Negro Americans in the Civil War: From Slavery to Citizenship*, 93.

20. Smith, *Black Soldiers in Blue: African American Troops in the Civil War Era*, 59.

21. *Ibid.*, 62.

22. Benjamin F. Butler, *Autobiography and Personal Reminiscences of Major General Benjamin F. Butler: A Review of His Legal, Political and Military Career* (A.M. Thayer Publishers: Boston, 1892), 742.

23. *Ibid.*

24. *Ibid.*, 743.

25. "The Mettle of Butler's Soldiers," *The Baltimore Sun* (August 2, 2001), http://articles.baltimoresun.com/2001-08-02/features/0108020166_1_medal-of-honor-butler-fought. Accessed June 30, 2018.

26. Joseph T. Wilson, *The Black Phalanx: African American Soldiers in the War of Independence, The War of 1812, and the Civil War* (Project Gutenberg EBook, February 21, 2010), 183–192. http://www.gutenberg.org/files/31339/31339-h/31339-h.htm.

27. Korda, *Clouds of Glory*, 647.

28. Freeman, *R.E. Lee: A Biography*, 58.

29. Patrick A. Schroeder "Out of the Checker-board," *Civil War Times*, Vol. 54, No. 2 (April 2015), 62.

30. Freeman, *R.E. Lee: A Biography*, 59.

31. Freeman, *R.E. Lee: A Biography*, 67.

32. *Ibid.*, 68.

33. Korda, *Clouds of Glory*, 650.

34. Andrew A. Humphreys, *The Virginia Campaign of 1864 and 1865: The Army of the Potomac and the Army of the James* (Charles Scribners' Sons: New York, 1883), 383–384.

35. Korda, *Clouds of Glory*, 651.

36. *Ibid.*, 651.

37. *Ibid.*, 655.

38. *Ibid.*, 658.

39. *Ibid.*, 667–668.

40. Schroeder, "Out of the Checker-board," 62. In 2013-2014 the Appomattox 1865 Foundation, the friends group for Appomattox Court House National Historical Park, obtained a grant so a researcher could look through the Compiled Military Service Record of each soldier in the nine USCT regiments that participated in the Appomattox Campaign and account for each soldier present in April 1865. The count resulting from that research found that the six USCT regiments on the battlefield the morning of April 9, 1865, numbered between 4,000 and 5,000 men.

41. Chernow, *Grant*, 510.

42. National Archives, *Letter from William Syphax to President A. Johnson*, RG 60 NAID 6782945.

43. *Ibid.*

44. 39th United States Congress, *An Act for the Relief of Maria Syphax, 1865-1867*, Vol. 14, Chapter 121, 589.

Chapter 11

1. Dennee, "African-American Civilians in Section 27 of Arlington National Cemetery, 1864–1867," 2–3.

2. *Ibid.*, 8n14.

3. *Ibid.*, 7.

4. Dennee, "African-American Civilians in Section 27 of Arlington National Cemetery, 1864–1867," 24.

5. Jim Downs, *Sick from Freedom* (Oxford University Press: New York, 2012), 72–73, 120–121.

6. Dennee, "African-American Civilians in Section 27 of Arlington National Cemetery, 1864–1867," 11.

7. *Ibid.*, 7–8.

8. *Ibid.*, 40.

9. *Ibid.*, 202.

10. *Ibid.*, 204.

11. *Ibid.*, 205.

12. *Ibid.*, 211.

13. *Ibid.*, 221.

14. Dennee, "A District of Columbia Freedman's Cemetery in Virginia?" 123.

Chapter 12

1. Joseph T. Wilson, *The Black Phalanx: African American Soldiers in the War of In-

dependence, The War of 1812, and the Civil War 199. See also James Parton, *General Butler in New Orleans: History of the Administration of the Department of the Gulf in the Year 1862, with an Account of the Capture of New Orleans, and the General, Civil and Military* (Mason Brothers: New York, 1864), 521–522.

2. Kristin E. Holmes, "Mayor Kenney References Starbucks Arrests at Ceremony Honoring African American Civil War Troops," *Philadelphia Inquirer* (Philadelphia, PA, April 24, 2018) http://www.philly.com/philly/news/starbucks-arrests-african-american-civil-war-troops-philadelphia-20180421.html. Accessed June 30, 2018.

3. "Travel Over the Bridges," *Evening Star* (Washington, D.C., May 29, 1868), 1.

4. "Decorating the Graves," *New York Herald* (June 1, 1868), 4.

5. "Decoration Day—Ceremonies at Arlington," *New Era* (Washington, D.C., June 2, 1870), 2.

6. Poole, *On Hallowed Ground*, 80–81.

7. *Ibid.*, 81.

8. Mitch Landrieu, *In the Shadow of Statues: A White Southerner Confronts History* (Viking: New York, 2018), 161–207.

9. Harry Shannon, "The Rambler," *The Evening Star* (Washington, D.C., August 17, 1912), 11.

10. Landrieu, *In the Shadow of Statues*, 172.

11. Poole, *On Hallowed Ground*, 84.

12. Dennee, "African-American Civilians in Section 27 of Arlington National Cemetery, 1864–1867," 13.

13. *Ibid.*

14. "The Rambler," *The Evening Star* (Washington, D.C., August 17, 1912), Part I., 11. *Chronicling America: Historic American Newspapers*. Lib. of Congress. http://chroniclingamerica.loc.gov/lccn/sn83045462/1912-08-17/ed-1/seq-11/.

15. Charles W. Hanna, *African American Recipients of the Medal of Honor: A Biographical Dictionary, Civil War Through Vietnam War* (McFarland:, Jefferson, NC, 2002), 3.

16. "Civil War Medal of Honor Recipients." United States Army Center of Military History. August 6, 2009, https://history.army.mil/html/moh/indianwars.html#SHAW. Accessed September 26, 2019.

17. *Ibid.*

18. Smith, *Black Soldiers in Blue: African American Troops in the Civil War Era*, 62.

19. George W. Dodge, "The Burial of United States Colored Troops at Arlington National Cemetery," *Arlington Historical Magazine*, Vol. 11, No. 1. (October 1997), 43.

20. *Ibid.*, 45.

21. *Ibid.*

22. Smith, *Black Soldiers in Blue: African American Troops in the Civil War Era*, 58.

23. Kenneth Chelst, *Exodus and Emancipation: Biblical and African-American Slavery* (New York, NY, 2009), 264. ISBN 978-9655240207.

24. William Gladstone, *Men of Color* (Thomas Publications: Gettysburg, PA, 1993), 50.

25. *Freedom: A Documentary History of Emancipation 1861–1867, Series II Black Military Experience*, 93.

26. *Ibid.*, 93–94.

27. Gladstone, *Men of Color*, 202.

28. *Ibid.*, 49. See also: Rayford, Logan W. and Winston, Michael R., eds., *Dictionary of American Negro Biography* (W.W. Norton & Co.: New York, 1967), 19; and Morais, Herbert M., *The History of the Afro-American in Medicine* (The Publishers Agency: Cornwells Heights, PA, 1978), 37.

29. Logan, *Dictionary of American Negro Biography*, 19.

30. *Freedom: A Documentary History of Emancipation 1861–1867, Series II Black Military Experience*, 356–357.

31. Pension of Alexander T. Augusta, widow application number 49875, National Archives.

32. Herbert M. Morais, *The History of the Afro-American in Medicine* (The Publishers Agency: Cornwells Heights, PA, 1978), 37.

33. Wesley and Romero, *Negro Americans in the Civil War*, 103–104.

34. Morais, *The History of the Afro-American in Medicine*, 37.

35. *Freedom, A Documentary History of Emancipation 1861–1867, Series II Black Military Experience*, 356–357.

36. *Dictionary of American Negro Biography*, ed. Logan W. Rayford and Winston, Michael R Winston (W.W. Norton & Co.: New York, 1967), 19. See also: Morais, Herbert M., *The History of the Negro in Medicine, International Library of Negro Life and*

History (Publishers Company: New York, 1968), 37. ASIN: B000NYXP1O.

37. Wesley and Romero, *Negro Americans in the Civil War: From Slavery to Citizenship*, 103–104.

38. *Freedom: A Documentary History of Emancipation 1861–1867, Series II Black Military Experience*, 356–357.

39. Gladstone, *Men of Color*, 49.

40. *Dictionary of American Negro Biography*, 19.

41. *Ibid.*

42. Morais, *The History of the Afro-American in Medicine*, 213.

43. *Ibid.*, 57.

44. Henry Louis Gates, and Evelyn Brooks Higginbotham, *African American National Biography*, Vol. 1 (Oxford University Press: New York, 2008), 199–200.

45. Lewis F. Emilio, *A Brave Black Regiment: History of the Fifty-Forth Regiment of Massachusetts Volunteer Infantry, 1863–1865* (The Boston Book Company: Boston, 1894), 336.

46. Brian Pohanka, *Carnival of Death: America's Civil War* (Empire Press: Leesburg, VA, 1991), 30–36.

47. Gladstone, *Men of Color*, 58.

48. *Ibid.*

Chapter 13

1. United States Department of the Interior, National Park Service, *National Register of Historic Places Registration Form*, February 24, 2014, 43.

2. *Congressional Record*, 43rd United States Congress, 2nd Session, March 2, 1875, 2054.

3. *Ibid.*

4. *Ibid.*

5. *National Register of Historic Places Registration Form*, 43.

6. National Archives and Records Administration Freedman's Bureau Preservation Project, 2002. https://www.archives.gov/files/research/microfilm/m1902.pdf.

7. James M. McPherson, *Ordeal by Fire: The Civil War*, Vol. 2 (McGraw Hill: New York, 2001), 435. ISBN 0-07-231736-1.

8. *Ibid.*, 39.

9. Milton Lomask, *Andrew Johnson: President on Trial* (Octagon Books: New York, 1973), 142. ISBN0-374-95082-2.

10. Foner, *A Short History of Reconstruction*, 77.

11. *Addresses and Ceremonies at the New Year's Festival to the Freedmen on Arlington Heights and Statistics and Statements of the Educational Condition of the Colored People in the Southern Sates and Other Facts* (McGill & Witherow: Washington, D.C., 1867), 7.

12. *Ibid.*, 8.

13. *Ibid.*, 9.

14. Foner, *A Short History of Reconstruction*, 68.

15. McElya, *The Politics of Mourning*, 128.

16. *Ibid.*, 102.

17. "Arlington House Woodlands," http://vnps.org/conservation/virginia-native-plant-registry-sites-3/arlington-house-woodlands/. Accessed June 30, 2018.

18. J.A. Commerford, Superintendent of the National Cemetery, *Letter to Lt. Colonel George B. Dandy, Deputy, November 12, 1887.* NARA RG 92, Office of the Quartermaster General, 1.

19. Liebertz, *A Guide to the African American Heritage of Arlington County*, 8.

20. "John Brice Syphax," http://syphaxfamily.com/The_People.html. Accessed June 30, 2018.

21. John B. Syphax, *Letter to William C. Endicott, January 18, 1888.* NARA RG 92, Office of the Quartermaster General, 1.

22. *Ibid.*, 1–2.

23. *Ibid.*, 2.

24. *Ibid.*

25. *Ibid.*, 2–3.

26. *Ibid.*, 3.

27. Poole, *On Hallowed Ground*, 98.

28. *Ibid.*

29. *Ibid.*, 99.

30. *National Register of Historic Places Registration Form*, 6.

Chapter 14

1. National Archives, "General Robert E. Lee's Parole and Citizenship," *Prologue Magazine*, Spring, 2005, Vol. 37, No. 1.

2. Nelligan, *Arlington House*, 418–419.

3. Walter Clark, Ed., *Histories of the Several Regiments and Battalions from North Carolina, in the Great War, 1861–1865* (E.M. Uzzell: Raleigh, NC, 1901), 242.

4. Congress adopted the Fourteenth Amendment (Amendment XIV) to the

United States Constitution on July 9, 1868, as one of the Reconstruction Amendments, in response to physical and administrative violence being perpetuated against the newly freed enslaved all across the south. Southern states were forced to ratify it in order to regain representation in Congress.

5. Mickey McElya, *The Politics of Mourning: Death and Honor in Arlington National Cemetery* (Harvard University Press: Cambridge, Massachusetts, 2016), 17–24.

6. Judith Pizarro, Roxanne Cohen Silver, and JoAnn Prause, "Physical and Mental Health Costs of Traumatic War Experiences Among Civil War Veterans," *Archives of General Psychiatry* (Chicago, Vol. 62, No. 2, February 2006), 193–200.

7. Holzer, *Lincoln and the Power of the Press*, 555–566.

8. Benjamin R. Justesen, Ed., *His Own Words: The Writings, Speeches, and Letters of George Heny White* (iUniverse: Lincoln, NE 2004), 167.

9. Stephen Middleton, Ed., *Black Congressmen During Reconstruction: A Documentary Sourcebook* (Greenwood Press: Westport, CT, 2002), xi.

10. John Warwick Daniel, "Oration of Senator Daniel," *Proceedings of the Third Annual Meeting and Reunion of the United Confederate Veterans*, held at New Orleans, LA, April 8–9, 1892, 24–46.

11. "The Best That Could Be Under the Circumstances" *Lexington Gazette* (Lexington, VA, June 13, 1902), 1.

12. Tarter, "Disenfranchisement," *Encyclopedia Virginia*, Accessed March 31, 2018.

13. Robert E. Lee, *Paper of the Lee Family*, Lee Papers (University of Virginia Archives, Charlottesville, December 13, 1866).

14. Abraham Lincoln's Second Inaugural Address, Saturday, March 4, 1865.

15. Ibid.

16. Heather Cox Richardson, *West from Appomattox, the Reconstruction of America after the Civil War* (Yale University Press, New Haven, Connecticut, 2007), 41. ISBN 978-0-300-11052-4.

17. Ric Murphy, *Freedom Road: An American Family Saga from Jamestown to World War*, Franklin Pearson Publishing, Alexandria, VA, 2019, 216.

18. Murphy, *Freedom Road*, 219.

19. Avery Craven, *Reconstruction: The Ending of the Civil War* (Holt, Rinehart & Winston: New York, 1969), 88–89. ISBN 03-073245-X.

20. National Archives, General Robert E. Lee's Parole and Citizenship, *Prologue Magazine*, Spring, 2005, Vol. 37, No. 1.

21. Foner, *A Short History of Reconstruction, 1863–1877*, 110.

22. Ibid., 106–113.

23. Ibid., 146.

24. Grant Ron Chernow, (Penguin Press: New York, 2017), 613.

25. Ibid., 147.

26. Chernow, *Grant*, 609–612.

27. "Another Democratic Murder," *The New Era* (Washington, D.C., June 2, 1870), 2.

28. McElya, *The Politics of Mourning*, 133.

29. *National Register of Historic Places Registration Form*, 19.

30. Ibid., 25.

31. William A. Blair, *Cities of the Dead: Contesting the Memory of the Civil War in the South, 1865–1914*. (University of North Carolina Press: Chapel Hill, 2004), 177. ISBN 0-8078-2896-3.

32. Ibid., 180.

33. Lloyd Robinson, *The Stolen Election: Hayes versus Tilden—1876* (Tom Doherty Associates: New York, 2001.) ISBN 978-0-7653-0206-9.

34. Bellesiles, *1877: America's Year of Living Violently*, ix–x.

35. McElya, *The Politics of Mourning*, 129.

36. Blair, *Cities of the Dead*, 182.

37. Landrieu, *In the Shadow of Statues*, 171–200.

38. Michael B. Chesson, *Richmond After the War, 1865–1890* (Virginia State Library: Richmond, 1891), 205. ISBN 0-88490-085-1.

39. Richmond's Growth," *Richmond Dispatch* (Richmond, VA, April 27, 1890), 8.

40. David D. Ryan *Richmond Illustrated: Unusual Stories of a City* (Dietz Press: Richmond, VA, 1993), 68.

41. "Partisan Fury, *Alexandria Gazette* (Alexandria, VA, May 31, 1890), 2.

42. "The Memory of Lee," *Richmond Dispatch* (Richmond, VA, February 9, 1890), 8.

43. "The Lee Statue," *Peninsula Enterprise* (Accomac Court-House, Virginia, May 10, 1890), 2.

44. Louisa May Alcott, *Civil War: Hospital Sketches* (Dover Publications: Mineola, NY, 2006), 54. ISBN-13: 978-0-486-449005.

45. Schultz, *Women at the Front: Hospital Workers in Civil War America*, 53.
46. McElya, *The Politics of Mourning*, 129.
47. *Ibid,*. 163, quoting Anita Newcomb.
48. Blair, *Cities of the Dead*, 188.
49. Kevin Phillips, *William McKinley* (Times Books: New York, 2003), 24. ISBN 0-8050-6953-4.
50. Murphy, *Freedom Road*, 278.
51. *Ibid.*, 279.
52. *Ibid.*
53. *Ibid.*
54. *Ibid.*
55. Blair, *Cities of the Dead*, 182.
56. Cynthia Mills, and Pamela Simpson, *Monuments to the Lost Cause, Women, Art, and the Landscapes of Southern Memory* (University of Tennessee Press: Knoxville, 2003), 150. ISBN 1-57233-272-7.
57. Blair, *Cities of the Dead*, 187.
58. Harriet A. Washington, *Medical Apartheid: The Dark History of Medical Experimentation on Black Americans from Colonial Times to the Present* (First Anchor Books, New York, 2006), 192. ISBN 978-0-7679-1547-2.
59. McElya, *The Politics of Mourning*, 169.
60. "Another Case of Death," *Alexandria Gazette* (Alexandria, VA, March 19, 1890), 2.
61. Blair, *Cities of the Dead*, 188.
62. "The New Virginia Law To Preserve Racial Integrity," *Virginia Health Bulletin* (Richmond, VA, March 1924), 1.
63. Washington, *Medical Apartheid*, 193.
64. *National Register of Historic Places Registration Form*, 25.
65. *National Register of Historic Places Registration Form*, 25.
66. "Captain Edwin Belcher," *Colored American* (Washington, D.C., November 2, 1900), 2.
67. Edmund L. Drago, *Black Politicians and Reconstruction in Georgia: a Splendid Failure* (Brown Thrasher Books: Athens, GA, 1992), 69-70.
68. Kathryn Allamong Jacob. *Testament to Union: Civil War Monuments in Washington, D.C.* (Johns Hopkins University Press: Baltimore, 1998), 165. ISBN 0-8018-5861-5.
69. Mills and Simpson, *Monuments to the Lost Cause*, 149-150.
70. *National Register of Historic Places Registration Form*, 25.
71. Recent interpretations of the monument have been changed to refer to it as a memorial, and the 1906 commemorative committee is now being referred to as the Arlington Confederate Memorial Association instead of its correct title, which was the Arlington Confederate Monument Association, as evidenced by period documentation.
72. Hillary A. Herbert, *History of the Arlington Confederate Monument at Arlington, Virginia* (United Daughters of the Confederacy, 1914), 77.
73. *Ibid.*
74. *Ibid.*
75. *Ibid.*
76. Chernow, *Grant*, 758-60.

Epilogue

1. *National Register of Historic Places Registration Form*, 1.
2. Gates and Higginbotham Vol. 3, 213-214.
3. *Ibid.*
4. Gates and Higginbotham, Vol. 5, 407-410.
5. Fitzpatrick and Goodwin, *The Guide to Black Washington*, 226.
6. Chase, "Ancient Custis Slave Remembers Brilliant Arlington Events," 5.
7. *Ibid.*
8. Dennee, 10.
9. Chase, "Ancient Custis Slave Remembers Brilliant Arlington Events," *The Sunday Star*, 5.
10. "Deaths," *Evening Star* (Washington, D.C., August 22, 1929), 9.
11. Enoch Aquila Chase, "The Mystery of Arlington," *Sunday Star Magazine* (Washington, D.C., December 15, 1929), 101.
12. "Former Custis Slave Buried in Arlington," *Evening Star* (Washington, D.C., August 23, 1929), 9.

Appendix II

1. Alexandria City Court Records, Virginia Deeds, Orders and Wills, January 1, 1858, 369-371. Certified by Alexandria County Court, September 11, 1858.

Appendix IV

1. Population of the States and Counties: 1790 to 1990, U. S. Department of Com-

merce Bureau of the Census. See Also, The Statistics of the Population of the United States, Class of Occupations, 1850, 1860 and 1870, U. S. Department of Commerce Bureau of the Census.

Bibliography

Books

Alcott, Louisa M., *Hospital Sketches and Camp and Fireside Sketches*, Roberts Brothers: Boston, MA, 1892.

Applebaum, Stanley, Ed., *Abraham Lincoln's Great Speeches*, Dover Thrift Editions, Toronto, Canada, 1991.

Atkinson, Rick, *Where Valor Rests: Arlington National Cemetery*, National Geographic Society: Washington, D.C., 2007.

Balogh, Brian, *A Government Out of Sight: The Mystery of National Authority in Nineteenth Century America*, Cambridge University Press: Cambridge, England, 2009.

Baptist, Edward E., *The Half Has Never Been Told: Slavery and the Making America*, Basic Books: New York, 2016.

Barber, James G., *Alexandria in the Civil War*, H.E. Howard, Inc.: Lynchburg, VA, 1988.

Bearss, Sara B., Ed., "Custis, George Washington Parke," *Dictionary of Virginia Biography*, Vol. 3, Library of Virginia: Richmond, 2006.

Beckert, Sven, *Empire of Cotton: A Global History*, Vintage Books: New York, 2014.

Bellesiles, Michael A., *1877: America's Year of Living Violently*, The New Press: New York, 2010.

Benbow, Mark E., "Holding the Line," *Arlington Magazine*, Arlington, VA, October 21, 2013.

Bentley, George, *A History of the Freedman's Bureau*, Octagon Books: New York, 1974.

Berlin, Ira, *Freedom's Soldiers: The Black Military Experience*, Cambridge University Press: New York, 1992.

Berlin, Ira, Steven F. Miller, Joseph P. Reidy, and Leslie S. Rowland, Eds., *Freedom: A Documentary History of Emancipation*, Series 1, Vol. 2, The Wartime Genesis of Free Labor, Cambridge University Press: New York, 1993.

Binkin, Martin, Mark Eitelberg, Alvin Schexnider, and Marvin Smith, *Blacks and the Military*, Brookings Institute: Washington, D.C., 1982.

Blair, William A., *Cities of the Dead: Contesting the Memory of the Civil War in the South, 1865-1914*, University of North Carolina Press: Chapel Hill, 2004.

Blassingame, John W., Ed., *Slave Testimony: Two Centuries of Letters, Speeches, and Interviews, and Autobiographies*, Louisiana State University Press: Baton Rouge, LA, 1977.

Blight, David, *Race and Reunion: The Civil War in American Memory*, Belknap Press of Harvard University Press: Cambridge, MA, 2001.

Brady, Patricia, *Martha Washington*, Penguin Press: New York, 2005.

Brandt, Lydia Mattice, *First in the Homes of His Countrymen: George Washington's Mount Vernon in the American Imagination*, University of Virginia Press: Charlottesville, 2016.

Brasher, David Glenn, "The Myth of Robert E. Lee and the Good Slave Master," *Daily Beast* (www.dailybeast.com), September 23, 2017.

Bryan, Helen, *Martha Washington: First Lady of Liberty*, Wiley: New York, 2002.

Burch, Thomas, *Catalogue No. 712: Relics of General Washington and a Variety of Historical Chinaware to Be Sold at 2:30 O'Clock*, at Thos. Birch Son's Book Auction Room, 1100 Chestnut Street, Philadelphia, PA, December 14, 1893.

Butler, Benjamin F., *Autobiography and Personal Reminiscences of Major General Benjamin F. Butler: A Review of His Legal, Political and Military Career*, A.M. Thayer Publishers: Boston, 1892.

Butts, Heather, *African American Medicine in Washington, D.C.: Healing the Capital During the Civil War Era*, History Press: Charleston, SC, 2014.

Campbell, Douglas E., and Thomas B. Sherman, *On the Potomac*, Lulu Publishing Services: Morrisville, NC, 2014.

Chelst, Kenneth, *Exodus and Emancipation: Biblical and African-American Slavery*: New York, 2009.

Chesson, Michael B., *Richmond After the War, 1865-1890*, Virginia State Library: Richmond, 1891.

Clark, Walter, Ed., *Histories of the Several Regiments and Battalions from North Carolina in the Great War, 1861-1865*, E.M. Uzzell: Raleigh, NC, 1901.

Codell, Carter, *The Rise of Causal Concepts of Disease: Case Histories*, Ashgate: Burlington, VT, 2003.

Cooling, III, Benjamin Franklin and Walton H. Owen II, *Mr. Lincoln's Forts: A Guide to the Civil War Defenses of Washington*, White Mane Publishing: Shippensburg, PA, 2009.

Coss, Stephen, *The Fever of 1721: The Epidemic That Revolutionized Medicine and American Politics*, Simon & Schuster: New York, 2016.

Craven, Avery, *Reconstruction: The Ending of the Civil War*, Holt, Rinehart & Winston: New York, 1969.

Crifts, Daniel W., *Lincoln and the Politics of Slavery: The Thirteenth Amendment and the Struggle to Save Slavery*, University of North Carolina Press: Chapel Hill, 2016.

Denny, Robert E., *The Civil War Years: A Day-by-Day Chronicle*, Gramercy Books: New York, 1998.

Devine, Shauna, *Learning from the Wounded: The Civil War and the Rise of American Medical Science*, University of North Carolina Press: Chapel Hill, 2014.

Dieterle, Lorraine Jacyno, *Arlington National Cemetery: A Nation's Story Carved in Stone*, Pomegranate Communications: Rohnert Park, California, 2001.

Dittmer, John, *The Good Doctors: The Medical Committee for Human Rights and the Struggle for Social Justice in Health Care*, Bloomsbury Press: New York, 2009.

Douglass, Frederick, *The Life and Times of Frederick Douglass by Himself: His Early Life as a Slave, His Escape from Bondage and His Complete History to the Present Time*, DeWolfe, Fiske & Co.: Boston, 1895.

Dowdey, Clifford, *Lee*, Bonanza Books: New York, 1965.

Downs, Jim, *Sick from Freedom: African-American Illness and Suffering During the Civil War and Reconstruction*, Oxford University Press: New York, 2012.

Drago, Edmund L., *Black Politicians and Reconstruction in Georgia: A Splendid Failure*, Brown Thrasher: Athens, GA, 1992.

Dunbar, Erica Armstrong, *Never Caught: The Washingtons' Relentless Pursuit of Their Runaway Slave, Ona Judge*, Atria Books: New York, 2017.

Ellis, Joseph J., *His Excellency George Washington*, Alfred A Knopf: New York, 2004.

Emilio, Lewis F., *A Brave Black Regiment: History of the Fifty-Forth Regiment of Massachusetts Volunteer Infantry, 1863-1865*, The Boston Book Company: Boston, MA, 1894.

Faust, Drew Gilpin, *This Republic of Suffering: Death and the American Civil War*, Vintage Books: New York, 2008.

Fett, Sharla, *Working Cures: Healing, Health, and Power on Southern Slave Plantations*, University of North Carolina Press: Chapel Hill, 2002.

Fitzpatrick, Sandra and Maria Goodwin, *The Guide to Black Washington*, Hippocrene Books: New York, 1990.

Foner, Eric, "Lincoln and Colonization," *Our Lincoln: New Perspectives on Lincoln and His World*, W.W. Norton: New York, 2009.

Foner, Eric, *Reconstruction: America's Unfinished Revolution, 1863-1877*, HarperCollins: New York, 1988.

Foner, Eric, *A Short History of Reconstruction*, Harper & Row: New York, 1990.

Forbes, Robert Pierce, *The Missouri Compromise and Its Aftermath: Slavery and the Meaning of America*, University of North Carolina Press: Chapel Hill, 2007.

Freeman, Douglas Southall, *Lee: An Abridgement in One Vol.*, abridged version of four-

Vol. *R.E. Lee* by Richard Harwell, Charles Scibner's Sons: New York, 1961.

Freeman, Douglas Southall, *R.E. Lee: A Biography*, Vol. IV, Charles Scribner's Sons: New York, 1935.

Freemon, Frank R., *Gangrene and Glory: Medical Care During the American Civil War*, Fairleigh Dickinson University Press: Madison, NJ, 1998.

Fuller, James, *The Election of 1860 Reconsidered*, Kent State University Press: Kent, Ohio, 2013.

Gale Group (creator), *Who's Who Among African Americans*, Gale Group: Farmington Hills, MI, 2000.

Gates, Henry Louis, and Evelyn Brooks Higginbotham, *African American National Biography*, Oxford University Press: New York, 2008.

Gerteis, Louis, *From Contraband to Freedman: Federal Policy Toward Southern Blacks 1861–1865*, Greenwood Press: Westport, CT, 1973.

Gladstone, William, *Men of Color*, Thomas Publications: Gettysburg, PA, 1993.

Gorman, Kathleen, L., "Civil War Pensions," *Essential Civil War Curriculum*, Virginia Tech University Press: Blacksburg, 2012.

Hanna, Charles W., *African American Recipients of the Medal of Honor: A Biographical Dictionary, Civil War Through Vietnam War*, McFarland: Jefferson, NC, 2002.

Hargrove, Hondon B., *Black Union Soldiers in the Civil War*, McFarland: Jefferson, NC, 1988.

Hays, J.N., *The Burdens of Disease: Epidemics and Human Response in Western History*, Rutgers University Press: Piscataway, NJ, 2009.

Herbert, Hillary A., *History of The Arlington Confederate Monument at Arlington, VA*, United Daughters of the Confederacy: Washington, D.C., 1914, 77.

Holzer, Harold, *Lincoln and the Power of the Press*, Simon & Schuster: New York. 2014.

Holzer, Harold, *Lincoln President Elect: Abraham Lincoln and the Great Secession Winter of 1860–1861*, Simon & Schuster: New York, 2008.

Hoptak, John David, *First in Defense of the Union: The Civil War History of the First Defenders*, AuthorHouse: Bloomington, IN, 2004.

Horn, Jonathan, *The Man Who Would Not Be Washington: Robert E. Lee's Civil War and the Decision That Changed American History*, Scribner's: New York, 2015.

Humphreys, Andrew A., *The Virginia Campaign of 1864 and 1865: The Army of the Potomac and the Army of the James*, Charles Scribners' Sons: New York, 1883.

Hunter, Tera W., *Bound in Wedlock: Slave and Free Black Marriage in the Nineteenth Century*, Belknap Press: Cambridge, MA, 2017.

Jacob, Kathryn Allamong, *Testament to Union: Civil War Monuments in Washington, D.C.*, Johns Hopkins University Press, Baltimore, 1998.

Janke, Lucinda Prout, *A Guide to Civil War Washington, D.C.: The Capital of the Union*, The History Press: Charleston, SC, 2013.

Jones, David, S., *Rationalizing Epidemics: Meanings and Uses of American Indian Mortality Since 1600*, Harvard University Press: Cambridge, MA, 2004.

Justesen, Benjamin R., Ed., *His Own Words: The Writings, Speeches, and Letters of George Henry White*, iUniverse: Lincoln, NE, 2004.

Keckley, Elizabeth, *Behind the Scenes, or, Thirty Years a Slave, and Four in the White House*, G.W. Carleton: New York, 1868.

Keegan, John, *The American Civil War: A Military History*, Alfred A. Knopf: New York, 2009.

Klingaman, William K., *Abraham Lincoln and the Road to Emancipation, 1861–1865*, Viking Penguin Books: New York, 2001.

Korda, Michael, *Clouds of Glory: The Life and Legend of Robert E. Lee*, HarperCollins: New York New York, 2014.

Lande, R. Gregory, *Psychological Consequences of the American Civil War*, McFarland: Jefferson, NC, 2016.

Landrieu, Mitch, *In the Shadow of Statues: A White Southerner Confronts History*, Viking: New York, 2018.

Larson, Kate Clifford, *Bound For the Promised Land: Harriet Tubman, Portrait of an American Hero*, Random House: New York, 2004.

Lee, Henry, *Funeral Oration on the Death of General Washington, Delivered at the Request of the Congress*, Printed for Joseph Nancrede and Manning & Loring: Boston, 1800.

Levine, Bruce, *Half Slave and Half Free: The Roots of the Civil War*, Hill & Wang: New York, 2005.

Litwak, Leon, *Been in the Storm So Long: The Aftermath of Slavery*, Vintage: New York, 1979.

Logan, Rayford W., Ed., *Dictionary of American Negro Biography*, W.W. Norton & Co.: New York, 1967.

Lomask, Milton, *Andrew Johnson: President on Trial*, Octagon Books: New York, 1973.

Long, A.L., *Memoirs of Robert E. Lee: His Military and Personal History*, The Blue and Grey Press: Secaucus, NJ, 1983.

Long, Gretchen, *Doctoring Freedom: The Politics of African American Medical Care in Slavery and Emancipation*, University of North Carolina Press: Chapel Hill, 2012.

MacDonald, Rose Mortimer Ellzey, *Mrs. Robert E. Lee*, Robert B. Poisal, Publisher: Pikesville, MD, 1973.

Manarin, Louis H., Ed., "Record of Council Minutes November 9, 1863," *Richmond at War: The Minutes of the City Council, 1861–1865*, University of North Carolina Press: Chapel Hill, 1966.

Manning, Chandra, *What This Cruel War Was Over: Soldier, Slavery and the Civil War*, Alfred A. Knopf: New York, 2007.

Martinez, Jaime Amanda, "Slavery During the Civil War," *Encyclopedia Virginia*, Richmond, 2015. Available at: https://www.encyclopediavirginia.org/slavery_during_the_civil_war

Masur, Kate, *An Example for All the Land: Emancipation and the Struggle Over Equality in Washington, D.C.*, University of North Carolina Press: Chapel Hill, 2012.

McElya, Micki, *The Politics of Mourning: Death and Honor at Arlington National Cemetery*, Harvard University Press: Cambridge, MA, 2016.

McGirr, Lisa, *The War on Alcohol: Prohibition and the Rise of the American State*, W.W. Morton Company: New York, 2016.

McPherson, James M., *For Cause and Comrades: Why Men Fought the Civil War*, Oxford University Press: New York, 1997.

McPherson, James M., *Ordeal by Fire: The Civil War*, Vol. 2, McGraw-Hill: New York, 2001.

Meier, Kathryn Shively, *Nature's Civil War: Common Soldiers and the Environment in 1862 Virginia*, University of North Carolina Press: Chapel Hill, 2003.

Middleton, Stephen, Ed., *Black Congressmen During Reconstruction: A Documentary Sourcebook*, Greenwood Press: Westport, CT, 2002.

Miller, David W., *Second Only to Grant: Quartermaster General Montgomery C. Meigs*, White Mane Books: Shippensburg, PA, 2000.

Mills, Cynthia, and Pamela Simpson, *Monuments to the Lost Cause: Women, Art, and the Landscapes of Southern Memory*, University of Tennessee Press: Knoxville, 2003.

Morais, Herbert M., *The History of the Afro-American in Medicine*, The Publishers Agency: Cornwells Heights, PA, 1978.

Morgan, H. Wayne, *William McKinley and His America*, Syracuse University Press: Syracuse, NY, 1963.

Murphy, Ric, *Freedom Road: An American Family Saga from Jamestown to World War*, first edition, AuthorHouse: Bloomington, IN, 2014.

Murray, Daniel, *Addresses and Ceremonies at the New Year's Festival to the Freedmen on Arlington Heights and Statistics and Statements of the Educational Condition of the Colored People in the Southern States and Other Facts*, McGill & Witherow: Washington, D.C., 1867.

Neely, Mark E., Jr., *The Civil War and the Limits of Destruction*, Harvard University Press: Cambridge, MA, 2007.

Nelligan, Murray H., *Arlington House: The Story of the Lee Mansion, Historical Monument*, Chatelaine Press: Burke, VA, 2005.

Nicolay, John G. and John Hay, *Abraham Lincoln: A History*, New Century Press: New York, 1890.

Nolan, Alan T., *Lee Considered: General Robert E. Lee and Civil War History*, University of North Carolina Press: Chapel Hill, 1991.

Oates, Stephens B., *A Woman of Valor: Clara Barton and the Civil War*, The Free Press: New York, 1994.

Osterholm, Michael T., and Mark Olshaker, *Deadliest Enemy: Our War Against Killer Germs*, Little Brown & Co.: New York, 2017.

Painter, Nell Irvin, *Sojourner Truth: A Life, a Symbol*, W.W. Norton: New York, 1996.

Parton, James, *General Butler in New Orleans: History of the Administration of the Department of the Gulf in the Year 1862, with an Account of the Capture of New Orleans, and the General, Civil and Military*, Mason Brothers: New York, 1864, 521–522.

Parzych, Cynthia, *Arlington National Cemetery: Trace the Path of America's Heritage*, Rowman & Littlefield: Guilford, CT, 2015.

Peters, James Edward, *Arlington National Cemetery: Shrine to America's Heroes*, Woodbine House, Kensington, Maryland 1986.

Phillips, Kevin, *William McKinley*, Times Books: New York, 2003.

Pohanka, Brian, *Carnival of Death: America's Civil War*, Empire Press: Leesburg, VA, 1991.

Poole, Robert M., *On Hallowed Ground: The Story of Arlington National Cemetery*, Walker & Co.: New York, 2009.

Poole, Robert M., *Section 60, Arlington National Cemetery: Where War Comes Home*, Bloomsbury Publishers: New York, 2014.

Provine, Dorothy S., *Alexandria County, VA, Free Negro Registers, 1791–1861*, Heritage Books, Inc., Bowie, MD, 1990.

Pryor, Elizabeth Brown, *Reading the Man: A Portrait of Robert E Lee Through His Private Letters*, Penguin Group: New York, 2007.

Rand McNally & Co., *Rand McNally & Co.'s Pictorial Guide to Washington*, Rand McNally & Co.: Chicago, Illinois, and New York, NY, 1904.

Richardson, Heather Cox, *West from Appomattox: The Reconstruction of America After the Civil War*, Yale University Press, New Haven, Connecticut, 2007.

Robinson, Lloyd, *The Stolen Election: Hayes Versus Tilden—1876*, Tom Doherty Associates: New York, 2001.

Ryan, David D., *Richmond Illustrated: Unusual Stories of a City*, Dietz Press, Richmond, VA, 1993.

Salmon, John S., *The Official Virginia Civil War Battlefield Guide*, Stackpole Books, Mechanicsburg, PA, 2001.

Sappol, Michael, *A Traffic of Dead Bodies: Anatomy and Embodied Social Identity in Nineteenth-Century America*, Princeton University Press, Princeton, New Jersey, 2004.

Savitt, Todd L., *Medicine and Slavery: The Diseases and Health Care of Blacks in Antebellum Virginia*, University of Illinois, Champaign, Illinois, 2002.

Schneider, Dorothy and Carl J. Schneider, *First Ladies: A Biographical Dictionary*, Infobase Publishing: New York, 2010.

Schultz, Jane E., *Women at the Front: Hospital Workers in Civil War America*, University of North Carolina Press: Chapel Hill, 2004.

Smith, John David, *Black Soldiers in Blue: African American Troops in the Civil War Era*, University of North Carolina Press: Chapel Hill, 2002.

Standiford, Lee, *Washington Burning: How a Frenchman's Vision for Our Nation's Capital Survived Congress, the Founding Fathers, and the Invading British Army*, Three Rivers Press: New York, 2008.

Steiner, Paul E., *Disease in the Civil War: Natural Biological Warfare in 1861–1865*, Charles C. Thomas, Springfield, Illinois, 1968.

Stowe, Steven, M., *Doctoring the South: Southern Physicians and Everyday Medicine in the Mid-Nineteenth Century*, University of North Carolina Press: Chapel Hill, 2003.

Taylor, Elizabeth Dowling, *The Original Black Elite: Daniel Murray and the Story of a Forgotten Era*, HarperCollins Publishers: New York, 2017.

Toler, Pamela D., *Heroines of Mercy Street: The Real Nurses of the Civil War*, Little Brown & Co.: New York, 2016.

Tomes, Nancy, *The Gospel of Germs: Men, Women and Medicine in American Life*, Harvard University Press: Cambridge, MA, 1999.

Trelease, Allen W., *White Terror: The Ku Klux Klan, Conspiracy and Southern Reconstruction*, Greenwood Press Publishers: Westport, CT, 1971.

Warner, John, *The Therapeutic Perspective: Medical Practice, Knowledge, and Identity in America*, Princeton University Press: Princeton, NJ, 1997.

Washington, Harriet A., *Medical Apartheid: The Dark History of Medical Experimentation on Black Americans from Colonial Times to the Present*, First Anchor Books: New York, 2006.

Washington, Margaret, *Sojourner Truth's*

America, University of Illinois Press: Chicago, 2009.
Waskie, Anthony, *Philadelphia and the Civil War: Arsenal of the Union*, History Press: Charleston, SC, 2011.
Wesley, Charles H., and Patricia W. Romero, *Negro Americans in the Civil War: From Slavery to Citizenship*, Publishers Company: New York, 1967.
Wiencek, Henry, *An Imperfect God: George Washington, His Slaves and the Creation of America*, Farrar, Straus & Giroux: New York, 2003.
Williams, George Washington and John David Smith, *A History of the Negro Troops in the War of the Rebellion, 1861–1865*, reprint edition, Fordham University Press: New York, 2012.
Wilson, Joseph T. *The Black Phalanx: African American Soldiers in the War of Independence, The War of 1812, and the Civil War*, Project Gutenberg EBook, February 21, 2010. http://www.gutenberg.org/files/31339/31339-h/31339-h.htm. Accessed June 30, 2018.
Yates, Bernice-Marie, *The Perfect Gentleman: The Life* and *Letters of George Washington Custis Lee*, Xulon Press: Maitland, FL, 2003.
Zeitz, Joshua, *Lincoln's Boys: John Hay, John Nicolay and the War for Lincoln's Image*, Viking Press: New York, 2014.

Newspaper Articles

"Another Case of Death," *Alexandria Gazette*, Alexandria, VA, March 19, 1890.
"Another Small-Pox Case," *Evening Star*, Washington, D.C., January 21, 1862.
"Arrest of the Mayor of Washington on Charge of Disloyalty," *Evening Star*, Washington, D.C., August 24, 1861.
"As Might Have Been Expected," *The Potter Journal*, Coudersport, PA, August 14, 1861.
"The Best That Could Be Under the Circumstances," *Lexington Gazette*, Lexington, VA, June 13, 1902.
"The Blacks at Washington," *Winchester Daily Bulletin*, Winchester, VA, February 7, 1863.
"Captain Edwin Belcher," *Colored American*, Washington, D.C., November 2, 1900.
Chase, Enoch Aquila, "Ancient Custis Slave Remembers Brilliant Arlington Events," *The Sunday Star*, Washington, D.C., November 4, 1928.
"Christening," *The Daily Republic*, Washington, D.C., August 6, 1853.
"Contrabands," *Evening Star*, Washington, D.C., February 13, 1862.
"Contrabands on a War Footing," *The National Republican*, Washington, D.C., January 1, 1862.
"Council Proceedings," *The Evening Star*, Washington, D.C., May 13, 1862.
"Death of Col. Ellsworth," *The National Republican*, Washington, D.C. May 25, 1861.
"Death of Mr. Custis," *Weekly National Intelligencer*, Washington, D.C., October 17, 1857.
"Deaths," *Evening Star*, Washington, D.C., August 22, 1929.
"Decorating the Graves," *New York Herald*, June 1, 1868.
"Decoration Day—Ceremonies at Arlington," *New Era*, Washington, D.C., June 2, 1870.
"Decoration of Soldiers' Graves," *Alexandria Gazette*, Alexandria, VA, May 27, 1874.
"Descent Upon a Ranche," *Evening Star*, Washington, D.C., November 4, 1861.
"The Effect of the Hatteras Affair on Naval Stores," *Newbern Weekly Progress*, New Bern, NC, September 17, 1861.
Enoch Aquila Chase, "The Mystery of Arlington," *Sunday Star Magazine*, Washington, D.C., December 15, 1929.
"Failure of the à Vache Colonization Scheme," *Alexandria Gazette*, Alexandria, VA, March 22, 1864.
Foner, Eric, "The Making and Breaking of the Myth of Robert E. Lee," *New York Times* (www.nytimes.com), August 28, 2017.
"The Funeral of G.W.P. Custis," *Evening Star*, Washington, D.C., October 13, 1857.
"Gen. Lee's Land," *The Liberator*, Boston, MA, July 15, 1864.
"General News," *Alexandria Gazette*, Alexandria, VA, October 25, 1862.
"George Washington Parke Custis Obituary," *Port Tobacco Times*, Port Tobacco, MD, October 12, 1857.
"Georgetown Affairs," *Evening Star*, Washington, D.C., October 12, 1857.
"The Greatest Memorial Service Is at Arlington Cemetery," *The Sunday Star*, Washington, D.C., May 26, 1912.

"A Horse Dealer," *Evening Star*, Washington, D.C., November 4, 1861.

"How the Proclamation Works in Virginia," *Chicago Tribune*, Chicago, Illinois, January 16, 1862.

"Howell Cobb on Resistance," *Keowee Courier*, Pickens Court House, SC, December 22, 1860.

"Hydrant Water," *The National Republican*, Washington, D.C., March 31, 1862.

"Jeff. Davis's Northern Conspiracy," *Chicago Daily Tribune*, June 25, 1861.

Kristin E. Holmes, "Mayor Kenney References Starbucks Arrests at Ceremony Honoring African American Civil War Troops," *Philadelphia Inquirer*, Philadelphia, PA, April 24, 2018. http://www.philly.com/philly/news/starbucks-arrests-african-american-civil-war-troops-philadelphia-20180421.html. Accessed June 30, 2018.

"The Lee Statue," *Peninsula Enterprise* Accomac Court-House, VA, May 10, 1890.

"Lemmon Case and the New York Tribune," *Richmond Enquirer*, Richmond, VA, October 9, 1857.

"Letter of John C. Underwood," *Alexandria Gazette*, Alexandria, VA, July 18, 1865.

"Manumission" *Evening Star*, Washington, D.C., December 11, 1857.

"The Memory of Lee," *Richmond Dispatch*, Richmond, VA, February 9, 1890.

"The Mettle of Butler's Soldiers," *The Baltimore Sun*, August 2, 2001, http://articles.baltimoresun.com/2001-08-02/features/0108020166_1_medal-of-honor-butler-fought. Accessed June 30, 2018.

"Mr. Hunter's Proposition," *Alexandria Gazette*, Alexandria, VA, January 8, 1861.

"Mortality of Federal Prisoners in Rebel Hospitals," *Soldiers Journal*, Camp Distribution, VA, May 13, 1864.

"Our Military Budget," *Evening Star*, Washington, D.C., February 26, 1862.

"Partisan Fury," *Alexandria Gazette*, Alexandria, VA, May 31, 1890.

Philips, Dave, "Arlington Cemetery, Nearly Full, May Become More Exclusive," *New York Times*: New York, May 28, 2018. Accessed at nytimes.com, May 28, 2018.

"President's Persistent Sorrow," *Evening Star*, Washington, D.C., May 27, 1861.

Proctor, John Clagett, "Master of Arlington House Striking Figure in Virginia History," *The Sunday Star*, Washington, D.C., February 26, 1928.

"The 'Protection of Washington'—Gen. Scott Carries Out the Black Republican Policy," *Richmond Enquirer*, Richmond, VA, January 18, 1861.

R.D.B., "Letter from Virginia," *New National Era*, Washington, D.C., June 8, 1871.

"Rebel Soldiers," *Alexandria Gazette*, Alexandria, VA, May 31, 1871.

"Reception of Col. Ellsworth's Remains at New York," *Evening Star*, Washington, D.C., May 27, 1861.

"Richmond's Growth," *Richmond Dispatch*, Richmond, VA, April 27, 1890.

"Senator Wilson's Description of the Jail," *The National Republican*, Washington, D.C., December 7, 1861.

Shannon, Harry, "The Rambler," *The Evening Star*, Washington, D.C., August 17, 1912.

"The Slaves of Mr. Custis," *New York Times*, December 30, 1857.

"Soldiers to the Front," The *National Tribune*, Washington, D.C., November 30, 1882.

"Southern Monitor," *Daily Dispatch*, Richmond, VA, May 28, 1857.

"Speech of A. Lincoln," *The Kansas News*, Emporia, KS, August 8, 1857.

"The Sufferings of the 'Contrabands,'" *Alexandria Gazette*, Alexandria, VA, November 12, 1863.

"Travel Over the Bridges," *Evening Star*, Washington, D.C., May 29, 1868.

"The Treachery of the Government," *The National Republican*, Washington, D.C., December 27, 1861.

"The Washington Star Says," *Alexandria Gazette*, Alexandria, VA, May 23, 1863.

"The Will of Mr. Custis," *New York Times*, January 8, 1858.

Electronic Sources

"Anderson Ruffin Abbot (1837–1913)," http://www.blackpast.org/aah/abbott-anderson-ruffin-1837-1913. Accessed October 19, 2017.

Burns, Stanley B., "Wound Infection," Technical Notes to PBS's *Mercy Street*, 2014. http://www.pbs.org/mercy-street/uncover-history/behind-lens/wound-infection/ Accessed June 7, 2017.

A Century of Population Growth: From the First Census of the United States to the Twelfth, United States Department of

Commerce and Labor, Bureau of the Census, Government Printing Office, Washington, D.C., 1909, 132.

Civil War Casualties, https://www.civilwar.org/learn/articles/civil-war-casualties. Accessed December 15, 2017.

Dennee, Timothy, "A District of Columbia Freedmen's Cemetery in Virginia? African-American Civilians in Section 27 of Arlington National Cemetery, 1864–1867," Friends of Freedmen's Cemetery. http://www.freedmenscemetery.org/resources/documents/arlington-section27.pdf. Accessed April 10, 2017.

Hanna, Jennifer (2001), *Arlington House: The Robert E. Lee Memorial* (PDF). Washington District of Columbia: U. S. Department of the Interior. p. 62. Accessed January 26, 2017.

"Museum of the American Revolution Names Theater in Honor of $8 Million Gift from Alan B. and Jill Miller," *Museum of the American Revolution Press Release*, March 15, 2018. https://www.amrevmuseum.org/press-room/press-releases/museum-american-revolution-names-theater-honor-8-million-gift-alan-b-and. Accessed June 28, 2018.

Slawson, Robert G., "African American Physicians in the Civil War Era," *National Civil War Medicine Museum*, http://www.civilwarmed.org/africanamericandrs. Accessed September 21, 2017.

Tarter, Bren "Disenfranchisement," *Encyclopedia Virginia* (Virginia Foundation of the Humanities, Richmond, VA, July 19, 2016. Accessed 31 March 2018.

"U.S. Census for 1860 and 1870," www.census.gov. Accessed March 15, 2018.

Voyages Database. 2017. *Voyages: The Trans-Atlantic Slave Trade Database, Assessing the Slave Trade, Estimates*. http://www.slavevoyages.org/assessment/estimates. Accessed February 24, 2017.

Williamson, Samuel W., and Louis P. Cain, *Measuring Slavery in 2016 Dollars*, Loyola University, Chicago, Illinois, and Northwestern University, Evanston, IL. Accessed May 4, 2017. https://www.measuringworth.com/slavery.php.

Government Publications

Adjutant General's Office Report: *Mount Vernon Relics*, 41st Congress, 2nd Session, House of Representatives, Report No. 36, Washington, January 29, 1870.

"Arlington House Woodlands," http://vnps.org/conservation/virginia-native-plant-registry-sites-3/arlington-house-woodlands/. Accessed June 30, 2018.

Hanna, Jennifer (2001). *Arlington House: The Robert E. Lee Memorial* (PDF). Washington, D.C., U. S. Department of the Interior. Retrieved January 26, 2017.

"John Brice Syphax," http://syphaxfamily.com/The_People.html. Accessed June 30, 2018.

Liebertz, John, *A Guide to the African American Heritage of Arlington County, VA*, Department of Community Planning, Housing and Development, 2016.

MacGregor, Morris J., Jr., *Integration of the Armed Forces, 1940–1965*, Center of Military History, United States Army, Washington, D.C., 1981. Superintendent Documents Number D-114.2: In 8/940-65.

United States Department of the Interior, National Park Service, *National Register of Historic Places Registration Form*, February 24, 2014.

United States War Department, *The War of the Rebellion: A compilation of the official records of the Union and Confederate armies*.

Magazine Articles

"The Contrabands at Fort Monroe," *Atlantic Monthly*: New York, Vol. 0008, Iss. 49 November 1861.

Daniel, John Warwick, "Oration of Senator Daniel," *Proceedings of the Third Annual Meeting and Reunion of the United Confederate Veterans*, held at New Orleans, Louisiana, April 8–9, 1892, 24–46.

Dodge, George W., "The Burial of United States Colored Troops at Arlington National Cemetery," *Arlington Historical Magazine*, Arlington Historical Society, Inc., Arlington, VA, Vol. 11, No.1, October 1997.

Douglass, Frederick "How to Win the War," *Douglass Monthly*, Rochester, NY, May 1861. Transcript at http://rbscp.lib.rochester.edu/4373. Accessed June 25, 2017.

Douglass, "What Shall Be Done with the Slaves If Emancipated," *Douglass Monthly*, Rochester, NY, January 2, 1862. Transcript at http://rbscp.lib.rochester.edu/4373. Accessed June 25, 2017.

Hacker, David, "A Census-Based Count of the Civil War Dead," *Civil War History*, Vol. 57, No.4, December 2011, Project MUSE, Baltimore, Maryland.

Hitt, Jack, Ed., "Making the Case for Racila Reparations: Does America Owe a Debt to the Descendants of Its Slaves?" *Harpers Magazine*, New York, November 2000.

James, Felix, "The Establishment of Freedman's Village in Arlington, Virginia," *Negro History Bulletin*, Washington, D.C., Vol. 33 Number 4, April 1970.

"Monthly Record of Current Events," *Harpers New Monthly Magazine*, Vol. 0023, Iss. 134, July 1861.

"The New Virginia Law to Preserve Racial Integrity," *Virginia Health Bulletin*, Richmond, VA, March 1924.

Reidy, Joseph, P., "Coming from the Shadow of the Past: The Transition from Slavery to Freedom at Freedman's Village," *The Virginia Magazine of History and Biography*, Vol. 95, No.4 October 1987.

Robinson, Harry S., "Anderson Ruffin Abbott, MD, 1837–1913," *Journal of the National Medical Association*, Silver Spring, MD, 1980, Vol. 72, Iss. 2.

Rose, C.B., Jr., "The Map of Arlington in 1878—Places and People," *Arlington Historical Magazine*, Arlington Historical Society, Arlington, VA, Vol. 2, No.2, October 1962.

Schildt, Roberta, "Freedman's Village: Arlington, VA, 1863–1900," *Arlington Historical Magazine*, Arlington Historical Society, Inc., Arlington, VA, Vol. 7, No.4, October 1984.

Schroeder, Patrick A., "Out of the Checkerboard," *Civil War Times*, Leesburg, VA, Vol. 54, No. 2, April 2015.

Warner, John Harley, and Lawrence Rizzolo, "Anatomical Instruction and Training for Professionalism from the 19th to the 21st Centuries." *Clinical Anatomy*, Vol. 19, 2006.

Welch, Graham D., "Ile À Vache and Colonization: the Tragic End of Lincoln's 'Suicidal Folly,'" *The Gettysburg College Journal of the Civil War Era*, Gettysburg, PA, Vol. 4, Article 5, April 2014.

"Where Will the Rebellion Leave Us?" *Atlantic Monthly*: New York, Vol. 08 Iss. 46, August 1861.

Index

Abbott, Anderson Ruffin 86–88
Abbott, Ellen (Toyer) 86
Abbott, Wilson Ruffin 86
Abbott Hospital 101
Abolitionist 10, 36, 46, 50, 52–54, 65, 71–72, 95, 98–99, 113, 148
Act for the Collection of Taxes in the Insurrectionary Districts 179–180
Adams, John 132–133
African American Civil War Memorial 136
Alabama 18; Mobile Bay 139, 188; Montgomery 57, 178
Alcott, Louisa May 163
Aleshire, William 119
Alexander, Stephens 57
Alexandria 2, 20, 27, 29–32, 34, 39–41, 44, 50–51, 62, 64, 73, 82–84, 90, 101, 108, 117, 146–147, 152, 167, 178–179; Canal 90; city jail 50; police 50
Alexandria Cemetery 64
Alexandria Gazette 100
Alexandria-Georgetown Turnpike 27
Allen, James 171
Amendments to the U.S. Constitution: 13th 159; 14th 154, 158–159, 162; 15th 154, 159, 162
American Colonization Society 29, 40, 94
American Constitution 9
American Legion 176
American Missionary Association 97, 100
American Revolution 9, 29–30, 40, 172
American Tract Society 97
Amnesty Oath 153, 158–159, 180–181
Andersonville 105
Anglo-Saxonism 165
anti-lynching bill 155
Antietam Cemetery 135

Arkansas 18
Arlington, Clarence 27
Arlington House 2, 3, 7, 10–13, 25–28, 30–35, 38, 39–46, 48–54, 59–62, 92, 106–108, 110–111, 138, 122, 135, 145, 152, 172, 175–180, 191; Rose Garden 181
Arlington National Cemetery: Section 8 191; Section 15 3, 176, 182; Section 16 156; Section 17 171; Section 23 113, 140, 170–171; Section 24 165; Section 26 160; Section 27 4–7, 9–11, 14, 16, 18, 20, 43, 76, 78, 108–109, 113–114, 116, 118–119, 122, 128–132, 134, 136–140, 152–154, 172–173, 176, 180, 188
Arlington Plantation *see* Arlington House
Atlanta Peach Jubilee 165
Atlantic slave trade 16
Augusta, Alexander Thomas MD 87–88, 140, 142–144, 189

Baker, Frank 66–67
Bank of England 9
Barton, Clara 4, 83, 163
Battle of Antietam 75, 92, 103, 106, 126
Battle of Ball's Bluff 103
Battle of Baltimore 19
Battle of Bull Run 13, 63, 70, 103, 160, 179, 181
Battle of Chaffin's Farm 119, 139–140, 189
Battle of Crater 118
Battle of Fredericksburg 84
Battle of Gettysburg 103, 106, 126, 139, 154, 164, 171, 179, 188
Battle of Manassas *see* Battle of Bull Run
Battle of New Market Heights 118–119, 140
Battle of Normandy 173, 192
Battle of Saltville 88
Battle of Wilderness 102

219

Index

Battle of Yorktown 24, 177
Battlefield of Solferino 105
Beauregard, Gen. Pierre Gustave Toutant 103, 162
Belcher, Capt. Edwin 167
Belknap, Secretary of War William 6, 112, 161
Bell, Dennis 164, 192
Bell, John 18
Biddle, Nicholas 19
Bingham, Austin 49–50, 183–184
Bingham, Caroline 49, 183–184
Bingham, Reuben 50, 183–184
Birney, Brig. Gen. William 143
Black Horse Harry *see* Lee, Henry, IV
Black Republicanism 36
Blair, Francis P. 178
Blair, William A. 161, 164
Board of Protection 151
Boston Traveler 46–48
Brady, Matthew 74
Breckenridge, John 18
British Army 28, 84
USS *Brooklyn* 139, 188
Brown, Brig. Gen. Hazel (Johnson) 192
Brown, Orlando 148
Brown, Landsman William H. 139, 188
Brown vs Board of Education, 173, 190
Buchanan, Pres. James 18, 57
Bureau of Colored Troops 113, 141
Bureau of Refugees, Freedmen and Abandoned Lands 96, 147, 180
Burk, the Rev. Herbert 29
Burke, Agnes 49–50, 183
Burke, Caroline 49–50
Burke, Catharine 49–50, 183
Burnside, Gen. Ambrose 117
Butler, Gen. Benjamin 12, 19, 66–68, 118–120, 134, 137, 140, 147, 159–160, 167, 179; medal of bravery 68, 119

Carter, Ann 30
Carter, Ariana 39
Carter, Charles 30
Carter, Maria *see* Syphax, Maria
Cemetery Hill 117
Charles I of England (king) 23
Charles II of England (king) 23
Chase, Enoch Aquila 10–12, 175
Chesapeake and Ohio Canal 107, 175
Chimbarazo hospital 90
Christman, Private William Henry 4–5, 108–109, 134, 153, 180, 188
civil rights 6, 23–24, 36, 55, 90, 98, 120, 153–155, 158, 173, 190, 192

Clark, George 41, 175, 183
Clark, Lawrence 40
Clark, Patsy 40
Coats, Robert 171
Cobb, Treasury Sec. Howell 56
Columbia Harmony Cemetery 128
Commerford, John A. 149–150
Confederate: constitution 57, 178; Fort Morgan 139, 188; graves 5–6, 111–112, 161, 166; headstones 162; hospitals 90
Confederate Army 19–20, 57, 63–64, 104, 107, 115, 120–121, 123, 125, 158, 166, 172–173, 218
Confederate Memorial 168–169, 173, 182
Confederate States of America 3, 7, 12, 14, 19, 56–57, 78, 92, 137, 165–166, 178–179, 191
Confiscation Act 12–13, 179
Congressional Record 145
Connecticut National Guard 144
Consolidated Statement of Contraband Tax 94–95
Constitutional Convention 25, 156
Continental Army 30, 89
contraband: camp 13, 72, 74–78, 80, 82, 84, 88, 90, 94, 96, 99; cemetery 5, 116, 128–129, 131, 133, 135, 137; of war 12–13, 66, 70, 118, 137, 179
Cooper Union Address 65
Cornerstone Address 57
Costin, Ann Dandridge 24
cotton 17–18, 29, 54, 56, 58, 80, 94
Crimean War 84–85, 105, 119
Cuba 155, 164–165, 182, 192; Santiago Harbor 164
Custis, Daniel 38, 39
Custis, Daniel Parke 24, 39
Custis, George Washington Parke 2–3, 9–10, 12–14, 25–29, 31–35, 39–41, 44–45, 49–54, 59, 64, 92–94, 108, 126–127, 149, 174–175, 177–178, 180–181, 184, 191
Custis, John 38–39, 177
Custis, John "Jacky" Parke 24, 39, 177
Custis, Maria Carter *see* Syphax, Maria Syphax
Custis, Martha Dandridge *see* Washington, Martha
Custis, Mary *see* Lee, Mary Custis
Custis, Mary Anna Randolph 28, 31, 39
Custis Mansion *see* Arlington House

Dandy, Col. George B. 149
Dandy, Daniel, John Warwick 155
Davis, Gen. Benjamin O., Jr. 190

Davis, Gen. Benjamin O., Sr. 174, 190
Davis, Confederate Pres. Jefferson 5, 7, 58, 84, 120, 162, 168
Declaration of Independence 36–37
Decoration Day 5, 111, 135, 161–162, 181
Delaware: Sussex County 15
Democratic Party 18, 156
Dennee, Timothy 129
Dix, Dorothea 4
Doubleday, Col. Ulysses 121
Douglas, Frederick 5, 67–68, 72, 111–112, 135
Douglas, Sen. Stephen A. 18, 35–37
Dowdey, Clifford 48
Dred Scott Decision 18, 35–37, 49, 178
Dunant, Henry 105
Dye, Superintendent Robert 10
Dyer, Frederick H. 88

Eisenhower, Pres. Dwight D. 174
Electoral College 18, 26, 162
Ellsworth, Col. Elmer 73
Emancipation Proclamation 12, 15, 78–79, 92, 179
Endicott, Sec. of War William C. 150–151
England: Arlington Row Bibury 26; Commonwealth 23; Parliamentarians 23; Royalists 23
Eugenics Records Office 166
The Evening Star 32–33
Evers, Medgar 173, 192
Ewell, Gen. Richard S. (CSA) 122
Ezekiel, Moses J. 167–168, 170

Florida: Pensacola 189
Ford, Pres. Gerald R. 153
Fort Albany 63, 73
Fort Aquia 103
Fort Bennett 73
Fort Cass 63
Fort Corcoran 73
Fort Ellsworth 73
Fort Fisher 120
Fort Haggerty 73
Fort Lee 191
Fort McPherson 13
Fort Monroe (aka Fortress Freedom) 13, 20, 66, 68–69, 95, 133, 138, 179
Fort Morgan 139, 188
Fort Myer 7–8, 13, 40, 63, 107, 150, 176
Fort Pickens 68
Fort Pillow 89
Fort Runyon 73
Fort Sumpter 56–57, 178

Fort Wagner 115, 121, 144, 180, 189
Fort Ward 20
Fort Washington 57
Fort Whipple *see* Fort Meyer
Foster, Col. C.W. 141–142
Francis, Thomas 170
Franklin and Armfield 54
Freedman Hospital 72, 86–88, 131, 133, 143–144, 163, 189
Freedmen and Southern Society Project 82
Freeman, Douglas Southall 121
Front Street Methodist Church 141
Fugitive Slave Act 12

Gardiner, Private James 140
Garfield, Pres. James A. 164
Geneva Convention 105
Georgetown Corporation 135
Gettysburg Address 180
Georgia 24, 105, 165, 168; Oglethorpe Plan 24; Savannah 57
Gettysburg Cemetery 135
Gibbon, Maj. Gen. John 121
Giesboro Cemetery 22, 130
Gordon, Maj. Gen. John B. (CSA) 122
Grand Army of the Republic (GAR) 6–7, 135–136, 160, 181
Grant, Gen. Ulysses S. 5–6, 75, 102, 107, 111, 116–117, 120–121, 123–126, 144, 158–160, 171, 180
Gray, Selena 60–61, 1761 183–184
Gray, Thornton 61, 176, 183–184
Greeley, Horace 52
Green, Benjamin 129
Green Spring Plantation 23
Greene, Col. Elias M. 90, 92, 179
Grindel, Coombs 130
Guam 164–165

Haiti 94–95, 150; Ile-À-Vache 95
Harmony Cemetery 22
Harris, Sgt. James H. 119, 139–140, 189
Harris, William 134
Hartford Fire Insurance Company 34
Hatfield, George 26
Hayes, Pres. Rutherford B. 91, 155, 162, 164
health: access to cadavers 85; amputations 85; anatomy lessons 84; antiseptic principles 85; Boston smallpox outbreak 80; brothels 22; clean water 4, 20–21, 70, 75, 82; counting the deaths 104; embalming 4, 82; homemade, remedies 77; hospital capacity 4; infections 85, 89, 137; inocu-

lation 80–81, 89; life expectancy 20; malnourishment 13, 21, 70; measles 4, 21, 78, 80, 108–109; medical care 82, 84, 86, 89; medical innovation 3, 86; military medicine 75; morality laws 21; mortality rate 13, 77, 88, 113; nurses 3, 63, 86, 94, 163, 186; potable water 95; public health crisis 2, 71; public health emergency 4, 75, 90, 101–102, 154; public health police powers 81; refugees' health 69; rubella 4; self-care 86; smallpox 74–75, 80–81, 89, 95–96; surgical techniques 82; typhus 24, 80, 83; vaccine 80; whooping cough 4, 21, 78, 80; wound care 85; yellow fever 4, 78, 163
Heintzelman, Gen. 73
Herbert, Hillary A. 168–170
Hinds, Congressman James 158
Hines, Benjamin 170
Hoar, Edward 171
Holabird, Gen. 152
Holland, Milton 140, 192
Hollywood Cemetery 112
Horner, Caleb 81
Howard University 190; Hospital 88, 101, 144
Howard, Gen. C.H. 148
Howard, Gen. Oliver Otis 147, 150
Hoyer, Rep. Steny 119
Huckster, Mrs. Fleming 50
Humphreys, Andrew A. 122
Hunter, Sen. Robert 19
Hunter, William H. 140–141, 189

Illinois, Springfield 58, 65, 73
Indian Wars 9, 139, 189–190

Jackson, Stonewall 107
Jefferson, Pres. Thomas 5–6, 133
Jenner, Edward 80
Jim Crow 7, 36, 160, 175
Johnson, Pres. Andrew 120, 126, 147, 153–154, 157–160, 180–181
Johnson, Henry 192
Johnson, Lucy Ellen 96

Kansas-Nebraska Act 18, 36
Keckley, Elizabeth 20
Kendall, Samuel 171
Kennedy, Pres. John F. 172
Kentucky 17, 190
Kilmer, Col. George L. 118
Kock, Bernard 94
Korean War 82, 189–191
Ku Klux Klan 90, 120, 158–160, 173, 191

Lafayette, Marquis de 27–28, 41, 63, 149, 177
Lee, Agnes 44
Lee, Ann 44
Lee, George Washington 6–7, 33, 44–45, 122, 147, 145, 182
Lee, Henry III 30–31, 39
Lee, Lee, Henry IV 30–31, 39
Lee, Mary Ann Randolph (Custis) 2–4, 6, 13, 29, 32, 39–40, 44, 50, 59–60, 120, 126, 145, 175, 178–179, 181, 191
Lee, Matilda 30
Lee, Mildred 44, 160
Lee, Gen. Robert E. (CSA) 2, 4–5, 7, 14, 29–31, 33–34, 37, 39, 41–42, 44–47, 49–51, 53–54, 58–59, 65, 92–93, 101, 107, 115, 120–121, 124–126, 145, 153, 156, 158, 160, 171–172, 174, 178–181, 184–185, 191; amnesty oath 159; oath of allegiance 153
Lee, Robert E., Jr. 44
Lee, William Fitzhugh (Rooney) 44
L'Enfant, Pierre 182
Letterman, Dr. Johnathan 84–85
Lewis, Dr. Samuel 165–166
Lexington Gazette 156
The Liberator 111
Liberia 29, 40
Liebertz, John 40
Lincoln, Abraham 3–4, 12, 15–16, 18–21, 33, 35–36, 55–58, 63, 65, 73–74, 78, 79, 92, 95, 99, 107–109, 113, 126, 132, 134, 137, 142–143, 148, 154, 156–158, 160, 178–180
Lincoln, Mary Todd 20
Lister, Joseph 85
Longstreet, Lt. Col. James, Jr. 171
Longstreet, Maj. Robert Lee 171
Louis, Joe 173, 190
Louisiana, Governor Kellogg 172
Louisiana: New Orleans 18, 120, 162, 171

Madison, Pres. James 56
USS *Maine* 165–166
Mallory, Sheppard 66
Marshall, Justice Thurgood 174, 190
Maryland: Annapolis 68; Baltimore 67, 139, 142–143, 188, 190; Bowie 119; Charles County 15; Chesapeake 20, 107; Nottingham 16; Saint Mary's County 139, 189; Talbot County 15; Westminster 51; Worcester 15
Massachusetts: 5th Cavalry 113–114; 54th Regiment 113–115, 121, 144, 180, 189; 55th Regiment 114

Mather, Cotton 80
McClellan, Gen. George B. 24, 84
McClerkin, Walter P. 134
McDowell, Brig. Gen. Irvin 4, 19, 60, 62, 179
McGuire, Overseer 61
McKinney, Private William H. 109, 188
McLean, Wilmer 125
Medal of Honor 118–119, 138–140, 165, 188–190, 192
Meigs, Lt. John Rodgers 111, 149, 160
Meigs, Brigadier Gen. Montgomery 4–5, 14, 63, 102, 106–108, 110–112, 134–136, 149, 153, 160–162, 165, 174, 176, 180, 182
Memorial Day 1, 5, 135, 172
Mexican War 82
Michigan 18; Detroit 191
Middle Passage 17
military camp 8, 13, 74, 78, 82, 84, 96, 164, 175–176, 191; Barker 71, 72, 74, 92, 143, 189; Convalescent 83; Meigs 114; Misery 83; Stanton 143
Mills, Cynthia 165
Minié, Claude-Étienne 85
Mississippi 18, 75, 105, 135, 156; Decatur 192; Natchez 18
Mississippi River 17, 119
Missouri Compromise 18, 36, 178
Monroe, Pres. James 133
Morris Island *see* Fort Monroe
Moulton, Rep. Samuel 148
Mt. Olive Baptist Church 152
Museum of the American Revolution 29

National Association for the Advancement of Colored People 174, 191
National Cemetery 153
National Cemetery System 1, 48
National Civil War Medicine Museum 86
National Freedman's Relief Association 74, 99
New Mexico 139; Carrizo Canyon 139
New York 3, 10, 34, 52, 55, 62, 65, 73, 118, 133, 191; Cold Harbor Spring 166; New York City 73; West Point *see* United States Military Academy
New York Times 34, 47
New York Tribune 52
Nightingale, Florence 163
Norris, Mary 51–52, 55, 61
Norris, Wesley 3, 51–52, 55, 61, 176
North Carolina 17, 103, 120–121, 154; Rockingham 189; Winston-Salem 192

Ohio 2, 65, 106, 143, 164; 3rd Regiment 140; 8th Regiment 139, 189; 18th Regiment 140; 92nd Regiment 140; 127th Regiment 140
Orange and Alexander Railroad 52
Ord, Gen. Edward 5, 121, 129, 134
Owens, Thomas 129

Paine, Gen. Charles J. 118, 139
Parks, Amanda 40
Parks, George 40, 59
Parks, James 3, 7, 10–14, 32–33, 40–42, 59, 63, 108, 129, 149, 152, 174–176, 178, 182
Parks, Lawrence 40
Parks, Leanna 40
Parks, Martha 40
Parks, Matilda 40
Parks, Patsy 40
Parks, Perry 40, 59
Parks, Robert 40
Pennsylvania: coal miners 117; First Defenders 19; Gettysburg *see* Battle of; Lehigh County 108; Philadelphia 9, 25, 29, 80, 113, 118, 135, 144, 167, 189; Volunteer Infantry 4, 167, 188
Pentagon 8, 27, 107
Philadelphia National Cemetery 135
Philippines 155, 165
Pryor, Elizabeth Brown 37, 108
Puerto Rico 164–165

Quakers 40

Reconstruction 5, 24, 36, 90, 101, 120, 154, 158, 160, 162, 175
Republican Party 6, 18, 36–37, 90, 101, 147, 149, 159–160, 162, 171
Richmond, Private James 139, 188
Richmond and Danville Railroad 121
Richmond Enquirer 36
Romancoke Plantation 34, 44, 185
Roosevelt, Pres. Franklin D. 174
Rush, Benjamin 80

Savage, Edward 25
Scott, Dred 18, 35–37, 49, 178
Scott, Gen. Winfield 3, 55
secession 3, 14, 19, 51, 55–57, 62–63, 65, 73, 163
segregation 5, 7, 35, 111, 119, 126, 134, 136, 160, 166; race purity 155; Racial Integrity Act 167; racial segregation 5, 162; separate but equal 155, 166, 173
Shannon, Harry 138

Shaw, Col. James, Jr. 121
Shaw, Col. Robert Gould 115, 144, 180, 189
Shaw, Sgt. Thomas 139, 189
Sherman, Gen. William T. 84–86, 120, 160
Sibley-tents 93
Simpson, Pamela 165, 168
Skinner, Randall 171
Soldiers' Journal 105
South Carolina 17, 24, 56–57, 67, 115, 142–143, 158, 167; Beaufort 144; Charleston 115, 120, 142; Morris Island 115, 144, 189
Spanish American War 163–165, 182
Stanton, Sec. of War Edward 4, 75, 87, 107, 110–111, 159
Stevens, Congressman Thaddeus 159
Stewart, Brigade Surgeon 81, 89
Syphax 2, 5–6, 10, 35, 111, 126, 150–152; Act for Relief of Maria 181
Syphax, Austin 49–50
Syphax, Carter 39–41
Syphax, John B. 149–150, 152
Syphax, Maria Carter (Custis) 2, 14, 39–41, 53, 93, 127, 149, 176, 178, 181
Syphax, Shorter 176
Syphax, William 100, 126, 145, 180

Taft, Pres. William Howard 172
Tennessee 17, 75, 105, 139, 157; Memphis 18, 75; Shiloh 85
Texas: Austin 140; Carthage 192; San Antonio 42
tobacco 17, 23, 105
Tomb of Civil War Unknowns 160
Tomb of the Unknown Soldier 131
Townsend, James 66
Truman, Pres. Harry 7, 171
Truth, Sojourner 4, 99–100

Uncle Tom's Cabin 36, 168
Underwood, John C. 99
United States Army 1, 3–4,-9, 13–14, 19, 25, 47, 55, 58, 62–63, 68, 73, 77, 84, 86–89, 103–105, 107, 112–113, 135–136, 139, 149, 158, 160, 174, 179, 181, 188–192; Ambulance Corps 83; Continental 30, 59; Nurse Corps 163; Surgeons 3
United States Capitol 28
United States Colored Troops 5, 10, 84, 88, 99, 111, 113–118, 121, 129, 134, 140–141, 170, 172, 180, 188; 4th Regiment 118, 140, 189; 5th Calvary 121; 5th Regiment 117–118, 140, 192; 6th Regiment 118, 140, 164; 7th Regiment 121, 142, 164, 189; 27th 1 Regiment 21, 140; 27th Regiment 141, 172; 29th Regiment 121; 31st Regiment 121; 36th Regiment 118; 38th Regiment 118, 139, 189; 41st Regiment 121; 45th Regiment 118, 121; 104th Regiment 142, 189; 107th Regiment 98; 109th Regiment 121; 116th Regiment 121
United Confederate Veterans 155
United States Congress Committees: Judiciary 146; Memorialize African Americans in the Civil War 136; Reconstruction 120
United States Corps of Engineers 106
United Daughters of the Confederacy 7, 164, 168
United States Marines 57
United States Military Academy, West Point 31, 60, 63, 107, 190
United States Patent Office 28, 60
United States Soldiers Cemetery 64
United States Supreme Court 7, 35–37, 147, 152, 156, 173, 178, 181, 190; *Brown vs Board of Education* 173, 190; Dred Scott Decision *see* Dred Scott
USCT *see* United States Colored Troops

Van Buren, Pres. Martin 18
Van Vorhes, Col. Nelson 140
Vietnam War 131, 189–191
Virginia: Accomack 15; Alexandria 27, 31–32, 34, 39, 47, 61–62, 73, 178; Amelia County 121–122; Appomattox Court House 124–126, 180; Appomattox River 122; Arlington County 7–8, 40, 63, 101, 149; Constitution (1870) 101; Fairfax County 107; Fredericksburg 70, 84; Hampton 20, 70; Henrico County 92; House of Burgesses 30, 179; House of Delegates 150; James River 28, 118, 140; King George County 15; King William County 45; Lancaster County 15; Lynchburg 181; Manassas Junction 64; Mount Vernon 24–26, 29, 32, 34, 39, 41, 133, 152; New Kent County 24, 44–45, 177; Newport 20; Norfolk 88, 142, 189; Potomac River 2, 7, 19, 24, 26–27, 42, 59, 62, 82, 106, 109, 172, 179; Richmond 3, 5, 13, 45, 46, 50, 52–54, 59–61, 63, 67, 77, 86, 90, 92–93, 102, 105, 107, 112, 115–118, 120–121, 125, 157, 162–163, 167, 179, 181, 185; Rosslyn 3, 27; Sayler's Creek 122–123; Spotsylvania 107, 109, 154, 185; Stafford County 103; Suffolk 70; Vicks-

burg 85, 126; Virginia Military Institute 167; Westmoreland County 45; Wheeling 17

Wadsworth, Military Gov. James 74
Walker, Confederate Secretary LeRoy Pope 3
Wall, Orandatus Simon Bolivar 114, 140–141, 189
Wanton, George H. 165, 190
War of 1812 28–29, 82, 172
Washington, Bushrod 40
Washington, Pres. George 1–2, 6–7, 9–10, 24–26, 30, 34, 38–39, 44, 53, 60, 89, 162–163, 175, 178, 180; as civilian 132
Washington, Martha Dandridge Custis 1–2, 9, 25–26, 29, 34, 38–39, 177; as civilian 132
Washington, D.C. 1, 6, 16, 21–22, 27, 57, 64, 70–71, 78, 82, 84, 90, 128, 134, 136, 144, 178–179; Barry Farm 147; Camp Barker 71–72, 92, 143, 189; Duff Green's Row 72–74, 77; Logan Circle 74; Medical Society 144
Washington Evening Star 71, 81, 138
Washington Star 175
Weitzel, Gen. Godfrey 6, 120–121, 129, 134
Welch, Frank 113, 140, 144, 189
Welles, Navy Sec. Gideon 66
Wells, John 129
Whiskey Rebellion 30
White Citizen's Council *see* Ku Klux Klan
Whitney, Eli 18
Wilson, Pres. Woodrow 7
World War I 9, 82, 131, 190, 192
World War II 83, 131, 173–174, 189–190, 191–192

www.ingramcontent.com/pod-product-compliance
Ingram Content Group UK Ltd.
Pitfield, Milton Keynes, MK11 3LW, UK
UKHW041947140426
5217IPUK00014B/686